Abstracts from

The Connecticut Gazette

(Formerly The New London Gazette)

*Covering
Southeastern Connecticut*

1777-1779

Richard B. Marrin

HERITAGE BOOKS
2014

HERITAGE BOOKS
AN IMPRINT OF HERITAGE BOOKS, INC.

Books, CDs, and more—Worldwide

For our listing of thousands of titles see our website
at
www.HeritageBooks.com

Published 2014 by
HERITAGE BOOKS, INC.
Publishing Division
5810 Ruatan Street
Berwyn Heights, Md. 20740

Copyright © 2010 Richard B. Marrin

All rights reserved. No part of this book may be reproduced or transmitted in any form or by any means, electronic or mechanical, including photocopying, recording or by any information storage and retrieval system without written permission from the author, except for the inclusion of brief quotations in a review.

International Standard Book Numbers
Paperbound: 978-0-7884-5017-4
Clothbound: 978-0-7884-8397-4

Table of Contents

Introduction. 1

Abstracts from 1777. 5

Abstracts from 1778. 105

Abstracts from 1779. 185

End Notes 261

Indices 273

Introduction

Welcome to Eastern Connecticut from 1777 through 1779. In this, the fourth in a series of news abstracts from the *Connecticut Gazette* [formerly *The New London Gazette*], can be viewed both the everyday life of the colonists of Eastern Connecticut and extraordinary event of the American Revolution. The Country and Connecticut were in rebellion against the greatest power in the world.

Make no mistake about it. Eastern Connecticut was no longer frontier. The 1,200 square miles that made up New London and Windham Counties had been settled already for more than a century and a half. Courts and schools, shops and taverns, churches and meetinghouses, all flourished. Pre- Revolution eastern Connecticut could boast of some thirty seven towns and twenty nine villages and boroughs. Its first citizens –the Mohegans and Pequots of the Alogonquin language stock, whose ancestors had lived there ten thousand years, remained in their ancestral homes at peace with the Colonists.

Its citizens were productive. Those outside of the towns were engaged in farming or in maritime matters. Good harbors, easy access to the interior for trade and a nearby ocean, full of fish, allowed commerce to flourish. Mills and factories were built on the waterways, providing necessities like flour and lumber for local consumption. .

While the Town of New London, a port city on the Sound, was the home of the *Gazette*, it was only one of a number of equally ancient colonial towns in the region. The citizens too of Groton, Stonington, Norwich, Saybrook, Lyme, Colchester, Preston, and Lebanon were served by, and reported on, by *The Gazette*. So also were the long settled towns of neighboring Windham County - Windham, Canterbury, Voluntown, Pompret, Woodstock, Killingly, Plainfield and Ashford.

Glimpse of daily life back then, from what the stores in town had to sell to who died and from what, abound in *The Gazette*. Published weekly, it was four pages long, on two folded sheets of laborious made paper. The first page was given over to political and international news. The second page reported on other colonies. The third and fourth pages, however, had items of interest for the readers of Eastern Connecticut, deaths and weddings, accidents of every sort imaginable, talk at town meetings and much more. In the classifieds, one could buy or sell nearly everything, personal property, real estate, even slaves. There were legal notices to creditors of the estates of both the dead and the bankrupt; notices of horses and livestock that "strayed or were stolen" and lists of letters left at the Post Office etc.,

History, of course, views these years 1777 through 1779 as more than as just another chapter in America's long history. We find ourselves in the midst of the American Revolution. To the northeast, Britain occupied Newport and, to the south and west, New York City. While Connecticut was not invaded by large forces of the enemy during these three years, 1777-1779–sadly that would come later in the War –it and its people were nonetheless very much involved in the Revolution. Silas Deane of Windham and Eliphalet Dyer of Groton were delegates to the First Continental Congress. Many of it citizens enlisted in the Continental Army and Navy and fought throughout the fledgling United States. Others joined the State Militia, drilled regularly and mustered, more than once, to repel expected invasions. Some local boys were heroes. At Bunker Hill, General Israel Putnam is famed for ordering his troops not to fire "until you see the whites of their eyes" Nathan Hale of Coventry, a spy for Washington and hung in New York City, of course, uttered the "I regret that I have but one life to give for my Country." There was a traitor too,. Benedict Arnold of Norwich, who is secondly only to Judas Iscariot in infamy.

But most were common every day Americans, largely unrecognized in the fight for Liberty but nevertheless deeply involved too. The citizens of Connecticut's towns and counties unified and formed Committees of Inspection and Observation as ordered by the First Continental Congress. They made certain the boycott against British goods was enforced. They exposed and rooted out residents with views considered "inimical" to the interests of the State and Nation. Each town took on the obligations of clothing and fitting out their soldiers and to assure that the families left behind would be fed. It produced many of the necessities of the war, gunpowder, cannon, salt, foods stuffs and clothing --Washington called Connecticut the "Provision State". Her vessels continued the commerce of the Nation, trading especially with the West Indies and Europe. But now, they risked capture by the British warships that patrolled the Long Island Sound. The citizens were aggressors as well in protecting their Liberty. Its privateers, specially fitted and privately owned ships of every sort, including whaleboats, preyed British shipping whenever the opportunity. Cargos from England intended for the British and Hessian soldiers ended up instead in Colonial hands. Everywhere the resolve of the People to gain their freedom was evident.

1777

From *The Gazette*, January 3, 1777

Battle of Trenton
Yesterday, at about one o'clock, the flag of truce, mentioned in our last to have sailed from this port (New London) to New York, returned from thence with 40 prisoners (seamen only) in exchange for a number of British prisoners. They chiefly belong to the state of Rhode Island.

Mr. Nathaniel Shaw Jun., who went in the above flag, was on his return in New Haven where an express had arrived on Wednesday with the following interesting and important intelligence - that on the 26th of December George Washington, with about 3,000 men, crossed the Delaware, and at about 8 o'clock in the morning engaged the enemy at Trenton, who were about 1600 in number and in 35 minutes routed the whole, taking 919 prisoners, exclusive of killed or wounded. [1]

died
at Killingsworth, Elnathan Stevens in the 74th year of his age.

submit bills
Notice by Robert Niles that all persons that have any bills against the Schooner *Spy* are desired to render them to the subscriber for payment.

stolen or went adrift
from the beach at the Harbor's [New London'] mouth, in the evening of the 29th ult, a Moses boat about 11 feet of keel, marked on the stern "SH No. 12", a small hole broke under her larboard bow; notice given by Job and Samuel Tucker.

administration of estates
Samuel Hefford, Amos Wells, Elias Worthington, appointed Commissioners by the Court of Probate for the District of East Haddam for the estate of Samuel Tozer, Jun., late of Colchester, deceased and being represented insolvent, hereby give notice of a meeting of creditors to be held at the house of John Tainter, Inn Holder in Colchester;

Notice by Ralph Stoddard, Nathan Gallup, Amos Geer, Commissioners appointed by the Court of Probate of Stonington, to the creditors of the estate of David Lester, late of Groton, deceased and represented insolvent, that a meeting will be held at the house of Jonas Belton of Groton.

broke into the enclosure [2]
of Zapaniah Lathrop of Norwich, a black and white heifer;

of Nathaniel Williams in Lebanon, a year old heifer of reddish brown color;

of John Tinker 3rd, a steer;

of Thomas Strickland in Chesterfield Society in Lyme, a dark red steer;

of Elisha Miller of Lyme, a heifer, marked with a crop upon the right ear;

of Thomas N. Niles of Groton, a white sow;

of Samuel Bradford of New London, North Parish[3] a brown and white heifer.

taken up
by Joseph Harvey in Lyme, a light bay horse.

****

From *The Gazette*, January 10, 1777

assault
About ten days ago, some differences occurring between John Dennis of this Town (New London] and – Perkins, belonging to the ship *Oliver Cromwell*. Dennis struck Perkins on the head with a hoe which fractured his skull and he lies dangerously ill. Dennis is committed to goal.

accident
Wednesday se'nnight,[4] the following accident happened - *viz*, as some guns were sealing on board a privateer, which lay at the Wharf in this town [New London], Mr. Thomas Lester was struck in the head by a wad and died of the wound last Friday. He lately removed here from Long Island because of the troubles there; he was an inoffensive man and sustained a good character.

suffering in Long Island
The transports, which in our last were said to be in the East End of Long Island, taking in wood for the ministerial army, still continue there under the protection of a man of war. It is said the inhabitants have suffered much from the soldiers who robbed them of their effects.

troops in town
Since our last, part of Col. Ely's Regiment of newly raised troops have arrived in Town.

Committee of Inspection and Observation meeting called
Notice to the members of the Committee of Inspection and Observation[5] of the Town of Groton to meet at the house of Capt. Jonas Belton, to consider and act, respecting sundry complaints made to said Committee. Capt. Hubbard Burrows, Jun., Mr. Elisha Williams, Ensign Henry Williams, Jun., Mr. Jonathan Randal and Mr. Nathan Gallup Jun, as friends of the free United States, are desired to attend said meeting as witnesses to sundry matters to be considered; notice by John Elderkin, Clerk.

died
on the 20th of last month died, at Stonington, Capt. Thomas Holms Jun, aged 32, leaving a disconsolate widow and five children. By a kind and affable behavior, he gained the respect and esteem of his neighbors and acquaintance who sincerely regretted his loss. He was taken sick in the Western Army about three weeks previous to his death. When called into the field in defense of his injured country, he cheerfully undertook the arduous task and was deservedly esteemed a good Officer;

Lord Day's morning last, died suddenly in Norwich, Gershom Breed of that Town, Merchant;

Last Wednesday, died in Groton, Luke Perkins of that Town.

claims from evacuation of Long Island
Notice by Hearing Officers Thomas Dering, John Foster and Thomas Wickham that a meeting will be held at the dwelling house of Ephraim Fenno, Inn Holder at Middletown, for all those with claims against the State of New York for transporting families, stock and effects from Long Island to Connecticut.

traitor escapes
Notice by Jabez Huntington, Sheriff of Windham County that one John Sheppard, a noted Tory who had been enlisting men for Gen. Howe's army, broke out of Windham goal; he is about 6 feet high; has straight brown hair; is thin and something gray; supposed to be about 50 years old.

ran away
from Pierpont Bacon of Colchester, an apprentice boy named Peregrine Dodge, about 16 years of age.

help wanted immediately
a number of journeymen nail makers. Good wages and constant employment will be given by Edmund Darrow;

an active boy between 12 and 15 years old, as an apprentice to the tailor's trade; in New London; enquire of the Printer.

for sale
immediately, for cash, by Roswell Saltonstall at the Distilhouse[6] in New London, flax seed, where may be had a small quantity of salt and Indian corn;

just published and to be sold by T. Green, *Freebetters New England Almanac* and Gentleman's and Lady's Diary for the year 1777.

choice liver oil to be sold by Jeremiah Clement at Norwich Landing; he also wants two or three apprentices in the nailing, blacksmith business.

sloop for sale
a sloop 75 tons burthen, well found; enquire of William Stewart of New London.

farms for sale
At Norwich West Farms, an elegant new dwelling house, very pleasantly situated at the parting of two roads; together with new barn; horse shed and 24 acres; enquire of Nathan Stedman at Norwich West Farms;

to be sold a convenient dwelling house at Poquatanuk Village, three miles from Norwich Landing, with a good garden adjoining, nicely situated for a merchant or mechanic; enquire of Daniel Hall of Norwich Landing;

a farm in Hopkinton adjoining the Great Road from Connecticut to Rhode Island, one mile from the Meeting House; 90 acres, well wooded and watered; 3 good orchards and 400 apple trees; good meadow and pasture; large dwelling house, barn and other out buildings; enquire of Henry Tew on premises.

a good cash price given
for clean cotton and linen rags at the Printing Office;

for live geese by Noble Hinman in New London;

for old brass copper pewter by Richard Collier at his shop near the Meeting House in Norwich; all sorts of copper and brass ware are made, mended and tinned – a few warming pans to be sold.

pay up
Ebenezer Backus of Windham wishes all those indebted to him to settle accounts; he has for sale a quantity of good English writing paper by the ream or quire; pork and grain will be received in payment;

William Woodbridge of Stonington wishes all those indebted to him to settle accounts.

administration of estates
Notice by Daniel and Benjamin Hyde to those indebted to the estate of Walter Hyde, late of Lebanon to make payment;

Notice by Samuel Hyde, Jun to all those indebted to the estate of Samuel Hyde of Lebanon to make payment;

Notice by John Howell Wells and Eliphalet Bill to creditors of the estate of Benajah Bill, late of Lebanon, that a meeting will be held at the house of Eliphalt Bill in Lebanon;

Notice to creditors by Solomon Safford and Elisha Lathrop, Commissioners for the estate of Lt. Samuel Bingham of Norwich, that a meeting will be held at the house of Widow Joanna Perkins;

Oliver Crary has been appointed Administrator of the estate of Capt. John Brewster, late of Preston.

lost
a hunting saddle; reward, if found; enquire of Printer.

stolen
from Samuel Jeffery of Fairfield, a bay colored horse;

from the saddle bag of Samuel M'Clellan, outside Mr. Tainter's Tavern in Colchester, shirts and stockings.

broke into the enclosure
of Ichabod Stoddard, a black calf;

of Walter Harris of New London Harbor's mouth, a light colored mare;

of John Henry of Colchester, a small, 2 year old heifer.

strayed or stolen
from Eleazer Bates in Haddam, a black cow;

from Roger Bulkley in Colchester, a last spring colt;

from Matthew Leffingwell of Chelsea in Norwich, a 2 year old mare;

from Andrew Griswold of Lyme, a 2 year old steer;

from Robert Robbins in Colchester, a red yearling heifer. It was last Spring brought off from Gardiner's Island by Mr. Marson of Lyme;

from David Jewett, East Haddam, a yellow heifer;

from Nathan Scovell of Lebanon, an 8 year old mare; please return to Anderson Martin of Lebanon Village or said Scovell in Colchester;

from Thomas Pelton of Chatham, forty sheep.

taken up
by Solomon Dart of New London, a 3 year old heifer;

by Morris Fowler of New London, a young steer;

by David Latimer of New London, two black cows;

by Rustford Rogers in Millington in East Haddam, a black 2 year old heifer;

by Levi Crosby Hadlyme in East Haddam, a sorrel horse;

****

From *The Gazette*, January 17, 1777

a letter from a prisoner in New York
The distress of the prisoners cannot be communicated by words; twenty or thirty die every day; they lie in heaps unburied.[7] What numbers of my countrymen have died of cold and hunger, perished for the want of the common necessaries of life. This is the boasted British Clemency! The New England people can have no idea of such barbarous policy; nothing can stop such treatment but retaliation.

day of fasting and prayer
The last day of January is appointed a day of fasting and prayer throughout this State.

veterans
Notice by Richard Sill, Paymaster of the 10th Regiment to the officers and soldiers belonging to the two companies of the 10th Regiment, commanded by Capt. Christopher Darrow and Capt. David Nevins that he will attend at the house of Jason Allen, Inn Holder in New London, North Parish, to settle with them on wages due for the last campaign.

deserter
Notice by William Coit of the armed ship *Oliver Cromwell*, belonging to the State of Connecticut, a mulatto fellow, named John Short, sometimes calls himself John Smith; is about 20 years old; 5 feet, 6 or 7 inches tall; poorly clothed.
N.B. Whoever may apprehend him is desired to secure what money he may have about him, as he has stolen from Roger Gibson a considerable amount of cash as he went off.

died
At Groton last night, departed this life in comfortable hopes of a better one, Luke Perkins, aged 81. A gentleman possessed of superior powers and endowments which qualified him for uncommon public service. While very young and for many years, he served the Town as a Representative;

Daniel Brainerd of East Haddam, for a number of years past, one of the representatives of this Town; was suddenly struck with an apoplectic disorder, which deprived him of his reason, locked up his senses and put an end to his life, last Friday in the 55th year of his life.

blubber for sale
choice liver oil and blubber to be sold by Joshua Starr in New London.

books for sale
Samuel Loudon has opened at the store of Col. Jedidiah Huntington; he has a few books for sale among them *Essays on the Character, Manners and Genius of Women,* Johnson's Plays, the renowned *Don Quixote, Wilks' Jests, The Free Mason's Companion,* and Baley's *Ovid.*

administration of estates
Notice by John Deshon, Winthrop Saltonstall and Marvin Wait, Commissioners appointed by the Probate Court of New London for the estate of Christopher Christophers, late of New London; deceased and represented insolvent, that a final meeting will be held at Marvin Wait's Writing office in New London;

Notice by Edward Chapman that all who are indebted to David Chapman, deceased, late of East Haddam, to settle accounts.

lost and found
out of Subscriber's pocket, somewhere on the road between Hebron and New London, a pair of flowered silver shoe buckles. Whoever will return such buckles will be handsomely rewarded by

Nathaniel Darby of Marlbrough Society in Hebron;

out of Subscriber's (Noble Hinman of New London) pocket, somewhere between his house and Capt. Joseph Harris' at Town Hill between 15 and 20 pounds;

Notice by Mrs. Champlin that she found, lying on a wall near the house of Mr. Samuel Taber of New London, a boy's homespun gray surtout,[8] partly worn with a pair of black breeches.

broke into the enclosure
of Thomas Stanton 4th of Stonington, a small black mare, two years old, one of her hind feet white.

****

From *The Gazette,* January 24, 1777

died
Last Friday died here, New London, William Garrick of the wounds he received from John Dennis. In our last paper, the deceased's name was called Perkins, through wrong information.

list of officers
of companies appointed to the first of the eight battalions of troops to be raised within the state of Connecticut, commanded by Col. Jedidiah Huntington:

Captains:
James Elridge;	David Nevins
Christopher Darrow Jun.	Eliphalet Holmes
Christo Ely	William Belcher
Benj. Throop Jun.	
Stephen Keyes	

1st Lieutenants:
Daniel Collins	Eben. Perkins
William Raymond	William Richards
Enoch Reed	Thomas Avery

Isaac Spencer
Marcus Cole

2nd Lieutenants:
Elisha Brewster   Henry Hill
Richard Douglas   Th. U. Fosdick
David Dorrance   Ez. P. Belden
John Tracy
Ezra Selden

Ensigns:
James Lord   Simeon Mouse
Simon Avery Jun.   David Spencer
Elijah Selden   Abidiah Fuller
Wm.Colfax
Ezra Lee

Committee of Inspection meeting
Notice by John Elderkin, Clerk, to the Civil Authority and Selectmen of the Town of Groton to meet the Committee of Inspection of said Town on the 30th instant at the house of Capt. Jonas Belton in said Groton at 1 o'clock pm to act on some matters of importance.

sale of prize vessels and cargo
Notice given by Winthrop Saltonstall, Register, that the trial of the libel[9] filed before Richard Law against the prize ship *Adelgonda Louissa,* her boats, tackle, apparel, furniture and cargo, taken on the high seas by armed vessels Schooner *Eagle,* commanded by Isaac Fields and the Sloop *True Blue,* commanded by Oliver Allen, in New London Courthouse on the 10th of February.

wife eloped
Whereas Lucy Latham of Groton, wife of the Subscriber, James Latham, has deserted and refuse to cohabit with me, this is to

forewarn all persons not to trust her on my account for I will pay no debt of her contracting, from the date hereof.

****

From *The Gazette*, January 31, 1777

prisoner exchange
Last Lord's Day, a flag of truce that lately went from Saybrook in company with several others with prisoners for New York, returned here.[10] They were not permitted to tarry but one night and were not allowed to go within some leagues of the city.

prize taken
The *American Revenue* Privateer, Capt. Champlin of this port, New London, has sent into Bedford a brig from Quebec which he took at windward of Barbados; her loading was chiefly fish.

runaway
from Francis Clark in Middletown, a Negro man servant named Dick; is very black; 21 years old; 5 feet, 6 inches tall; has a scar on the instep of one foot, occasioned by a cut of the ax; return to Subscriber or to Deacon Joseph Clark in said Town.

administration of estates
Notice by Administrator John Patten of New London, North Parish, to creditors of the estate of William Patten of Groton, deceased, to settle up;

Notice by Administrators Rhoda Harvey and Joseph Harvey to those indebted to the estate of John Harvey, deceased and late of Lyme, to settle up.

taken up
by Martin Southworth, in Saybrook, Chester Parish, a black horse with a white face;

by Isaiah Bolles in New London, a brown steer.

strayed
from Eleazar Bates of Haddam, a black cow.

clock and watch maker
Joel Atkins, clock and watch maker, has opened his shop next south to Mrs. Bigelow's Tavern in Middletown.

lost
by Edward Chapman on the road between East Haddam and North Bolton, 120 dollars in bills wrapped in newspaper.

dissolution of partnership
Notice by Silas Church and Edward Hallam that they have dissolved their partnership of Church & Hallam and would expect people to settle accounts.

****

From *The Gazette,* February 7, 1777

ship driven ashore by enemy
A ship of war, supposed to be the *Niger* of 36 guns, has lain just within the west end of Fisher's Island most of the time since our last. On Monday, she came to sail and, on the same day, drove on shore on Narraganset Beach a large schooner, the prize to the *American Revenue* Privateer, Capt. Champlin of this port, New London. The schooner was from Ireland and was bound for the West Indies with flour, bread, butter and other provisions and had two bales of linen on board, which the privateer took out. After the prize was on shore several attempts were made by boats from the ship to set her on fire which they once effected, but it was soon extinguished by the vigilance of the inhabitants who collected on the occasion and drew to the shore several field pieces, with the help of which they preserved the vessel.

administration of estates
Notice by Andrew Wheatley and Jane Wheatley, Administrators to the creditors of the estate of John Wheatly, late of Norwich, to file claims.

from imprisonment on the 8th of the month and was taken with the small pox on the 10th, of which distemper he died leaving a widow and three small children.

deserted
from Capt. Jeremiah Halsey's Company in Col. Ely's Regiment, two soldiers:
James Alsworth of the state of Rhode Island, of a light complexion, of 5 feet, 9 inches high; about 35 years old;

John Wompey, an Indian, belonging to Groton, about 25 years old; about 5 feet, 8 inches high.

administration of estates
Notice from both Ethan Clarke, Administrator of the estate of Samuel Ward, deceased, late of Westerly and from Job Bennet and Phineas Clarke, Commissioners to the said estate to those obligated to it to settle up and to creditors to file claims.

strayed
from Amaziah Spencer of East Haddam, a blackish mare.

prize taken
Tuesday last, a prize schooner laden with coal was carried into Stonington. She had been taken by a Boston privateer.

****

From *The Gazette,* February 21, 1777

arrests for treason
On Monday last, a number of persons belonging to the Great Neck[12] of this Town, New London, were discovered to have been concerned in sundry transaction, inimical and dangerous to the State and were accordingly taken into custody, one of whom ,viz. Pardon Taber, is committed to goal on the statute made for the punishment of High Treason against the State. The others are now confined under safeguard to be dealt with according to the just demerits of their crimes.

ship escapes the enemy
Last Sunday, Stephen Cly, belonging to Connecticut River, in 23 days from Hispaniola, was drove ashore on Narragansett Beach by two frigates, who fired a number of shots at his vessel and attempted to send a barge to take possession of her, but the inhabitants appeared for his assistance, beat off the boat and assisted in getting off the vessel, which is since arrived safe at Stonington. The two ships afterward bore for Newport.
Capt. Cly in the latitude of Cape Hatteras spoke with Capt. Nathan Moore of this town, New London, from St. Eustatia bound to North Carlina, who informed that it was a current report when he left Statia,, which was the 25th of January, that France had declared War against England.

accident
Last Saturday, between nine and ten in the evening, Mr. John Hall of this Town, New London, Rigger, fell out of a canoe into the river and was drowned.

public beware
The Public are cautioned to be aware of counterfeit 36 shilling Massachusetts bills.

prisoner exchange
Last Sunday morning, a flag of truce with prisoners went from this place, New London, to the *Amazon* Frigate, lying near Gardiner's Island, to be exchanged for Capt. Palmer's people, lately taken. We hear a general exchange of prisoners is soon to take place over the whole continent.

died
Mrs. Mary Lucas, a widow;

At Killingsworth of the small pox, the Rev. Eliphalet Huntington;

at Saybrook Mr. Jonathan Leigh, Inn Holder.

reimbursement
The officers of the late Col. Selden's Regiment are desired to call upon Edward Hallam, the late quartermaster of such Regiment, for their rations and men's mileage.

list of officers in Col. Durkee's Regiment
Captains:

Stephen Brown Elisha Lee
Jed Hyde John Harman
Nathaniel Webb Jn. McGregory;
Nathan Peters

First Lieutenants:
Wm Adams
Robert Hammam Beriah Bill
Andrew Fitch Seth Phelp
Jno Waterman L. Cleft
Daniel Wait

Second Lieutenants:
James Holt Po. Demming
Edward S. Coleman John Boell
Tim Cleveland Jno. Durkee, Jun;
Charles Fanning

Ensigns
Benj. Holt Ezeckiel Smith
Jabez Smith Jun. Nathan Nobles
Eben. Wales John Abbot
Andrew Griswold
Robert Williams

Staff Officers
Rev. Andrew Lee, Chaplain Master
Elihu Marvin Adj. Wm. Adams, Post Master
Andrew Wheatley, Quarter

The officers are desired to be as expeditious as possible in recruiting and to make returns immediately to the Colonel of the names of the men they recruit, dates of enlistment, terms for which they enlist, place of abode, age, stature, color of their eyes, hair, complexion and countenance.

for sale
by Messrs. Rodulphus & Co., ten double fortified 3 lb carriage guns with carriages.

sale of prize vessels and cargo
Notice given by Winthrop Saltonstall, Register, that the libel filed before Richard Law against the prize schooner *Britannia,* her boats, tackle, apparel, furniture and cargo taken on the high seas by armed vessels *Schooner Eagle* commanded by Isaac Fields and the Sloop *True Blue,* commanded by Isaac Field in the armed schooner *Eagle,* fitted out as vessel of war by John Matthews and Associates, that the trial of such ship will be in New London on the 14th of March next.

lost
Notice by Ephraim Miner that he lost on the road between New London and Norwich, a pair of saddle bags.

administration of estates
Notice by Joseph Peck and Elizabeth Peck, Executors, to those indebted to the estate of Joseph Peck, late of Norwich, to settle accounts;

Notice by Timothy Lester, Roger Sterry and Samuel Leonard to the creditors of the estate of Jonas Brewster of Preston that a meeting of creditors will be held at the house of Robert Crary, Inn Holder in Preston;

Notice by Samuel Tracy and Elisha Lathrop to the creditors of the estate of Reuben Bishop, of Norwich deceased and represented insolvent, that meeting of creditors will be held at the house of Azariah Lathrop, Inn Holder in Norwich, and a second meeting at the house of Benjamin Burnham in said Norwich;

Notice by John Barstow and Josiah Dewey, Commissioners, to the creditors of the estate of John Dodge, late of Canterbury, deceased and represented to be insolvent, that a meeting of creditors will be held at the house of John Parks Jun , Inn Holder in Canterbury;

Notice by Roger Sherry, Administrator, to the those indebted to the estate of Mrs. Grace Frink, late of Preston, deceased, to make speedy payment;

Notice by Cady Allen, Administrator, to the creditors of the estate of Phineas Allen, late of Mansfield, deceased, to file claims.

Notice by Nathaniel Eaton, Administrator, to the creditors of the estate of Ebenezer Eaton, late of Pompret, deceased, to file claims; a meeting will be held at the house of Ephraim Ingals on Tuesday and Wednesday, March 3 and 4th, and at house of Jacob Siminds, Inn Holder in Windham, on the 5th and 6th.

****

From *The Gazette,* February 28, 1777

clothes for soldiers
Andrew Huntington of Norwich continues to give hard money for homemade cloth for coats, flannel, tow cloth, blankets, linen, felt hats, shoes and stockings for the army. He flatters himself that every friend of the Country will exert himself to furnish as many of the said items as is in his power.
It is recommended to everyone to make their flannel white, a full yard wide and the stockings also white, as that color may be most agreeable. The cloth for coats should be blue, brown or red.

jailed
Last Monday, Benjamin Jorem and Pardon T. Tabor of New London, Great Neck were confined to goal for sundry acts inimical to the State.

died
at Killingsworth of the small pox, the Rev. Eliphalet Huntington, Pastor of the First Church and Congregation of that Town at the age of 40 years, in the 14th year of his Ministry.

married
Dr. Thomas Barber of Middletown in New Jersey to Miss Polly Darrel of Stonington.

small pox inoculation for soldiers
By order of his Excellency Gen. George Washington and a Resolve of Governor Trumbull of this State and the Council of Safety that hospitals are provided in New London, Norwich and Pomfret for the inoculation of the Continental troops under the superintendence of Brigadier General Parsons. The soldiers are to produce certificates of their enlistment to the Director of the Hospital before they are inoculated. Cols. Huntington and Durkee are to inspect the hospital at Norwich; Lieutenant Colonels Prentice and Russell those of New London and Major Grosvenor that of Pomfret; by order of General Parsons by Col. Jed Huntington.

to be sold
three carriage guns, three pounders; enquire of Nobel Hinman;

a vessel of 170 tons, now on stocks in Westerly; she is well molded for sailing and can be enhanced in a short time. Enquire of George Sheffield of Stonington.

farm for sale
by Samuel Parsons, a dwelling house and 17 acres of upland and meadows adjoining in Lyme less than a half a mile from the Connecticut River and adjoining a navigable creek; good for a merchant or mechanic.

administration of estates
Notice by Richard Chapman, Administrator, to those indebted to the estate of Major James Chapman, Jun. of New London to

speedily settle accounts.

lost
on the 17th instant between the New London Meeting House and Robert Douglas's house, a broadcloth cloak; enquire of James Douglas of New London.

taken up
by Henry Bishop of New London, a hog.

stolen
from the enclosure of Thomas Wait of Lyme, a mare.

****

From *The Gazette,* March 7, 1777

close call
Last Monday, a sloop, James Latham, Master, sailed from New London bound for the West Indies. She went through Fisher's Island Sound within a gunshot of a Man of War which took no notice of him.

died
of the small pox, Mr. Nathan Heward;

Mrs. Bolles, Widow of John Bolles;

sailors wanted on Ship Trumbull
Sailors willing to serve their country aboard the Ship *Trumbull,* Dudley Saltonstall Master, lying in the Connecticut River are hereby informed that she is an excellent ship, upwards of 700 tons burthen, and mounting 32 guns and will certainly sail on a Cruise after the River opens, as having a considerable part of the crew already engaged. Apply to the Commanding Officer on board; Gilbert Saltonstall of New London, Jacob White of Middletown or Mr. Jonathan Sabin of New Haven.

restriction on small craft movements
Notice by Nathaniel Shaw, Jr., Marvin Wait, Thomas Rogers and

Griswold Avery, Selectmen, to owners of boats and small vessels to convey their boats above Fort Trumbull, from which they shall not depart without the liberty of the Selectmen.

to be sold
a farm lying in Saybrook; 140 acres; by the river; there is a good dwelling house, barn and two orchards, well fenced, wooded and watered; enquire of Richard Sill on the premises.

ferry for lease
the ferry at New London to be let; enquire of the Selectmen.

if you are to be inoculated
Notice by Nathaniel Ames that all persons intended to be inoculated, bring with them some old tick to fill with straw, a pair of sheets and a blanket, otherwise but few can be accommodated for the existence of the hospital is so precarious that the Proprietors think it not proper to be a large expense for bedding.

horse stolen
Notice by Bezaleel Fisk that stolen from him was a sorrel mare by a person who called himself Hudson, who lately moved from Long Island and now lives in Colchester; he is a well built man; about 30 years of age; 5 foot 9 inches tall; has a scar under his right eye and has had the small pox.

runaway
from Samuel Mosely of Windham, an apprentice named John Vaugn, 13 years of age;

from Paul Tew of Woodstock, a Negro man named Cesar; about 5 feet, 7 inches high; middling well set; speaks tolerably good English; near 60 years of age; has gray hair.

****

From *The Gazette*, March 14, 1777

scare
On Saturday morning last, a fleet of 11 ships being part of the

British fleet from Rhode Island appeared just to the west of Fisher's Island, but the wind being small and the tide unfavorable, they drifted back to the Point and anchored.

The appearance of this force so near us occasioned the militia from the neighboring towns to be ordered in for the defense of the harbor, among which was the Norwich light infantry company, commanded by Col. Christopher Leffingwell[13] who made a genteel and martial appearance, being neatly dressed in uniform.

After the departure of the fleet, Col. Leffingwell with some boats went out to Fishers Island to make what discoveries they could. They learned the following from Mr. Brown who lives on the island. The fleet took off the island 108 sheep, 8 oxen, 11 cows, 22 yearlings, 26 swine 24 turkeys, 4 dozen fowls, 123 bushels of corn, 100 bushels of potatoes, 5 and 1/2 tons of pressed hay and three cords of wood; they also took a parcel of pork out of the cellar, some bed clothing such as blankets and sheets. The names of the ships were the *Amazon,* Capt. Jacobs; the *Greyhound,* Capt. Dickinson and the *Lark* with Capt. Smith. They landed three companies of British and three companies of Hessians. We learn that the stock taken off Fishers Island was principally paid for.

close call

Last Saturday three men went from hence (New London) in a sail boat to Fisher's Island for a load of corn, having a permit for that purpose from the Committee of this Town and being in the greatest strait therefor, there being none to be purchased here. But, before they loaded their boat, they noticed a number of troops had landed on the island. They thought it advisable to make their best way back to the boat. They accordingly set out, but soon found themselves being pursued and, by the time they on board the boat which lay within pistol shot of the shore, by about 300 men in two divisions had gotten to the shore. An officer called to them to come on shore, threatening to fire on them if they did not, but they, disregarding these threats, began to hoist sail when the enemy fired a volley at them which they repeated until the boat was out of their reach which was about 15 minutes, the wind being small. In the mean time, the enemy tried to get to them in a sail boat, but she happily ran aground on the Point. The three men say a 1000 rounds of shot or more were fired at them and about 100 struck the boat, but providentially none of them men were hurt.

Indian visitors
Last Tuesday, five warriors of the Oneida tribe arrived here on important business and were politely entertained by the officers of the army and the principal inhabitants of the Town. They appeared to be very pleased with the kind treated afforded them.[14]

taken up
by Joseph Lewis at the mouth of New London harbor, a canoe about 19 feet long and two feet wide;

by John Brown at the mouth of Groton harbor, a Moses boat.

settle accounts
Joshua Hempsted, late post rider, wants subscribers to settle accounts.

to be sold
in the Second Society of Lyme, near the head of the Niantic River, a farm of about 90 acres, well proportioned with plowing, pasturing and mowing land; with a fine new growth of wood; well watered with a large dwelling house and barn; also two orchards, cider mill and press; fine location for a merchant, mechanic or tavern, it being on the road between New London and Middletown; enquire of Benjamin Lee on the premises.

runaway
from Elisha Babcock of Ashford, Boston, a Negro man; very black; 5 feet, 6 inches high; about 28 years old; scar on his temple; very short hair.

administration of estates
Notice by Lydia Wright and Joel Wright to all those indebted to the estate of Capt. Seth Wright, late of Lebanon, to settle up and to creditors to file claims.

broke out
of the enclosure of Thomas Wait of Lyme, a mare
****

From *The Gazette*, March 21, 1777

execution
Last Wednesday, Moses Dunbar was executed in Hartford for High Treason against the State, pursuant to a judgment of the Superior Court.

sailboat seized
Last Thursday se'nnight, a sailboat belonging to Samuel Beebe of Stonington was taken in the Sound by the *Amazon*, Capt. Jacobs.

prisoner exchange
On Saturday, the *Amazon* came to came to anchor just outside the Light house and sent in a boat with a flag to propose a prisoner exchange. Saturday, they landed Mr. Bulkley, his first mate and Mr Cornelius Cunningham, a passenger of Capt. Bulkley's on Fisher's Island and, on Monday morning, the ship sailed for Rhode Island, her station off this harbor, we hear, being up. The above Mr. Cunningham sailed from New Haven for the West Indies and was taken up just two hours sail outside of Martinico.
We learn from the prisoners that they were treated with humanity and kindness by Capt. Jacobs, who appeared to be much of a gentleman, consequently he is of a much different disposition than most of his profession being stationed here, among whom the name of Wallace[15] will long be remembered by hundreds who have felt or been witness to his mean and savage conduct in firing on single defenseless houses, burning and destroying private property, abusing women and children and those whom age has made rendered incapable of resistance.

died
Mrs. Sarah Hillhouse, consort of William Hillhouse in the 49th year of her age; she was a person of many shining virtues, lead a pious and exemplary life and delighted in the study and practice of religion. She discharged the duties of a child, sister, wife and

mother with particular tenderness and affection and was cheerfully resigned to her death in the joyful expectation of blessed immortality;

in Pomfret on the 9th, of small pox, John Weld in the 28th year of his life; he left a sorrowful widow and two small children. He was the only surviving son the Rev. Aeljah Weld;

Saturday morning, after a short illness, died here in Charlestown, Rhode Island, the Rev. Mr. Joseph Park, the Congregationalist Pastor in Westerly and Charlestown, in the 72 year of his life, the 44th of his Ministry. His funeral was preached by Rev. Mr. Fish of Stonington.

for sale
Samuel Mather, Jun. has to sell at his ship in Lyme, a quantity of white Hollands at different prices, stripes, camblets, checked linen, handkerchiefs.

lost
Notice by Nathan Doboll of Groton, a blue duffle great coat.

administration of estates
Notice by Executors Abraham Burnap and Jabez Lewis of the estate of Ebenezer Leach, deceased and late of Coventry, to those obligated to it to settle up and to creditors to file claims.

Notice by Josiah Dewey and Daniel Foster, Commissioners of the estate of Abijah Read, deceased and late of Canterbury, to those obligated to it to settle up and to creditors to meet at the house of Mr. John Parks, Jun, Inn Holder in Canterbury.

****

The March 28, 1777 issue of the *Gazette* is not legible

****

From *The Gazette*, April 4, 1777

guilty of murder
At the Superior Court of Norwich held last week, one John Dennis

of New London was found guilty of the murder of William Garrick and received the sentence of death.

guilty of crimes against the State
Pardon Tabor of New London was found guiltily of crimes inimical to the State and was sentence to be imprisoned for one month, pay a fine of twenty pounds and bound to his good behavior to the next term;

Pardon Tillinghast Tabor was found guilty of the same crime and was sentenced to one month imprisonment and a twenty pound fine;

Benjamin Butler of Norwich was found guilty of defaming the Continental Congress and sentenced to be bound to his good behavior, be disarmed, and rendered incapable of hold any office, civil or military.

United States lottery tickets
to be sold by Samuel Gray of Windham, Charles C. Chandler of Woodstock, David Trumbull, Elianah Tildale of Lebanon, and from Andrew Huntington, Norwich.[16]

to be sold
a quantity of cherry tree boards and plank, lying at Mr. Lyons Wharf in East Haddam; notice by John Gelston.

deserted
Notice by Lt. John Buell that deserted from Col. Durkee's Regiment, a soldier named William Aegel; 25 years of age; middling stature; has short black hair;

Notice by Lt. Henry Hilliman of William Richard's Company in Col. Huntington's Regiment, Christopher Sherman of North Kingston, 5 feet, 7 inches high; blue eyes; light short hair.

to be let
a farm in Stonington, North Society 100 acres; enquire of Amos

Mains near the Premises.

administration of estates
Notice by Samuel Ball and Moses Bartlett, Commissioners of the estate of Lt. Samuel Cooper, late of Chatham, deceased and represented insolvent, to those obligated to it to settle up and to creditors to file claims; a meeting is to be held at house of Christopher Vanfant of Chatham, Inn Holder;

Notice by Elijah Hyde, Jr and Enoch White, Administrators to the estate of Simeon Gray of Lebanon, deceased, to those obligated to it to settle up and to creditors to file claims;

Notice by Enoch Lord, Executor of estate of Richard Lord, late of Lyme, deceased, to those obligated to it to settle up and to creditors to file claims.

stolen
Notice by Josiah Handy of Ashford that his horse has been stolen.

lost
on the road between Mansfield, Old Society and subscriber John Swift's home, a gold necklace and locket.

taken up
by John Brown at the mouth of the River at Groton, a Moses boat;

by Nathaniel Marsh Jun. in Plainfield, a black mare colt.

dissolution of partnership
The partnership of Champion and Deming of Colchester is being dissolved and all those indebted to it are asked to settle accounts.
****
From *The Gazette,* April 11, 1777

died
at East Haddam on the 29th *ult*, the Rev. Mr. Grindal Rawson in the 70th year of his life and the 44th of his Ministry

list of letters at New London Post office[17]

Beriah Bacon, Chatham
Wm. Browning, New London
Ezekiel Bailey, Groton
Abisha Chapman, New London
Jacob Conkling, New London
Libbeus Chapman, New London
Jedidiah Chapman, Col. Ely's Reg.
Edward Crowel, New London
Zacheus Chase, New London
William Dee, New London
Rudolf Esling, New London
Capt. Thomas Kennedy, New London
Abra. Lopez, Stonington
Emanuel Lewis, New London
Capt. John Morgan, Groton
Joseph Owens, New London
Samuel Powers, New London
William Prince, New London
Ebenezer Potter, New London
Capt Nathan Palmer, Stonington
Oliver Smith, Stonington
Christopher Smith, Long Island
William Skinner, New London
Henry Sherril, New London
Isaac Squire, New London
William Stark, New London
Edward Tinker, New London
Elisha Williams, Groton

New London Town Meeting

At a Town Meeting for the Town of New London, held on March 31, 1777, John Hempsted, Moderator
VOTED
That a committee be appointed and directed to promise and engage on behalf of the Town to provide necessaries on behalf of such soldiers belonging thereto, as shall enlist into any of the Continental battalions, now raising in the State, and during their continuing in such service, and to deliver the same to such families, at the price by law affixed, without any additional expense for such soldier on said Committee's receiving money from such soldier for said purpose, agreeable to a Proclamation by his Honor, the Governor
Committee of Supply will consist of:

Nathaniel Shaw, Jun.
Marvin Wait
Joshua Raymond
William Manawaring
Col. Jonathan Latimer

Guy Richards
James Rogers (Great Neck)
G. Avery

VOTED
That the inhabitants of this Town will, with zeal and unanimity, exert themselves into carrying into execution the Laws made for the defense of our Rights and Privileges and will in a special manner assist the Authority, Selectmen and all informing officers in punishing the violators of the Laws, lately made for regulating and affixing the prices of the various necessities of Life.
attest: Edward Hallam, Town Clerk

Norwich Town Meeting
At a Town Meeting of the Town of Norwich, held on April 7, 1777, Ebenezer Baldwin, Moderator

VOTED
That the Town will agree and unite strictly to adhere to and observe the laws of this State respecting the regulating of prices of the necessaries of Life.

VOTED
That this Town will and does hereby engage and promise to such men of this Town as have families and have enlisted for the term of three years or during the War that the Town will supply their families with the necessaries of life during said service, at the prices stated by law for those articles, upon such men lodging sufficient money in the hands of the Committee here appointed.
Committee of Supply:

Ebenezer Thomas
James Hyde
Thomas Hyde Jun.
Nathaniel Kingsbury
Samuel Griswold
Joseph Hyde

Daniel Bishop
John Perkins
Jeremiah Kinsman
Solomon Safford
Stephen Johnson
Alice Fitch

Elijah Lathrop	David Hough
Elazer Waterman
Nehimiah Huntington

ready to march
Notice by Col. Jed Huntington to the soldiers of his Regiment that any who do not hold themselves out as ready to march to the places of rendevous next Wednesday will be taken up and sent under guard to Camp, if not otherwise punished. This is not to prevent every officer's exertion to have his men ready and equipped.

deserted
Notice by Lt. Richard Douglas that deserted from Christopher Darrow's Company of Col. Huntington's Regiment, one Levi Davis; about 5 foot, 7 inches; short dark hair; something pitted with the small pox; speaks a little broken; says his friends live near Philadelphia where it is likely he has gone.

help wanted
Salisbury Furnace wants for such furnace a great number of workmen for several branches of business, especially for cutting wood and making coals. The best wage and pay may be expected. Those who engage here will serve this country as well as they can anywhere and may be encouraged that, while they are engaged in such service, they will be excused from all other service. Those who enter the service with a view to cutting wood are desired to bring their axe and blanket. Gentlemen farmers and others are earnestly desired to lend their aid as speedily, as possible as cannon to be made are much wanted.
Benjamin Henshaw and Wm. Whiting, Managers

Great encouragement for a number of Journeymen Paper makers; also for two or thee active boys, from 10 to 14 years old, who can read and write tolerably as apprentices to the paper making business in Norwich.

fishing
Timothy Tiffany carries on the Fishing business at Eight Mile River in Lyme, the usual place of fishing at Tiffany's Point where all persons, who may be pleased to favor him with their custom, may depend on the best usage.
For a direction to strangers, he informs those who come from eastward that they must ride 40 to 50 rods west of the usual place of turning where they may turn down by the house of Mr. William Harrison.

administration of estates
Notice by George Griffing, Administrator to the creditors of the estate of Mrs. Mary Dorr, deceased and late of Lyme to file claims;

Notice by Beriah Strong, Administrator of the estate of Elijah Bishop, deceased and late of Norwich to those obligated to it to settle up with Thomas Lathrop in Norwich;

Notice by John M. Breed, Executor of the estate of Capt. Gershom Breed, deceased and late of Norwich, to those obligated to it to settle up.

strayed or stolen
from Samuel Taber in New London, a reddish brown cow.

runaway
Notice by Jerusha Jonson of Walnut Hill, Lyme that some of the Selectmen of Lyme had enticed away his apprentice girl, Mary Mullendine, and have ever since detained her from his service and "I understand she has had a child since she last left me, I do hereby forbid them or any other person to detain her service any longer and, if any person will return her to me speedily with or without her child, they shall be paid 18 pence and no questions asked."

lost
out of Capt. Harris' store in Saybrook, sundry articles belonging to Mary King of Long Island, now living at Middletown South

Farms including two bags of wheat, one of corn, a bag of salt, a frying pan, a copper tea kettle.

****

From *The Gazette,* April 18, 1777

prize taken
A few days ago, a large prize ship taken by the *Defense* privateer, Capt. Smedley, belonging to this State, arrived at Bedford. She is said to have about 3,000 barrels of provisions on board.

sermon for elections
The Rev. John Devotion of Saybrook is appointed by His Honor, the Governor, to preach the annual Election Sermon, the 8th of May next.

married
Mr. Nathaniel Willis of Boston to Miss Lucy Douglas, daughter of Captain Nathan Douglas of this Town.

died
At Lyme, Benjamin Lee of the small pox.

notice to soldiers
The soldier in my Regiment, who have not marched to the rendezvous in East Haddam, by the 28th of this month, must be ready to march. The officers, as they would avoid the charge of indolence and pain of disgrace, are positively ordered to use their utmost activity in collecting their men and equipping them with blankets from their respective towns.
Col. Jed Huntington
N. B. It is much to be feared that some of the soldiers will be prevented from marching for want of blankets, as some towns do not supply their men.

to be sold
at public vendue near John Hempsted's in New London, a Black Smith's shop and a complete set of Smith's tools; also one small barn; likewise one case of drawers and two round tables. The

above articles may be seen by applying to Jedidiah Brown of New London.

to be let or sold
a farm of about 200 acres of good land lying in Lyme; enquire of John M'Curdy of said Lyme for further particulars.

left
at the house of Spera Douglass in New London, about a year since, three soldiers packs containing some clothing.

sailors and marines needed
The Ship *Oliver Cromwell* Seth Harding Commander, lying in the harbor of New London, is nearly ready to sail on a six month cruise, having a great part of her men engaged. Able seamen and Marines will meet with great encouragement and receive pay equal to those in the Continental service.
Apply to the Sign of the Golden Ball in New London or on board said ship.

escape
Notice by Jabez Huntington, Sheriff of Windham County that broke out of goal there, William Stewart, a short sandy faced Irishman sentenced to Newgate Prison for the crime of burglary; he is about 40 years of age; wears his own hair, of a yellow tinge; stole and carried with him one Dutch blanket, the property of Nathaniel Hebard.

for sale
In the ferry District in Saybrook, an exceedingly good house, almost new, consisting of two good rooms on the lower floor, with a bed room, milk room and a good cellar; two good rooms in the chamber, all well fixed; the whole building well painted; together with about 18 acres of land adjoining the house and about three acres of meadow, about a mile from said premises; with a considerable number of fruit trees; the whole in good fence; likewise a good barn and out buildings; enquire of Amos Williams on said premises. The above is situated on the country road about

a mile from Saybrook Ferry, very fitting for a tavern or a merchant.

administration of estates
Notice by Ephraim Kingsbury and Sarah Kingsbury, Administrators of the estate of Dr. Obidiah Kingsbury, late of Norwich, deceased, to those obligated to it to settle up and to creditors to file claims;

Notice by Martha Hyde, Administratrix of the estate of Mr. Silas Hyde, deceased and late of Norwich, to those obligated to it to settle up.

taken up
by William Wintworth in Norwich, a black mare.

deserted
notice by Lt. Daniel Wait that deserted from Capt. Lee's Company in Col. Durkeee's Regiment, one John Gills, 27 years of age; gray eyes; short black hair; much pock broken.

****

From *The Gazette*, April 25, 1777

enemy prize taken
The armed brig *Defense,* Captain Smedly, owned by the State, and the Sloop *American Revenue,* Capt Chamlin, belonging to this Town, New London, are arrived at a safe port from a cruise in which they have each taken four valuable prizes.
Since our last, Capt Wattles, in a small sloop letter of Marquee belonging to Norwich, arrived her from the West Indies. In his outward passage, he took a brig from Europe bound for the East Indies with a valuable cargo, which he sold in South Carolina.
Sunday a sloop, Captain Roland, arrived here from St. Croix with 1,300 bushels of salt.

American prize taken
We hear that Capts. Stilman, Lewis and Lay outward bound from this port, but leaving from Stonington with one other vessel, were

all taken by a British Frigate last Monday near Block Island.

Governor visits New London
His Honor, our Governor and the Council of Safety arrived in Town last Monday. Their arrival was announced by a discharge of cannon from the forts and shipping in the Harbor. Having finished the business they came on, they left the Town Wednesday.

Haddam Town Meeting
At a Town Meeting for the Town of Haddam New London, held on March 31, 1777, Jabez Brainerd Moderator:
VOTED unanimously by the inhabitants of the Town that they will join with, and support to the utmost of their power, the Authority, the Selectmen, the Committee of Inspection and all informing officers in carrying into execution the good and wholesome laws made for regulating and affixing the price of certain articles, as recommended by his Honor the Governor.

VOTED that the families of such soldiers, who have or shall engage in any of the Continental Battalions to be raised in this State, are to be supplied with the necessaries in their absence by a Committee appointed for that purpose at the price by law affixed, without any additional expense for such soldier, on said Committee's receiving money from such soldier for said purpose, the additional cost to be paid for by the Town, agreeable to a Proclamation by his Honor, the Governor.
Committee: Abraham Tyler, Nehimiah Brainerd, Jeremiah Hubbard, Elijah Brainerd, Ezra Brainerd, John Ventrus and Charles Smith
attest: Nemimiah Brainerd, Town Clerk

taxes due
Notice by Robert Hungerford and Joseph Fowler, Collectors for East Haddam, to the inhabitants to pay their taxes at the houses of Capt. Icabod Olmsted, of William Cone, of John Wiley; of Green Hungerford, of John Emmons; of Caleb Chapman and of Robert Hungerford on the days and times listed.

a genteel boarding house
Opened for gentlemen travelers and kept by Thomas Allen in the house here where Capt. Robinson Mumford lately lived, opposite the ferry wharf in New London;
price per week for breakfast dinner, supper. and lodging is five pounds, lawful money for a single person;
N. B. Horse keeping moderated by the immoderate price of hay and oats[18]

farms for sale
in East Haddam about 100 acres in Millington Parish, about two miles from the Meeting House and one mile and a half from Mr. Seare's Mill, with good house and barn and two orchards, well proportioned for mowing, pasturing and wood land; enquire of Levi Gates, living on the premises;

a farm lying in the East Society of Lyme on the road from Lyme to New London, consisting of a little more than 200 acres; is well watered and wooded; well proportioned for mowing, pasturing and wood; both upland and salt meadow; not one acre of waste land; has on it a large dwelling house and barn and three good orchards; enquire of Amos Lay, living on the premises;

a good farm in the North Parish of Coventry about 130 acres, lying on the Willimantic River; about 70 acres of land under good improvement with good orchard and very good fruit; for price, enquire of those living on the premises;

a convenient dwelling house and barn at Norwich about a half mile from Town House; with a good garden and well water; enquire of Joseph Post of Lebanon.

administration of estates
Notice by Asa Harvey and Mary Graves, Administrators of the estate of Benjamin Graves, deceased and late of East Haddam , to creditors to meet at the house of said deceased to file claims;

Notice by Israel Champion and Timothy Gates, Commissioners of the estate of Ebenezer Cone of Farmington, deceased and represented insolvent, to the creditors of said estate to meet at the house of Amos White, Inn Holder in East Haddam.

crockery ware for sale
by Stephen Russ at the store of Benjamin Huntington Jun. in Norwich, black and white, plain and fluted tea pots; white stone and creamed colored plates; earthen and glass, sugar dishes; beaker glasses, black cream colored and glass mustard; wine glasses, punch bowls, vinegar cruets; cream colored and white coffee bowls etc.

potatoes for sale
a quantity of good potatoes to be sold Noble Hinman.

strayed
from Joseph Post Lebanon, a black bull.

lost
by Aaron Horsford, near the dwelling house of Chauncey Bulkley's on the road between said Bulkey and Aaron Horsford, a leather pocket book containing nine or ten pounds; whoever finds it may leave it at Mr. Bulkey's or at Mr. Elisha Cornwell's or with Simon Arnold;

by Thomas Turner on road between New London and said Turner's house in New London, a leather pocket book.

runaway
from Samuel Gardner, living in Hopkinson in the State of Rhode Island, a Negro servant man name Prince, about 5 feet, 6 or 7 inches tall; well set; has three marks or scars on each temple (made in Guinea); speaks a little hoarse.

deserted
Notice by Lt. Nathaniel Bishop that deserted from Col. Durkee's Regiment, one Amos Green, 26 years of age; well set; short black hair; a brown eye; down look, something round shouldered;

Notice by Lt. Elisha Brewster that deserted from James Eldridge' Company in Col. Huntington's Regiment, a soldier who calls himself Robert Patterson of Ashford in the State of Connecticut; about 5 feet, 6 or 7 inches high; light eyes; light complexion and sandy hair; a pretty well set man.

****

From *The Gazette*, May 2, 1777

clothes cleaned
The public are hereby informed that William Fielding proposes to follow the worsted combing business in its nicest branches; likewise clothes cleaned and scoured and spots and stains taken out. Enquire at Capt. Noble Hinman's or at said Fieldings shop, opposite the Church in New London.

deserted
Notice by Capt. Nat. Webb that deserted from Col. Durkee's Regiment, Thomas Fitzgerald, a soldier about 5 feet, 6 inches high; brown hair; grey eyes; fair complexion; about 29 years old; very sprightly and active;

James Malony; 5 feet, 7 inches high; short black hair; black eyes; dark complexion; 25 years of age.

to stand stud
Stud services at the stable of William Waters in Norwich of his horse called the *Royal Hateen*, clear blooded of the Hateen and Heeler breed of horses, so called. He is a horse of great speed, strength, firmness, beauty, resolution, grace and carriage, perhaps equal to any raised in this government;

Charles C. Chandler of Woodstock the full blooded *Ranger,* an Arabian horse, formerly the property of Mr. Wyllys of Hartford and Capt. Nichols,

Robert Swan of Stonington, North Society, *Diamond*; he is a horse of about 15 hands high; on the sire side of the famous breed of Col. Williams old horse; bred on the farm of Elihu Chesebrough;

the horse was lately owned by Col. Seymour of Hartford and last season was owned by Charles Phelps;

by Collins Gorton, New London, Great Neck, the horse *Peacock;* he exceeds all for courage, beauty, activity and going.

Connecticut Insurance Office
The public is hereby informed that there is kept by the subscriber, Barnabas Deane at his house in Wethersfield, next door to the Meeting House, an Insurance office. The underwriters are Samuel Broome, John Broome, Jeremiah Platt and Joseph Webb. Any gentleman that wants insurance made may apply to any of the above gentlemen.

lost
on the road between New London and Norwich, a pair of empty saddle bags marked on the flaps "W. Ellery".

taken up
by Thomas Whipple in New London, living on the beach, a small white sow and five little pigs;

in Stonington harbor, a very good anchor, weighing about 400 pounds. Enquire of John Rathbun Jr., living at said harbor.

runaway
a mustee slave[19] named Jo; of a complexion lighter than common, having long bushy hair, short, thick and active; has a down look and large legs; deliver him to William Dyer on Tower Hill on south Kingston or Robinson Mumford in New London; he is the same slave that ran away from Mr. Stephen Hassard of South Kingston about 18 months ago.

to Captains of the 3rd Regiment
Notice by Col. Jonathan Latimer to the several Captains of the 3rd Regiment that they are required to make their returns of their Companies to the State by the 10th of this month, agreeable to the law.

From *The Gazette,* May 9, 1777

enemy warships
A British frigate has been plying up and down the Sound for several days since, and, on last Wednesday, several others were seen in the offing.
We learn from the western post that a considerable number of ships lay in the Sound off New Haven, last Tuesday night, but in the morning were gone.
We learn that about 100 of the enemy's horses and a number of wagons were left by them on the shore, when they embarked after the expedition to Danbury.

died
Major General Wooster died last night of the wound he received at the late skirmish with the enemy.

notice to march
Notice by John Mills, Captain, that four men enlisted with Capt. Lewis in Col. Webb's regiment, John Turner, Enos Blacksee, Asa Brunson and Norman Newell, supposed to belong to the County of New London, are ordered to march and join their respective regiments without delay, to rendevous at Danbury per the orders of Brig. General Parsons.

clothes, hats and shoes needed
Notice by Joshua Elderkin that he continues to purchase all sorts of woolen and linen cloths, felt hats, mens' shoes for the use of the Continental Army at his dwelling house in Windham at prices affixed by law.

small pox inoculations
The Directors of Mendon Hospital acquaint the public that those people who enter the hospital to be inoculated are requested to bring with them sheeting especially and, if possible, with blankets too. A generous price will be give them, if the possessors leave them. The scarcity of linen and woolen makes this notice

necessary, as it is impossible this present day to furnish a large hospital with those necessaries.

deserted
Notice from Capt. John Mills that deserted from Capt Robert Lewis' Company at Stratford, in Col. Webb's Regiment, about ten weeks past, one John Wright.

notice
The soldiers of my late Company, who joined their Regiment in New London or Providence are notified that they may receive their wages and billet by applying to Capt. Jonathan Calkins in New London.

administration of estates
Notice to creditor by Joseph Parker, Administrator of the estate of Capt. Samuel Parker, deceased and late of Coventry, to file claims;

Notice that all persons having any demand on the estate of Mrs. Bridget Chesebrough, deceased, late of Stonington, to bring their accounts to Thomas Stanton 2d and Elijah Palmer, Administrators.

farm for sale
Notice by James Braman, appointed by the Court of Probate for the District of Norwich, Administrator of the Estate of Mr. Jonas Brewster, deceased and late of Preston, that will be sold at Public Vendue, 70 acres of good land, a large dwelling house, barn, corn house and good orchard; the land is well proportioned for mowing, pasture and wood and is well watered.

deserted
Notice by Ebenezer Wales that deserted from Capt. Webb's Company in Col. Durkee's Regiment, William Brummicum; 34 years of age, 5 feet, 7 inches tall; dark eyes; dark complexion;

Notice by Captain Josiah Child that deserted from Col. Philip B. Bradley's Regiment, two men: John Bond and Joseph Carn, both

17 years of age, middling stature, both have had small pox and both from Mystic in Massachusetts.

runaway
from Benjamin Morgan of Preston, Asa Bowdish, 15 years of age; dark complexion; mid stature.

to stand stud
Notice by William Bulkley of Colchester that his *Young Ranger* will cover at his stable; he was got by the famous Arabian horse kept in Hartford. The price is five dollars for the season and $1.25, the single leap.

strayed or stolen
from Elisha Rice of Chesterfield in Lyme, a 2 year old colt;

from Joseph Lewis of Groton, a sorrel mare;

from Simeon Cobb of Chesterfield in New London, sorrel mare.
****
From *The Gazette*, May 16, 1777

to the Tories
Wanted for His Majesty's Servant, as an Assistant to his Excellency General Howe and Hugh Gaine, Publisher and printer of the *New York Gazette*, a Gentleman who can lie with ingenuity. Enquire of Peter Numbskull, Composer and Collector of Lies for their Excellencies in New York.
N.B. a good hand will receive the honor of Knighthood.[20]

administration of estates
Notice by Elisha Lathrop 3d of the estate of Robert Avery, deceased and late of Lebanon, to those obligated to it to settle up;

Notice by Joshua Babcock and Mercy Babcock, Administrators of the estate of Lt. Oliver Babcock, deceased and late of Stonington, to those obligated to it to settle up and to creditors to file claims;

Notice by Jane Wheatley and Andrew Wheatley, Administrators to the estate of John Wheatley, deceased and late of Norwich, to those obligated to it to settle up;

Notice by Christopher Ely, Executor of the estate of Major Daniel Ely, deceased and late of Lyme, to those obligated to it to settle up with Christopher Ely or, in his absence, with Ezra Selden;

Notice by Joseph Lover and John Soper, Commissioners appointed by the Probate Court of New London, to the the estate of Thomas Manwaring, deceased and late of New London, to those obligated to it to settle up and to creditors to file claims. There will be a meeting at the house of Lydia Manwaring, Widow, in said New London;

Notice by David West, Executor of the estate of Amos Randal, deceased and late of East Haddam, to those obligated to it to settle up forthwith to prevent being put upon in a more disagreeable way.

deserted
Notice by Lt. Silas Goodell that from Capt. Cleft's Company in Col. Eyllys' Regiment, Abraham Parkhurt; 5 feet, 9 inches tall, 23 years of age, has straight black hair; dark eyes; lately lived in Killingly.

witness statement
I certify that I was nurse to P. Webster in his last sickness and heard him apply to Doctor Bulkley to take care of him through his illness, which he refused on account of his having too many patients under his care. I understand that Dr. Bulkey did not innoculate Webster for I heard Webster say he would not depend on Dr. Bulkey as his physician.
Israel Webster of Lebanon

for sale
For the benefit of the weak and sickly by Thomas Allen at his boarding house, in New London, choice Madeira wine, claret and

a soldier named Caley More; 24 years of age; 5 feet, 8 inches tall; brown hair; grey eyes; light complexion;

Notice by Samuel Richards that deserted from Captain Champion's Company of Col. Wylys' Regiment, a soldier named Charles Wiempay; born in Farmington; 6 feet high; straight and well proportioned; dark complexion; black long hair; black eyes;

Notice by Capt. Wills Clift that deserted from Col. Wylys's. Regiment, a soldier named Jedidiah Green; 5 feet, 11 inches high; black hair; dark eyes and complexion; about 24 years old; a well built fellow, slow of speech; belongs to Coventry and has left family there;

Notice by Capt. Jedidiah Hyde that deserted from his Company of Col. Durkee's Regiment, a soldier named John Rogers; 5 feet, 6 inches high; 19 years old; dark complexion; black hair and eyes; has had the smallpox; said he belonged to Updike's New Town in Rhode Island.

to stand stud
will cover at the stable of R. Mumford, two miles from New London on the Post Road to New York, the horse *Standy*; apply to Hugh Miner living near the premises.

administration of estates
Notice by Isaac Carrier, Administrator of the estate of Judah Saxton, deceased and late of Chatham, to those obligated to it to settle up;

Notice by Charles Eldridge, Jun. and Ebenezer Avery 3d, Commissioners appointed by the Probate Court of Stonington for the estate of Robert Dunlap, deceased and represented insolvent, late of Groton, to creditors that there will be a meeting to examine claims at the house of Edward Jeffery, Inn Holder in said Groton. All those indebted to the estate should make payment to John Williams, Administrator;

Notice by Thomas Johnson, Jun. and Joshua Johnson, Executors of the estate of Thomas Johnson, deceased and late of Middletown, to those obligated to it to settle up and to creditors to file claims.

strays
Notice by Jonathan Walker of Saybrook that two mares came into his enclosure.

to be sold
at public vendue all the real estate of Jonas Brewster, late of Preston; 70 acres of good land; a large dwelling house, barn, corn house and good orchard; the land is well proportioned for mowing, pasturing and woods; well watered; notice by James Braham, Administrator, Preston.

****

From *The Gazette*, May 30, 1777

enemy ships
Last Tuesday forenoon, one brig, two schooners and four sloops from the eastward went up the Sound.

prizes taken
Thursday se'nnight, Capt Conkling, in a privateer sloop from this port, New London, arriving at Bedford from a cruise and carried in a prize schooner with 7,000 gallons of rum, which he took on his passage from Dominica to Halifax.
Captain Conkling, sometime before, took another schooner loaded with fish bound from Halifax to the West Indies which he sent to Guadloupe where he sold her cargo.

died
Last Saturday died in Groton in the prime of his life, Lt. Jonathan Leeds of the State Brig *Defense*.

entertainment
The public are hereby notified that Daniel Hyde, late Inn Holder at Woodstock, has removed to Lebanon and opened house of

entertainment at the *Golden Ball,* just below the Meeting House where gentlemen travelers may be well accommodated with Diet, Liquor etc. as the present circumstances of the country will permit.

for sale
by John Gates in Groton, French indigo, pewter, fans, nutmeg, ribbons, snuff by the single pound or any other quantity for retailing, hard soap, allum, ginger, shoe buckles, sleeve buttons, coat and jacket buttons.

strayed or stolen
from Moses Peirce of Norwich Landing, a bay horse;

from Nathan Stedman, a light brown cow.

administration of estates
Notice by Capt. Thomas Holmes and Samuel Holmes, Administrators of the estate of Thomas Holmes, Jun., late of Stonington, to those obligated to it to settle up and to creditors to file claims.

deserted
Notice by Elisha Hinman that deserted from the Continental Ship *Alfred,* Perins Chapman; dark complexion; 4 feet and 5 and one half inches high; suppose to have gone to New London or Norwich as he has a wife in one of those places. He has received a considerable sum from me and lately enlisted in the Continental Army in Boston and deserted;

Notice by Elisha Hinman that deserted from the Continental Ship *Alfred,* Thomas Darby and James Little; supposed to have gone to New London as they married in that place;

Notice by Lt. Lemeul Clift in Plainfield that deserted from Captain John Megringer's Company of Col. Durkee's Regiment, a soldier named Oliver Plumbley; a straight built fellow; 26 years old; 5 feet, 10 inches high; dark complexion; short black hair and eyes; said he belongs to Uxbridge in Massachusetts.

found
40 shilling money in Hanover Parish Norwich; enquire of Nathan Bushnel, Jun., post rider.

****

From *The Gazette,* June 6, 1777

absconding Tories apprehended
A sloop, Daniel Rice, Master belonging to this place, New London, was last week taken off Fairfield by a boat from Capt. Hawley's privateer and carried into Fairfield on the presumption that the sloop was bound for New York. It appeared that the sloop had taken a cargo at Darby for this place but, when she was met by Capt. Hawley's boat, was standing for New York and had several Tory passengers on board. Rice and his passengers were committed to the Fairfield goal.
We hear that three other small vessels were taken about the same time and place and were carried into Black Rock and that 13 absconding Tories were found on board these vessels.

accidental shooting
Last Saturday, a young woman named Lydia Huntington was killed in Lebanon by the accidental discharge of a musket which was in the hands of another young woman.

lightning strike
Tuesday night, three cattle of Hez. Mitchell in Lyme were killed by lighting.

died
in Norwich, Mrs. Abigail Calkins, wife of Mr. Pember Calkins of that Town.

wanted
a couple of boys as apprentices for the nail making business; enquire of John Hertrell in New London.

strayed or stolen
from Andrew Wattles of Lebanon, a bright, white faced sorrel

mare;

from Daniel Dewy of Lebanon, a bay mare.

notice from Mendon Hospital
Samuel and Levi Willard advise all those who had applied to them for inoculation that there are no further inoculations until a more convenient season and return their hearty thanks to all those Gentlemen and Ladies who have obliged them by their custom.

farm for sale
52 choice acres for mowing and other improvement, lying in the parish of Millington; exceedingly well situated as a tavern, having been several years improved for that purpose; enquire of James Dickson on the premises.

found
on the road between Colchester and New London courthouse, a sum of money; apply to Asa Hendee of Bolton.

left
at the house of Nathan Douglas in New London, a pillow case, a riding hood and a pair of child's stockings.

deserted
Notice by Capt. Vine Elderkin that deserted from his Company of Col. Wift's Regiment, a soldier named Eleazer Wescot of Scituate in the state of Rhode Island; 5 feet, 7 inches tall; 23 years of age; light complexion; light colored hair and dark eyes;
also one James Wood of MarbleHead in Massachusetts; 5 foot, 4 inches high; between 20 and 30 years old; light colored hair and eyes and has a remarkable very long chin.

administration of estates
Notice by Freedom English, Administrator of the estate of Richard English, late of Lebanon, deceased, to those obligated to it to settle up and to creditors to file claims.

****

From *The Gazette,* June 13, 1777

report delinquents
The commanding officers of the military companies in the County of New London are notified to make returns of delinquents, which are by law returnable to the County Clerk, as soon as may be possible; by order of Winthrop Saltonstall, Clerk.

administration of estates
Notice by Eph. Carpenter, Administrator of the estate of Joshua Carpenter, late of Lebanon, deceased, to creditors to file claims and settle accounts;

Notice by Samuel Selden and Elisabeth Selden, Administrators of the estate of Samuel Selden, late of Lyme, deceased, to those obligated to it to settle up and to creditors to file claims;

Notice by Paul Wheeler, Executor f the estate of Cyrus Wheeler, late of Stonington, deceased, to those obligated to it to settle up and to creditors to file claims;

Notice by David Gardner, Executor of the estate of Benjamin Gardner, late of Norwich, deceased, to those obligated to it to settle up and to creditors to file claims.

primers for sale
wholesale and retail, to be sold at the Printing Office, near the store of Christopher Leffingwell in Norwich.

farm for sale
by order of the Probate Court of Stonington, all the personal and real estate of David Lester, late of Groton, deceased. The real estate consists of a good dwelling house, warehouse, wharf and shipyard; extremely well situated for ship building and has been for several years improved for that purpose; lying on the New London River, about a mile or so above the ferry; also about 24 acres, a barn, the house, the incumbrance of the Widow's Dower excluded; notice given by William Avery and Thomas Lester,

Administrators.

deserted
Notice by Lt. Dudley Wright that has deserted from Captain Allen's Company of Col. Wylys' Regiment, a soldier named William Hall, a native of Ireland, 5 feet, 9 inches tall; light complexioned; dark colored hair; blue eyes and about 25 years old.

strayed or stolen
from William M'Fall in Chesterfield in New London, a milch cow;

broke into the enclosure
of Joshua Raymond in New London, a heifer calf.

wanted
a large chaise horse, about 5 or 6 years old, for which a good price will be given; enquire of William Constant in New London.

****

From *The Gazette*, June 20, 1777

attack at Guilford
Last Tuesday, a party of men from three British ships, landed at Sachem's Head in Guilford, three or four miles from Town, where they burned a large dwelling house belonging to Mr. Leets; also two barns and carried off several cattle, calves and sheep. But the inhabitants being alarmed, the enemy made but a short tarry. The next morning, three ships from the westward passed this harbor and stood to the eastward. They doubtless were the same ships mentioned above and bound for Newport.

to gentlemen sailors and others
Now is the time for a fortune. There is bound on a cruise against the enemies of America, the Sloop of War *Two Brothers,* Thomas Chester, Commander, now laying at Groton and will sail in a few days; well known to be a prime sailor, completely equipped in a war like manner, mounting 12 carriage guns and furnished with

good provisions and stores. All suitable encouragement will be given to those inclined to enter by applying to said Capt. Chester on board at Groton.

bound
on a cruise against the enemies of America, the Sloop of War *Polly*, Eliphalet Roberts, Commander, now lying in the harbor New London; a great part of her men are engaged, but some able seamen and marines are still wanted, to whom all suitable encouragement will be given by applying to said Capt. Roberts at the *Golden Ball* in New London.

sale of prize vessels and cargo
Notice given by Winthrop Saltonstall, Register, that the libel filed before Samuel Coit, against the schooner *Britannia*, Obidiah Rogers; a sloop *Generous Friend,* and a schooner *Success,* Peleg Bordon, late master, Sloop *Polly,* late master James King; her boats, tackle, apparel, furniture and cargo, taken on the high seas by armed vessels and that the trial of such ship will be in Norwich on the 7th of July next.

administration of estates
Notice by Kezia Perkins, Executrix of the estate of Luke Perkins, late of Groton, deceased, to those obligated to it to settle up and to creditors to file claims;

Notice by John Felch and Wm. Bingham, Commissioners appointed by the Court of Probate of Plainfield for the estate of Andrew Lester, late of Canterbury deceased and represented to be insolvent, that a meeting of creditors will be held at the home of William Bingham in said Canterbury;

Notice by Samuel Dorrance and James Dorrance 3d, Commissioners appointed by the Probate Court of Plainfield for the estate of Stephen Jordan, late of Voluntown, deceased and represented insolvent, to those obligated to it to settle up and to creditors to file claims;

Notice by Eph. Carpenter Administrator of the estate of Joshua Carpenter, deceased, late of Lebanon, to those obligated to it to settle up and to creditors to file claims;

Notice by Ezra Selden, Administrator of the estate of Capt. Dan Marvin, deceased and late of Lyme, to those obligated to it to settle up and to creditors to file claims.

to be sold
at Public Vendue at the Court House in New London, a quantity of ivory, Irish linen, seamen's clothing, bean and ship bread;

Linseed oil to be sold at Printing Office;

by Joseph Knight in Enfield, Indigo, pepper, allspice and ginger.

found
in Killingworth, a bundle containing sundry articles of men and women's apparel; notice by Nathaniel Williams, Jun.

lost
Notice by Amos Stanton on the road from Preston to Groton between the house of Ebenezer Witter and Groton Ferry, 26 pounds, lawful money wrapped in paper. Please return to subscriber or Mr. Samuel Stanton 2d in Groton;

by Samuel Talman between Knox's and Eaton's on the Providence Road, a pocket book containing $60.

taken up
by Simeon Bingham of Norwich, below Waterman' Point in Norwich, a Moses boat, about 13 feet long.

strayed or stolen
from the enclosure of Dr. Elisha Tracy in Norwich, a black roan mare; notice given by Lydia Dorr;

from Patrick G. Pemberton of Preston, a chestnut colored horse.

broke into the enclosure
of Gideon Brokway of Lyme, a red yearling heifer;

of Joshua Raymond in New London, a heifer calf.

****

From *The Gazette,* June 27, 1777

New York prison ships
Last Wednesday evening, a flag of truce arrived from New York, Capt. Charles Bulkley was a passenger. He had been taken in a vessel belonging to this State and has been a prisoner in a guard ship at New York for the last three months past.

It appears that great numbers of our countrymen, who are so unhappy as to fall into the hands of the worse than savage Britons and put on board their guard ships, are forcefully taken and put on the cruising ships whenever they are wanted.. Twenty five were taken out of the ship that Captain was prisoner in, among them three who had been his hands.

trials of those disaffected
Last Tuesday, a special Superior Court was convened at Norwich to try number of person disaffected to the State.

died
after a long indisposition, Mrs. Elizabeth Deane, consort of Silas Deane, now in France, and daughter of Gen. Gurdon Saltonstall of this Town, New London.

administration of estates
Notice by Thomas Swift, Administrator of the estate of Elder Morgan, deceased and late of Mansfield, to those obligated to it to settle up and to creditors to file claims;

Notice by Asa Palmer, Administrator of the estate of Capt. Nathan Stanton, deceased and late of Stonington, to those obligated to it to settle up and to creditors to file claims.

wanted
a journeyman shoe maker; enquire of Thomas Jones in New London.

salt petre
At the Powder Mill in Windham, the Manufacturers and Inspectors of this important article are desired to be particularly careful that the same be pure, clean and dry as the Law directs.

to be sold
the hull of a brig, burthen about 100 tons; likewise her sails, rigging, cable, anchors etc; also a number of horses suitable for carriage or saddle; enquire of Oliver Smith of Stonington.

farms for sale
A large and commodious dwelling house, almost new and nearly finished; very convenient and well calculated for two families with a large blacksmith shop, a large barn, large and excellent garden; situated about 20 rods from the Court House in New London; enquire of Pember Calkins living on the premises;

At the house Oliver Helms, by the order of the Probate Court of Stonington, one half of a saw mill and a mortgage on a tract of land, 25 acres, lying in said Stonington near Pauquatuck Bridge and was under the estate of Lt. Samuel Brown, late of Westerly in the State of Rhode Island.

runaway
from Jonathan Lyon that a lad named Asa Lyon; 13 years of age; tall and slim for his age; dark complexion.

taken up
by John Lord, a black spotted sow in Lyme.

broke into the enclosure
of George Williams of New London, a black mare;

of Thomas Allen, Jun. on Mount Pleasant in New London, Great

Neck, a 4 year old steer;

of Noble Hinman, a horse; notice given by William Fielding;

of Thomas Wheeler of Stonington, a sorrel roan horse.

strayed or stolen
from Joel Phelps of Mansfield, a blackish or dark brown mare;

from Michael Foster of Sturbridge, twelve old sheep and ten lambs;

from John Wright in Colchester, 15 sheep;

from Samuel Bolles of New London, a 4 year old black horse.
****
From *The Gazette,* July 4, 1777

accident
Monday se'nnight, as a child of Ephraim Lyons of Canterbury was climbing an ash cart, which was leaning by a wall next to his father's house, the cart tilted forward and, falling on the child's head, killed him instantly.

notice to recruits
Notice by Ezra Lee of Lyme to all the Men in the Town of New London that are detailed to fill the Continental Army, that they must march by Monday, July 7, or they will be deemed deserters and treated accordingly.
If they want blankets or arms, they must apply to the Selectmen who are directed to furnish all such men with those articles that the other soldiers have.

ship seized
Last Wednesday, Captain Ezehiel Rogers in a small sloop returned from Huntington, Long Island. He was sent as a Flag from this port of New London and delivered a British prisoner on board the *Swan*. On his return, off Saybrook, he was boarded by a small

sloop tender to the British Sloop *Halifax*; the commander of which put Captain Rogers and his crew into the vessels's hold and preceded with it as far as Huntington. When they came in sight of the *Swan,* they let them go, after plundering him of six dollars, a pair of silver buckles and two pairs of breeches. This is piracy with a witness!

departure to England
The Flag of Truce mentioned in our last sailed from this port, New London, to New York last Wednesday, in which went passengers Duncan Stewart and Family, they having permission to remove to Great Britain.[22]

farm for sale
in Plainfield on the Country road, nigh the center of town, within about a quarter of a mile of the Meeting House; containing about 130 acres with a commodious dwelling house, two barns, corn house, chaise house; stock and farming utensils also for sale; apply to John Gady on the premises.

fire
Yesterday se'nnight, the dwelling house of Samuel Richards of this town, New London, took fire on the roof by a spark from the chimney, which grew a considerable head before it was discovered; the house with the greatest part of its goods was consumed.

list of letters
Nathaniel Adams, Jun. - Groton,
Simeon Burke, - Groton
Madam Chret, - Windham
Nathan Dubolt, Jun - Groton
William Havens - Stonington
Eliphalet Hobart - Stonington
Thomas J Jackson -

Stonington
William Morgan, - Norwich
Richard Masters, - Windham,
Joshua Raymond - New London
Capt. Amos Stockholm

administration of estates
Notice by Thomas Swift, Administrator of the estate of Elihu Morgan, late of Manfield, deceased, to those obligated to it to settle up and to creditors to file claims;

Notice by Thomas Williams, Administrator of the estate of Robert Dunlap, late of Groton, that there will be a sale of the estate of deceased consisting of wearing apparel and sundry other articles; the sale is to be at the Administrator's house.

wanted
a quantity of green or dry lamb or sheep skins with the wool, for which cash will be paid, or good felt hats given in exchange by Abilzer Smith at his shop at Norwich Landing.

found
by George Williams of New London, a large cedar battoe, supposed to have drifted away from its owner.

taken up
in New London, a Negro man who says his name is Primus and that he belongs to Abraham Case of West Simsbury.

runaway
from James Stedman in Windham, a Negro man named Sharper; about 17 years of age; 5 feet high.

broke into the enclosure
of Abraham Lomis in Lebanon, a black mare.

strayed or stolen
from Samuel Bolles of New London, a black horse
****

From *The Gazette*, July 11, 1777

lightning
Three sheep were killed by lightning near the house of Mr. Caleb Lomis in Colchester on the 8th inst.

execution set
The sixth of next month is set for the execution of John Dennis of this Town, who was convicted at the Superior Court held in Norwich of murdering one William Garrick.

troops arrive
Part of Col. Ely's Battalion of newly raised troops has arrived here since our last.

died
On the 30th ult., died in Norwich, after a tedious illness that was brought on by small pox, Mr. Simeon Lester in the 43rd year of his life. Mr. Lester has left a widow and seven children to lament him;

in New London, Mr. John Bolles. It is apprehended that he left a will in the hands of some people unknown to his heirs; whom they would like to come forward.

wool cards
will be given in exchange for sheep skins by Jeremiah Clement in Norwich.

deserted
Notice by Lt. Lemuel Clift that has deserted from Captain Megriegier's Company of Col. Durkee's Regiment, a soldier named John Clark; says he belonged to Saybrook; enlisted at Plainfield; appears to have been an honest fellow, about 20 years old; 5 feet, 10 inches high; light colored hair and eyes; dark complexion.

administration of estates
Notice by Benjamin Hoxsie, Jun., Administrator of the estate of John Goodbody, deceased and late of Charlestown, Rhode Island, to those obligated to it to settle up and to creditors to file claims.

to be sold
by Thomas Allen Jun. on Mt. Pleasant in Great Neck, New

London, three gentle saddle horses.

farm for sale
commodious and well situated dwelling house, with garden spot, barn, and horse shed, belonging to Zebulon Eliot; for many years it was the Ferry House and Tavern on the beach; all in good repair; also a boat, 22 feet keel, well found and a prime sailor.

prize vessels to be sold
Notice by Prosper Wetmore, Marshall, that to be sold at auction at Stonington Point, the following prize vessels: the sloops *Generous Friend, Happy Return, Britannia,* and *Success.*

lost
by Nathan Belcher between Mr. Leffingwell's shop in Norwich and Lt. Ebenezer Bishop's of Newent, a black leather pocket book;

on the road between New London and Norwich, a woman's white round hat; whoever returns it to General Parsons' house in Lyme will be well rewarded.

****

From *The Gazette,* July 18, 1777

American vessels seized
Captain Bigelow, belonging to the Connecticut River, is taken in the West Indies. Captain Palmer in a small privateer from Stonington is taken and carried into Newport. Captain Stilman from Connecticut River (Mr. Jacob Sebord, Jun., Supercargo) is taken and carried to New York.

enemy vessels taken
Last Friday, a prize brig was sent into this port (New London), taken by the sloop *Trumbull*, Capt. Henry Billings from this port. She had 5,000 or 6000 weight of coffee and some other articles on board. Another brig, taken at the about the same time by the same privateer, with 98 hogsheads of rum has arrived at Marble Head.

American success
Captain Samuel Champlin in the sloop *American Revenue* of this port, in company with a smaller privateer, has taken a large ship with 439 hogsheads of sugar which arrived in a safe port. The above privateers were in sight of 5 or 6 ships.

prisoner
Last Tuesday, General Prescott, who was lately taken prisoner at Rhode Island, was brought to Lebanon from Providence under guard.

Dutch shipping seized
By Captain Latham, we learn that all Dutch vessels having American produce on board, bound to Europe or elsewhere, are taken by the British cruisers, alleging that all such produce is British property.

rejoin Regiment
Notice by Col. John Ely to soldiers to rejoin their Regiment at New London.

administration of estates
Notice by Elias Worthington, John Henry and Asa Daniels Commissioners appointed by the Probate Court of the District of East Haddam for the estate of Deacon Thomas Gustin, late of Colchester, deceased and represented to be insolvent, that a meeting of creditors will be held at the house of the deceased. Accounts must be well attested.

deserted
Notice by Lt. Pownall Deming that John Smith, a transient person, has deserted from Captain Andrew Finch's Company of Col. Durkee's Regiment, about 26 years old, somewhat pock broken; 5 feet 9 inches tall, well built, blue eyes, light hair, almost bald; supposed to have enlisted on the *Cromwell* or gone off into the country in company of a large fat woman, light hair and complexion whom he called his wife.

Notice by Lt. Richard Chapman that has deserted from Captain Nathan Palmer's Company of Col. Ely's Regiment, a soldier named Joshua Wilson, a transient person; about 20 years old; 5 feet, 7 inches high; light complexion.

****

From *The Gazette,* July 25, 1777

sails on horizon
Last Sabbath, about six o'clock in the afternoon, twenty three sail appeared westward of this harbor, coming down the Sound with a fair breeze and it was apprehended that they may be bound into the harbor. Alarm guns were fired and the troop got under arms, but it soon appeared they were headed further east and, by sunset, they had passed the western point of Fisher's Island.
Capt. Niles in the armed schooner *Spy* had been watching the motion of the above fleet from the time they came through Hell Gate[23] and arrived at the harbor's (New London's) mouth just about the time the fleet moved past. He had several shots fired at him when near Goshen Reef, but at too great a distance to have injured him. Capt. Niles learned from a deserter in the fleet, whom he brought in with him, that the above were a fleet of victualers, bound for England under the convoy of *Niger* Frigate and that they had orders to touch on Newport. It is said there were a considerable number of invalids on board.

married
at Colchester Capt. Joseph Packwood of this Town, New London, Merchant to Miss Demise Wright, daughter of Capt. Dudley Wright, a young lady of most amiable disposition and great beauty, possessing every accomplishment that can tend to the felicity of the connubial state.

pay is ready
Notice to the officers of the Regiments, lately commanded by Col. Throop and by Col. Latimer that the money due them is ready for payment with the late quartermaster.

muster
Notice to officers and men in the Brigantine *Resistance*, Samuel Chew, Commander, are desired to repair on board as the brig will certainly sail with ten days. Any seaman with an inclination to serve on board should apply to said Chew or to Nathaniel Shaw, Continental Agent in New London.

just published and to be sold
by Green & Spooner, near the store of Christopher Leffingwell in Norwich, a new edition of Dr. Watt's *Divine Songs for the use of Children*, where also may be had Primers and a variety of pamphlets, wholesale or retail.

deserted
Notice by Robert Niles, Captain of the Schooner *Spy*, that a sailor, named Jonathan Rudd, deserted; he is about 22 or 23 years old; son of Samuel Rudd, Inn Holder in Norwich; he is of dark complexion, short black hair and dark colored eyes.
****
From *The Gazette*, August 1, 1777

ship movements
Saturday noon, seven sail of British shipping, under convoy of a Man of War, from Newport went up the Sound.
Saturday, Captain Niles of the schooner *Spy* returned from a cruise in the Sound and brought in with him an empty sloop, burthen about 80 tons, which was in company with the above fleet, bound to Long Island for wood and another sloop loaded with that article, both taken by Captain Niles and Captain Conkling.

died
last Wednesday in this town, New London, Capt. Benjamin Branson, late a prisoner who, a few days before, arrived here from Newport, in a flag of truce with a number of others. He appeared to be about 30 years old.

taken
from a stake in Fisher's Island, a two masted vessel; notice by

John Brown of New London.

wanted
a number of ship carpenters to work on the Continental ship building in the Norwich River; good wages will be given; apply at Joshua Huntington's store at Norwich Landing.

runaway
from Daniel Denison 3d of Stonington, a Negro man named Orford, belonging to the estate Capt. Daniel Denison, late of Stonington, deceased.

strayed
from Ephraim Miner of New London, a brown mare.

for sale
snuff and snuff boxes, taps, buckles, combs, pewter, coat buttons, pins, needles to be sold by Solomon Lord in Saybrook, near the Meeting House.

****

From *The Gazette*, August 8, 1777

abuse of prisoners
Last Saturday, a flag of truce arrived here with a number of poor emaciated languishing prisoners from Newport, whose deplorable condition, one would think, were sufficient to excite the commiserations of the most barbaric savage, but alas the hearts of our enemies seem to be callous to every sentiment of humanity. The more than brutal policies of our enemies is to debilitate the bodies and ruin the constitutions of their prisoners, only to leave enough life in them to answer an exchange, although many die in this unheard of operation which is performed by starvation. One of the above prisoners, Capt. Moses Parsons of Cape Ann, died in two hours after he was taken on the truce vessel and was buried in Stonington. Samuel Kilby of Cohasset in Massachusetts, Nathan Solly, and Francis Irons of Cape May, were carried to lodgings in this town, New London, where they lie dangerously sick. The others feeble as they were managed to crawl from town to town

until they might get home.

execution
Last Wednesday was executed in Norwich, John Dennis of this Town, Mariner, for the murder of William Barrick, as has been mentioned. He has left a widow and five small children.

prize taken
Capt. Champlin, in the *American Revenue* privateer of this Port, has sent into a safe port a prime schooner with 220 hogsheads of rum. This is the third prize, out of five taken by him, that arrived safe. The others are not yet given over.

prizes sold
Notice by John Hudson that a meeting will be held at the house of John Denison of Stonington Point for all persons who have any concern in the prizes taken by the Sloop *Revenge*, Joseph Conkling, Commander.

Libels filed before Hon. Samuel Coit in New London against the sloop *Ferguson*, Christopher Allen, late master, her cargo, boats, tackle, apparel and furniture, taken on the high seas by Robert Niles, Commander of the armed schooner *Spy* and Joseph Conkling, Commander of the armed sloop *Revenge*; notice by Wm. Saltonstall.

administration of estates
Notice by Asa Foot, Noah Pomroy and John Wright, Commissioners appointed by the Probate Court East Haddam, to the estate of Charles Clark, late of Colchester, deceased and represented to be insolvent, to those obligated to it to settle up and to creditors to file claims; a meeting will be held at the home of Dudley Wright of said Colchester.
N. B. The report of the last Commissioners on said estate being disapproved by said Judge.

****

From *The Gazette,* August 15, 1777

wanted immediately
by William Lax of Norwich, a journey man wheelwright who thoroughly understands the business. He also wants a smart active boy, about 14 years of age as an apprentice.

lightning
Last week, a barn belonging to Mr. Wheeler in Mohegan was struck by lightning and consumed.

taxes
Notice by Peter Strickland, Tax Collector, to advise all inhabitants of New London who are obliged to pay taxes, that the places for payment are set for the houses of:
Nathan Douglas on September 1
James Hughes on September 2
Dr. Seth Holmes on September 3
Jason Allen on September 4
Joseph Prentis on September 5
Benjamin Gorton on September 8
Capt. Stephen Prentis on September 9
Thomas Harris on September 10

deserted
Notice by Lt. Elisha Bottom that deserted from Captain James Smith's Company of Col. Ely's Regiment, a soldier named Isaac James, belonging to Voluntown; a pretty well set fellow; about 22 years of age; dark complexion; dark gray eyes; black hair.

broke into the enclosure
of John Hough of Canterbury, 3 two year old cattle.

taken up adrift
in Norwich River between Gales Ferry and Mammocock, an old chestnut canoe; apply to John Sheperd in New London.

runaway
from Christopher Newton, Jun. of Groton, an apprentice boy named Christopher Allyn; in his 15th year; light complexion; small of stature.

****

From *The Gazette*, August 22, 1777

lighting strikes
Friday evening, a severe thunderstorm passed over this town, New London, when a flask of lightning struck a tree standing at the door of Mr. Jonathan Starr's house and knocked to the ground sundry persons who were in that and the neighboring houses. Four soldiers at the same time passing over the Long Bridge were struck down. So severe was the shock that several persons at the distance of 30 rods from each other were considerably affected by it, but happily no lives were lost.
The same night, a barn at Stonington, belonging to Mr. Palmer, was consumed by lightning.

British blockade
Saturday evening, last Capt. Jehiel Tinker in a small privateer, belong to East Haddam, a small sloop, John Harris, Master, and a large boat belonging to Mr. Peter Rogers of this town, New London, were all drove on shore at Narraganset Beach by one of the enemy's ships. And, at about the same time, a sloop, John Keney, Master and Owner belonging to this place, New London, was taken by a boat from a British Man of War near Block Island; the people took to their boat and landed on that island and have since got to the main land.

notice to report
Whereas a number of soldier belonging to Col. Prentices's Regiment have not as yet joined the Regiment, this is to give notice to all such who belong to the towns of Lyme, New London, Groton, Stonington, Preston and East Haddam to appear in Lyme on the 27th instant and those in the other towns repair to Norwich and be ready to march. Those at Norwich are to apply Ens. Darius Peck for orders and those at Lyme to Lt. Enoch Reed; all these

who neglect to attend will be considered deserters; by order of Brig. General Parsons by Lt. Enoch Reed.

farm for sale
at Public Vendue in Groton on the Norwich River; just above Gale's Ferry; a commodious; dwelling house and orchards; well watered and fenced; was formerly owned by Jonathan Williams. For terms, apply to Nathan Avery in Groton.

administration of estates
Notice by John Richards, Samuel Latimer and Richard Deshon, Commissioners appointed by the Probate Court of New London of the estate of Maj. James Chapman, late of New London, deceased and represented to be insolvent, to those obligated to it to settle up and to creditors to file claims.

taken up
by Andrew Perkins at Norwich Landing, a small boar hog;

by Daniel Whitemore of Middletown, a chestnut colored mare.

deserted
Notice by Capt. Thomas Arnold that has deserted from his Company on the march from Coventry to Peek's Kill, Moses Smith; 17 years of age; 5 feet, 11 inches tall; blue eyes; brown hair; light complexion; a tanner by trade; born in Scituate, Rhode Island.

salt needed
Those who are manufacturers of salt are hereby informed that cash and a generous price will be given by Roswell Saltonstall at his Distilhouse in New London for that kind of salt usually known by the name of pudding salt.

settle accounts
All those who have an account open with the late Commissary John Deshon are desired to bring them in for settlement in New London, as he is removing to Boston.

ran away
from James Sheffield of New London, an apprentice named Asa Crandal.

****

From *The Gazette*, August 29, 1777

wants employment
in Town or country, a young man that can be well recommended, long practiced in teaching reading and writing the English tongue grammatically, vulgar and decimal arithmetic, extractions of the roots, surveying and navigation; also a new concise method of writing shorthand. For particulars, enquire of the Printer in New London.

linen yarn needed
Zurishhaddai Key, tape weaver from Manchester, is setting up his shop in Norwich and wants to purchase a quantity of linen yarn; apply to said Key or Elisha Lathrop3d at Norwich Landing.

warning
Notice by James Rogers of New London that, whereas there is a great quantity of stock, such as horses, cows, sheep, hogs, poultry and also a quantity of household furniture and farming utensils on my farm in Great Neck, New London, under lease to William and Collins Gorton, which stock I have attached for my security and, whereas I apprehend that said Gorton might attempt to sell such stock, furniture and utensils and thereby deprive me of my security. I do hereby forbid any person buying such stock, as I shall claim all the same from whomever shall purchase.

broke into
the enclosure of Jedidiah Beckwith in Chesterfield, Lyme, two cows.

runaway
from Stephen Potter of South Kensington Rhode Island, an Indian woman servant, about 25 years of age, about 5 feet high and something thick, has a remarkable scar under her jaw, occasioned,

as is supposed, by the King's Evil[24] and also a scar on the pit of her stomach; supposed to have been born somewhere in Lyme and Saybrook and called her name, when there, as Martha Occum.

taken up
on the South side of Fisher' Island by Paul Burrows of Groton, a cedar or pine canoe, 12 or 14 feet long.

stockings needed
Thomas Mumford of Groton continues to purchase yarn stockings for the army. They prefer white, which being the natural color, must be cheaper to the manufacturer.

hair needed
cash given for men and women' hair and for white horse hair by J. Jennings at his shop in Windham. Said Jennings carries on the business of making wigs as usual.

important meeting called
Notice by John Elderkin, Clerk, to the members of the Committee of Inspection and Correspondence for the Town of Groton that there will be a meeting at the house of Jonas Belton in said Groton to consult and determine on some matters of importance, respecting the welfare of the United States.

workmen wanted
Good encouragement will be given by Peleg Hyde and Edmund Barrow in Norwich to eight or ten journeymen nail makers and one who is acquainted with edge tools; also three or four boys wanted as apprentices to nail making business.

****

From *The Gazette*, September 5, 1777

prizes to be sold
Notice by Prosper Wetmore, Marshall that there will be sold at Norwich Landing three prize vessel and cargos, namely, the Brig *Generous Friend,* Sloop *Ferguson* and a sloop of about 70 tons, name unknown.

administration of estates
Notice by Ebenezer Spencer and Timothy Gates, Commissioners appointed the Probate Court of East Haddam to the estate of Joseph Sluman, deceased and represented insolvent, that a meeting will be held at Mr. Joseph Emons, Inn Holder in East Haddam;

Notice by Mary Mighells, Executrix of the estate of John Mighells, deceased, late of Chatham, to those obligated to it to settle up and to creditors to file claims.

trials
The County Court for the County of New London will sit in New London for the trial of those persons who were returned by the several militia officers for not complying with orders when detached; by order. Wm. Saltonstall, Clerk.

broke into
the enclosure of Caleb Lomis 2d, a gray horse.

strayed or stolen
from S. Juteson in Chatham 12 sheep; notice by John Ward, Chatham.

taken up
by Samuel Beckwith of East Haddam, a red heifer calf.

ran away
from George Beckwith of Lyme, a Negro man named London; about 25 years old; a pretty well set fellow; about 5 feet 5 inches tall; his fore teeth very much gone; speaks pretty good English; is naturally bashful.

left in the store
of Edward Hallam, sometime since, owner unknown, one barrel of flour and one bed. It is supposed to belong to an officer or soldier.

died at Groton
Mrs. Edridge, wife of. Mr. Charles Eldridge and daughter of Col. Ebenezer Avery.

list of letters left in New London Post office

Nathaniel Adams - Groton
John Barber - Groton
Amos Babcock - Voluntown
Simon Butler - Groton
– Bellows - Groton
Abiel Brown - Granville or Bedford
Timothy Beckwith - New London
Miriam Cheets - Windham
Elizabeth Davis - Mansfield
Rev Nathaniel Eels - Stonington
Daniel Eldridge - Groton
Christopher Eldridge - Stonington
Samuel Graves - Stonington
William Havens - Stonington
Ezckiel Hayes - New London
Elisha Lewis - Farmington
Thomas Lewis - Farmington
John Mott - Canterbury
Samuel Newton - Groton
Charles Phelps - Stonington
John Earle - Stonington
Zeb Sabin - Killingly
Wm. Turner - Ship *Trumbull*
Stephen Tinker - New London
Nathan Thompson - Windham
Capt. John Vail - New London

****

From *The Gazette*, September 12, 1777

traitors jailed
Saturday, two men, who were detected in transporting some Tories to Long Island, were sent from Killingsworth and committed goal in this town, New London.

representatives chosen
Last Tuesday, William Hillhouse and Winthrop Saltonstall were chosen to represent this Town (New London) in the General Assembly.

strayed or stolen
from the door of Mr. David Richards of New London; a white mare; reward to whoever brings it to William Skinner of New London or to the Printing Office;

from Thomas Hall in East Haddam, a bay mare;

from Robinson Mumford in New London, a dark sorrel mare. Mr Mumford also has to sell a cider mill and press; also a yoke of two year old steers;

from Joshua Grant of Stonington, a 2 year old heifer.

farm for sale
a commodious dwelling house, two stories high with very convenient rooms and a lot of 26 rods of land contiguous to it; also a large two story home, very convenient for a Merchant; also a stable next door to John Denison's Tavern upon Stonington Long Point; apply to Simeon Hiscox on the premises.

passage boat
Notice by Nathaniel Dyer that he will ply from Stonington Point to New London in a convenient boat for that purpose once a week, which will be on Friday; apply to the subscriber in Stonington or to Mr. Zebulon Elliot in New London.

administration of estates
Notice by William Avery and Thomas Lester, Administrators of the estate of David Lester, deceased and late of Groton, to creditors to meet at the house Mr. Edward Jeffrey in said Groton.

tax collector coming
Notice to all the inhabitants of the Town of Lyme, who are obliged to pay taxes, that they can be received on the dates specified at the houses of Col. Marshfield Parsons, Edward Champlin, Widow Mary Lee, Jesse Beckwith, Abner Griffing, Capt. Abner Comstock and Daniel Lord; notice by Nathaniel Matson, Tax Collector.

****

From *The Gazette*, September 19, 1777

prizes taken
Tuesday se'nnight, the ship *Oliver Cromwell*, Seth Harding, belonging to this State, arrived from Boston on a cruise and brought in a prize ship, which was bound from Jamaica to London, as a packet. She mounted 16 carriage guns, had about 50 men and several passengers among whom is the Captain of a 50 gun ship. She had on board a considerable number of dollars and a quantity of wrought plate.
Captain Conkling of the Privateer *Revenge* of this port, New London, has taken a brig from Dominica to Newfoundland with 30 hogsheads of rum on board, which is arrived in a safe port. This vessel, we learn, a few days before she arrived spoke with a snow with 427 hogsheads of rum on board, prize to Capt. Staples in a privateer from New Haven.

libels filed
before Hon. Samuel Coit in New London against a sloop, name unknown and her cargo, boats, tackle, apparel and furniture, taken on the high seas by Robert Niles, Commander of the armed schooner *Spy*; also a libel in favor of William Briggs, Commander of the Schooner *Charming Sally*, fitted out by Mr. Alex Roe and Co. against the Sloop *John* lately under the command of Remembrance Simons; notice by Wm. Saltonstall.

for sale
at Stonington Long Point by Andrew Brown, 40 new hogsheads and the same number of barrels;

officer hangers, made in the neatest manner and on hand to be sold by Samuel Buel, opposite the Town House in Middletown.

taken up
by Daniel Harris in New London on the east end of Fisher's Island, a white pine canoe.

lost
on road from New London courthouse and Collins Gorton's house in Great Neck, a good saddle; whoever returns it shall have a reward and a bowl of egg punch.

administration of estates
All persons having any demands on the estate of Simeon Lester are to bring their accounts to Mary Lester, Adminstratrix.

broke into the enclosure
of Nathan Baxter of Hebron, a dark brown 2 year old steer.

settle up
All those indebted to James Morton, late of the city of New York, Merchant, are requested to make payment to Pierpont Edwards of New Haven.

deserters
Notice by Lt. Asa Lyon that has deserted from Captain Keys' Company of Col. Ely's Regiment, a solder named Aholiab Branch, who lately lived in Killingly; he was supposed to have enlisted in Providence under Lt. Zedock Williams;

Notice by Lt. Simeon House that has deserted from Captain Wm. Richards' Company of Lt. Col. Prentice's Regiment, a soldier named John Wrightbee; 5 foot, 4 inches tall; brown hair and blue eyes, one leg crooked by being broke; a scar on one cheek; a weaver by trade.

****

From *The Gazette*, September 26, 1777

retraction
Whereas Mr. Lee Pech was advertised by Capt. Jabez Blebs as having deserted his Company, which was then stationed at Fort Trumbull in New London. The advertisement was caused by false information and his absence was occasioned by unavoidable sickness.

deserted
Notice by Samuel Chew that has deserted from the Brig *Resistance,* Samuel Culver; a lusty well set man and is supposed to be lurking around Groton.

administration of estates
Notice by Jonas Green of Milford, Executor of the estate of Samuel Green, deceased and late of New London, to those obligated to it to settle up and to creditors to file claims;

Notice by John Bolles, Administrator of the estate of John Bolles, deceased and late of New London, to those obligated to it to settle up and to creditors to file claims.

rags wanted
Cash given for clean cotton and linen rags at the Printing office.
****
From *The Gazette,* October 3, 1777

to taxpayers in East Haddam
All the inhabitants of the Town of East Haddam, who are obliged to pay taxes, are advised that they can make payment at the houses of Joseph Emmerson, Capt. Ichabod Olmsted, Capt. Cone and at Capt. John Hite on the dates and times specified; notice by Robert Hungerford, Collector of Taxes.

administration of estates
Notice by Powell Holmes, Executor of the estate of James Holmes, deceased and late of South Kingston, to those obligated to it to settle up and to creditors to file claims.

broke into the enclosure
of Amos Murdock of Lebanon, a 3 year old horse of a reddish color;

of Nodiah Fuller of East Haddam, a black colt.

strayed or stolen
from Thomas Hall of East Haddam, a bay mare;

in New London from Stephen Johnson of Lyme, a chestnut colored mare, a natural pacer

deserted
Notice by Lt. Nathaniel Chapman that has deserted from Captain Parsons' Company of Col. Webb's Regiment, a soldier named Nathaniel Rose of Coventry; 5 feet, 10 inches tall; well set; light hair; light complexion; 32 years old;

Notice by Lt. Daniel Wait that deserted from Captain Elisha Lee's Company of Col. Durkee's Regiment, a transient person who calls himself David Wilson; thick set fellow; 5 foot, 6 inches high; light hair and eyes; crooked nose; a tough looking fellow and much given to drink; is a Scotch man and has all the appearances of a sailor; by trade, a nailer.

****

From *The Gazette,* October 10, 1777

prize ship
A few days since, arrived at a safe port, a valuable prize ship loaded with sugar and cotton and said to be valued at 60,000 pounds, taken by the *Raleigh,* Capt. Tompson and the *Alfred,* Capt. Hinman, two ships of war belonging to the State.

British frigate damaged
We learn that the *Galactia,* a British Frigate arrived at Newport a few days since, in order to repair the damage she sustained in an engagement with the *Randolph* Continental Frigate, commanded by Capt. Biddle.

boat swamped
One day last week, a boat in which there were eight militia men from the State of Rhode Island was overset at Narraganset by running on a rock and all were drowned.

died
at Plainfield, the Rev. Mr. Fuller of that place.

letters left at New London Post Office

John H. Brown - Stonington
Ritner Chapman - New London
William Dunphy - New London
James Davis - Stonington
Betsy Dunlop - New London
Morris Fowler - New London
Capt. John Holmes - Stonington
Burnet Miller - Stonington
Thomas Manning - Stonington
Arthur Myers - Norwich
Charles Miner, Jun. - Stonington
Wait Rathbone - Stonington
Nathan Spicer - New London
Benj Stedmin - Groton
William Tinker - New London
John Wheeler - Stonington

for sale
by Abel Pierce of Plainfield, the Proprietors' Settling Right in the Township of Plymouth in the Susquehanna Purchase[25], one of the first towns settled on the river, containing upwards of 20 acres of intervale, a 10 acre plot for a house lot and two other divisions, in total 200 acres within 2 miles of river and which has for the past three or four years produced several hundred bushels of Indian Corn, besides other grains and grass.

broke into the enclosure
of Elisha Tyler of Preston, North Society, five cattle.

to be sold
in New London the prize Sloop *John* and her appurtenances; also a prize sloop laden with wood; per order of Prosper Wetmore, Marshall.

lost
Notice by Hezekiah Merril of Hartford that he lost on the road between Norwich and Plainfield, a small silver watch, watch

maker's name John Arthur, Liverpool.

stolen
out of the stable of Nicholas Miller at Kinderhock, a bay mare about 14 hands high; notice by Collins Gorton, New London, Great Neck.

libels
Notice given by Wm. Saltonstall, that a libel has been filed before Hon. Samuel Coit in New London in favor of Nathaniel Shaw Jun. against the ship *Amherst,* Jason Landon, Master, and its cargo. It was taken on the high seas by the armed Sloop *Revenge,* Capt. Conkling;
also a libel in favor of said Shaw and Joseph Conkling, Commander of the armed sloop *Revenge,* against the cargo, boats, tackle, apparel and furniture of the Brigatine *William,* Henry Davis, Master, taken on the high seas;
another libel also in favor of said Shaw and Conkling against cargo, boats, tackle, apparel and furniture of the armed Schooner *Halifax,* taken on the high seas.

rags
It is wished that more attention would be be paid by every family to the saving of rags for, without that article, our schools and the press would be destitute of paper[26]. There are rags in the country sufficient to answer every purpose, if those who throw them in their fire or sweep them out doors, could be prevailed to deposit them in a basket or bag and, when five or six pounds or any larger quantity is collected, a market is ready for them. Although the price is not high, the satisfaction of having served the country, as well as benefit to themselves, ought to be sufficient inducement to every family in the area.

farm for sale
in New Hartford by Elisha Russel 10, 20, 30, 40 or 50 head of horned cattle, also a dwelling house, 40 feet or thereabout, with one acre of land, well situated for a merchant or trader; situated in the town of Goshen, County of Litchfield, on the great road to

Albany.

runaway
from Matthew Tallcott of Middletown, a large Negro man; about 20 years of age.

****

From *The Gazette,* October 17, 1777

damaged ship returns
Last Lord's Day returned into port, the Privateer Sloop *Two Brothers*, Capt. Thomas Chester, having in latitude 34 suffered considerable damage to her rigging from a British Transport of much superior force and full of men. Capt. Chester had one man killed and three injured.

prisoner exchange
Wednesday last, about 30 seaman taken in the *Weymouth* Packet, by Capt. Harding in the ship, *Oliver Cromwell,* arrived in Town (New London), who, with 152 other prisoners, were put on board a flag of truce, which yesterday sailed from New York to be exchanged for a like number of our men.

administration of estates
Notice by William Stewart and Marvin Wait, Commissioners, appointed by the Probate Court of New London for the estate of Capt. Edward Palmes, late of New London, deceased and represented to be insolvent, for those obligated to the estate to settle up and to creditors to file claims.

runaway
from Daniel Shaw of East Haddam, Millington Society, a Negro man named Martin; about 28 years old; is very small for his age, not very black, walks very much catharpened; when he stands still, he stands bracing with knees close together.

strayed or stolen
from John Johnson of Lyme, a steer.

notice
by Lt. Col. Marshfield Parsons to all officers of the 3rd Regiment to receive new commissions.

just published and to be sold
by T. Green, Roman's *Map of the State of Connecticut and parts of New York, New Jersey and islands adjacent.*

clothier
notice by John Goold, clothier, that he is carrying on that business at the shop of Mr. Matthew Sears, about a half mile from Chapman's Ferry in East Haddam.
****
From *The Gazette*, October 24, 1777

mutiny
The flag mentioned in our last to have sailed for New York was, the night after, forced onto shore at Crane's Island, Long Island, by the prisoners, 37 out of 45 of whom, took the vessel from the Captain and, after robbing her provisions, made heir escape on the Island, purposely to avoid the man of war. The remainder were taken on board the *Scorpion*, Capt. Brown, the flag being stopped by him from proceeding to New York. If any of the prisoners should make their escape to the main land, it is hoped that they will be retaken and secured that they may still be sent to New York to redeem our unhappy country men confined there.
Misfortunes of this nature may be prevented by confining the prisoners to a prison ship, there to remain until our enemy should send a vessel to redeem them.

wanted
by Peter Mumford in Pomfret, a quantity of well cleaned flax seed for which will be given two dollars a barrel. The sooner it is delivered, the better. Said Mumford lives in the house lately belonging to Thomas Cotton.

taken up
in the Sound by Richard Deshon of New London, a wrecked or

damaged sloop about 40 tons burthen; towed into Stonington.

deserted
Notice by Capt. James Green that has deserted from his Company of Col. Hyde's Regiment, a soldier named Benjamin Gary of Lebanon; well built fellow; about 5 feet, 10 inches tall; dark complexion; brown hair; about 30 years old.

lost
on the road between Pomfret Church and Mr. Buchanan's tavern, an gold sleeve button with a basket of flowers engraved thereon;

by Elijah Dyar of Canterbury on the road between John Dyar's and James Cobb's, on the main road to Canterbury, a string of gold beads;

by Daniel Collins on the road between Palmer Meeting House and landlord Danielson's, a white linen coat and a jacket; please deliver to Landlord Bliss' in Palmer.

administration of estates
Notice by Daniel Brainerd and Prudence Brainerd, Administrators of the estate of Daniel Brainerd, deceased and late of East Haddam, to those obligated to it to settle up and to creditors to file claims.

strayed or stolen
from Jedidiah Strong of Lebanon, a bay horse;

from Matthew Adgain of Norwich, a bay mare;

from John Champlin in New London, a black horse.

runaway
from John Rose of South Kingston, Rhode Island, a Negro man named Ned; about 20 years of age; well built and very black; 5 feet, 10 inches tall; speaks hoarse; has a scar over his right eye.

broke into enclosure
of Morris Fowler in New London, Great Neck, a brindled colored bull.

****

From *The Gazette*, October 31, 1777

administration of estates
Notice by Samuel Ely, Nathaniel Matson and Abner Comstock, Commissioners appointed by the Probate Court of Lyme for the estate of Samuel Phelps, late of Lyme, deceased and represented to be insolvent, to those obligated to it to settle up and to creditors to file claims; a hearing is to be held at Samuel Phelps house in Lyme;

Notice by Samuel Ely, Nathaniel Matson and Abraham Pirkins, Commissioners appointed by the Probate Court of Lyme regarding the estate of Charles Phelps, late of Lyme, deceased and represented to be insolvent, to those obligated to it to settle up and to creditors to file claims; a hearing is to be held at the house of Charles Phelps in Lyme;

Notice by Ebenezer Hartshorn, Administrator of the estate of David Hartshorn 3d, deceased and late of Norwich, to those obligated to it to settle up and to creditors to file claims; a hearing to be held at the home of Ebenezer Hartshorn in Norwich.

farm for sale
in Chesterfield Parish in Lyme, half a mile from the Meeting house, a good grist mill, about 80 or 90 acres, well watered with springs of water; excellent soil for wheat and grass; dwelling house, barn; enquire of Eushbius Bushness, living on said premises.

to taxpayers of Chatham, East Haddam
All the inhabitants of the Town of Chatham, East Haddam who are obliged to pay taxes, are advised that they can be received at the houses of Thomas Williams, Gideon Arnold, John Wright, Jun., Captain Bush, Dr. Moses Bartlet and Jeremiah Goodmen on the

dates and times specified; notice by Samuel Taylor, Collector of Taxes.

strayed or stolen
from Waterman Clift in Plainfield, a black mare;

from Solomon Lord of Windham, a red yearling heifer.

broke into the enclosure of
Henry Curtis of Coventry, a sheep ram without horns;

Abner Ashley of Windham, Second Society, two cows.

boat stolen
Notice by Charles Jeffrey, Jun. that a two masted boat, about 15 feet keel, supposed to have been taken by some prisoners and gone to Long Island.

cheese
to be sold by Jedidiah Leeds of Groton by the dairy or single hundred.

****

From *The Gazette*, November 7, 1777

thanksgiving
Thursday, the 20th instant, is appointed to be observed as a day of Thanksgiving throughout this State.

sale of prize and cargo
Notice by Prosper Wetmore, Marshall, that there will be sold at Stonington, the prize vessel *Amherst* and her cargo, consisting of 40 tons of lumber and 20 tons of mahogany;

Notice by Prosper Wetmore, Marshall, that there will be sold at New London also the Prize Brig *William* and her cargo of rum, molasses, a few boxes of chocolate, barrels of sugar and dry goods.

broke into the enclosure
of John Hubbard Jun. of Chatham , a two year old heifer;

of William Matson of Lyme, a small year old ox.

taken up
by Levi Sholes in Groton, a sorrel mare.

strayed or stolen
from Joseph Bucklin Jun., a chestnut colored horse.

found
by Nathan Smith Jun. of New London, North Parish, a knapsack, pair of trousers and jacket which were were left at his house.

your help needed
for rugged, barefooted soldiers, to procure and send forward their several proportions to Elijah Hubbard of Middletown, Mr. Royal Flint of Beakman Patent or to Abel Higs of New Milford so that the soldiers may have them before the weather is severe.
The subscriber entreats the several towns in this State, which have not sent their quota of clothing according to the Resolve of His Excellency the Governor and the Council of Safety, to do so.

administration of estates
Notice by William Cone, Ichabod Olmsted and Levi Gates, Commissioners appointed by the Probate Court of East Haddam regarding the estate of Daniel Gates, late of East Haddam, deceased and represented to be insolvent, to those obligated to it to settle up and to creditors to file claims.

****

From *The Gazette*, November 14, 1777

for sale
six carriage gun, two pounders, 6 swivels 150 wt.; powder; a quantity of swivel and grape shot to be sold by John Rathburn, Jun. at Stonington Point.

wanted
by Peter Mumford, a quantity of well cleaned flax seed for which will be given two dollars a bushel; said Mumford lives in the house lately occupies by Thomas Cotton in Pomfret.

strayed or stolen.
from Asa Brewster of Windham, a speckled heifer, red and black.

farms for sale
at Public Vendue by the order of the General Assembly, a new dwelling house and garden belonging to the estate of John Lamb, late of Groton deceased; very conveniently situated near John Denison's tavern in Stonington, Long Point; notice by Allen Wightman, Administrator.

iron exchange
Managers of the Cannon Foundry at Salisbury, empowered and directed to exchange the pig iron for necessaries for carrying on said foundry and continuing the work, these therefore are to give personal notice that there is an immediate want for six or eight good teams and drivers for 3 or 4 months, with a good number of able bodied men for curing and coaling wood; woolen core cloths and checked flannel, tow cloth, woolen stockings, mens' shoes, sole leather and upper lather, pork, beef, wheat, rye, Indian corn, oats, hay, all sorts of West Indies goods; notice given by Managers Benjamin Henshaw and William Whiting.

notice regarding sale of prize
Notice by John Hudson to all persons who might have any interest in the prizes captured by the armed Sloop *Revenge*, Joseph Conkling, Master, on her first cruise to the West Indies, that there will be a meeting for settlement at the house of Nathan Douglas at New London;

administration of estates
Notice by William Lee and Mary Lee, Executors of the estate of Benjamin Lee, deceased and late of Lyme, to those obligated to it to settle up and to creditors to file claims;

Notice by William Avery and Ralph Stoddard, Commissioners appointed by the Probate Court of Stonington regarding the estate of John Anew, late of Groton, deceased and represented to be insolvent, to those obligated to it to settle up and to creditors to file claims;

Notice by William Avery and Ralph Stoddard, Commissioners appointed by the Probate Court of Stonington regarding the estate of John Avery, late of Stonington, deceased and represented to be insolvent, to those obligated to it to settle up and to creditors to file claims.

broke into the pasture
of Morris Fowler New London, Great Neck, a small yoke of oxen;

of John Marston of Lyme, a dark colored bull;

of Isaac Chapel of New London, seven cattle.

clothier business
Notice by Matthew Dorr that he has set up the clothier business in East Haddam at the place once occupied by John Chapman.

libels filed
before Hon. Samuel Coit in New London against an unnamed sloop, her cargo, boats, tackle, apparel and furniture, taken on the high seas by Thomas Scranton, Commander of the armed schooner *Retaliation* and in behalf of Richard Dershon, Commander of armed boat [not legible]; notice by Wm. Saltonstall.

lost
by Daniel Abbeon on the road between his house and the Town of Enfield, a leather pocket book;

about ten days since between New London and the Rope Ferry, a woman's silk mitt of a lightest peach color; enquire of Printer.

escaped
from on board the Brig *Betsy* in New London Harbor, William Case of Johnson, Rhode Island; 5 foot, 10 or 11 inches tall; well set; about 24 years old; return to Joseph William of Norwich or John Clark, Master of said brig.

runaway
from Noble Hinman of New London, a slave named Dick; 33 years of age; 5 foot, 8 inches high; very black; speaks good English; large mouth and feet; good teeth; is very fond of snuff; a chair maker by trade.

wanted immediately
a good workman and a steady person to carry on the card making business. Such a one will be met with encouragement (by being admitted as a partner or hired for wages) by applying to Ethan Clarke or George Thurston of Hopkinton, Rhode Island;

a good workman that understands making bloomery and foundry iron; also one good workman at country work as a blacksmith and two or three nailers by applying to Ethan Clarke of Hopkinton, Rhode Island.
N. B.: a German or English prisoner or deserter who understands either of the above branches of business and can be well recommended will be employed as above.

taken up
by James Stoddard of Groton, a dark brown mare
****
From *The Gazette*, November 21, 1777

farm for sale
by the order of the General Assembly, the dwelling house, where the late Capt. Jonathan Latimer, late of New London, dwelt, together with about 20 acres, pleasantly situated about one mile from the Meeting House in New London; likewise a lot of about 90 acres lying next to the Roacher Lot; also about 120 acres of

woodland lying in Chesterfield, adjoining the land of Col. Latimer; notice give by Jonathan Latimer and Daniel Latimer, Administrators.

weaver's shop moved
Robert Bennet, late of Colchester, Clothier and Weaver has removed to Lyme here he intends to carry on the business of weaving plaid in the neatest manner at the house of James Gold in Lyme, North Quarter.

thief stopped
Notice by Joseph Budd that, near Mr. Horton's Tavern in New London, he stopped a supposed thief with 16 and ½ yards of fine white flannel, supposed to be stolen from a nearby fulling mill, as it is was still wet; the supposed thief is a thick well, set fellow; about 40 years old.

libels filed
before Hon. Samuel Coit in New London in favor of Thomas Scranton, Commander of the armed boat *Retaliation* and on behalf of Richard Deshon, Commander of the armed boat *General Mifflin* against a dismasted sloop, name unknown, and her cargo, boats, tackle, apparel and furniture, as taken on the high seas; notice by Wn. Saltonstall.

Notice by John Hudson in New London to all persons claiming an interest in the prizes captured by the armed sloop *Revenge*, Joseph Conkling, Commander, in her first cruise to the West Indies to come for settlement at the house of Nathan Douglas.

notice to report
Notice by Col. John Ely that all those belonging to the Second Battalion of Continental soldiers out on furlough are required to immediately return to their Regiments.

lost
Notice by Eliza. Williams of Pomfret that he lost on the road between Inn Holder Griffin's of Wndham, Canada Society and

Joseph Fuller, clothier, of that place, a 10 yard long linen. If found, please return to Landlord Ingel's of Pomfret or the Widow Elizabeth Williams.

****

From *The Gazette*, November 28, 1777

prize cargo to be distributed
Notice by John Denison 2d in Stonington and New London to all persons claiming an interest in the prizes captured by the armed sloop *Revenge*, Joseph Conkling, Commander in her second cruise to the West Indies to come for settlement at the house of Mr. John Denison 4th in order to deliver them their share of rum coffee, sugar and chocolate.

pay
Notice by Capt. Elijah Avery to those of his company in Groton to meet at Capt. Jonas Belton of Groton; those at Preston to Mr. Amos Avery; those at Norwich at Mr. Azariah Lathrop; those at Stonington to Mr. Giles Russel to receive wages for their services.

please settle accounts
Notice from Barnard Phillips, Postmaster, at Pomfret, to those indebted to him for the *New London Gazette* to make payment.

strayed or stolen from
Eliplez Hunt in Coventry, a dark brown yearling heifer;

from James Griffeth of Richmond, King County, Rhode Island, a sorrel horse.

broke into enclosure
of Charles Putnam, a brown horse with some white in his face;

of Joseph Tyler in Preston, a red yearling bull;

of Theohpilus Baldin, Jun. of Stonington, a bull.

found
by David Whipple on the road from New London to Rope Ferry, a pocket book.

for sale
by Thomas Robinson at his store in Stonington Long Point, a quantity of rigging sails, blocks and sea coal.

****

From *The Gazette*, December 5, 1777

administration of estates
Notice by John Griffing Executor of the estate of Mr. William Huntley, deceased and late of Lyme, to those obligated to it to settle up and to creditors to file claims.

strayed
from Allen's Wharf in New London, a sorrel mare; reward if delivered to Jonathan Douglas in New London, Capt. Dudley Wright in Colchester or Elijah Parsons, post rider.

broke into the enclosure
of Peter Chapman of New London, a black and red boar pig.

lost
by Elijah Starr of Groton on the road between New London Ferry and Stonington, a leather pack.

farm for sale
at the house of Seth Smith in Stonington, the real estate of Mr. Ephraim Smith, late of Stonington, deceased; notice by Jeremiah Halsey of Preston.

clothier business
David Yeamons informs the public that he is carrying on the clothier business in Colchester. He has a workman from Europe long experienced in the business; he takes country produce.

snuff and pigtail tobacco for sale
by Emanuel Boix in New London.

settle up
Nathan Bushnel, Jun. desires all persons indebted to him to make payment;

Ebenezer Hovey desires all persons indebted to him to make payment;

Amos Main and David Belding desire all persons indebted to them to make payment.

****

From *The Gazette,* December 12, 1777

letters left at New London Post office

Capt. Roger Billings - Preston	James Panniman - New London
Joshua Babcock - Stonington	Abraham Loper - Stonington
James Davis - Stonington	Prudence Russel - Stonington
Jeremiah Halsey. Esq. - Stonington	Thomas Stanton Ens. - Lebanon
John Holmes - Stonington	
Thomas Hiscock - Stonington	Capt. Jabez Wescott - Sloop *Victory*
Amos Main - Stonington	Ensign John Wylie - New London
Thomas Manning - Stonington	Hosea Wheeler - Stonington
Asher Meyers - Norwich	
John Philipps - Norwich	

to be sold
for cash only, one hundred hogsheads of Muscavado sugar; for price apply to Thomas Mumford of Groton or David Mumford at Bedford, where such goods are stored;

by James Tilly of New London, one new 15 inch cable, 120 fathoms new and 120 fathoms part worn.

strayed
from Lemuel Scovel in Chatham, a sorrel horse colt.

taken up
by Stephen Brainerd in Chatham, two yearling heifers.

broke into the enclosure
of Francis Percival, a white faced yearling steer.

administration of estates
Notice by Jonathan Philips in Preston, Executor of the estate of Joshua Philips, to those obligated to it to settle up and to creditors to file claims.

to be published
in a few days *Freebetterer's New England Almanac.*

****

From *The Gazette,* December 19, 1777

explosion
Last Friday, the powder mill in Windham blew up, by which accident the principal workman was so much hurt that his life is despaired of.

for sale
by James Hubbard at his store in Norwich Landing, for cash or country produce choice Jamaica spirits by the hogshead or barrel, brandy by hogshead or barrel, pepper, allspice, nutmeg, ginger, brimstone, white lead and Spanish brown, Philadelphia and Spanish steel; said Hubbard wants to purchase a quantity of hogshead hoops, also 40 to 50 staves, four feet and four inches long; it will answer to have them made in oak, walnut or chestnut, for which pay will be made one half in cash and one half in West India goods;

a few warming pans and small brass kettles may be had in exchange for old brass, copper or pewter by Richard Collier, near the Meeting House in Norwich;

by John Denison 2d at the house of John Denison, Inn Holder at Stonington Point, nine or ten double fortified four pounders, two anchor and cables.

administration of estates
Notice by Joshua Ransom, Israel Newton and Amos Jones, Commissioners appointed by Court of Probate of East Haddam to receive and examine the claims to the estate of Benjamin Rathborn, deceased and late of Colchester, to those obligated to it to settle up and to creditors to file claims.

broke into enclosure
of James Comstock of Lyme, a black to year old heifer;

of Elisha Wales of Ashford, two yearling heifers;

of John Henry in Colchester, a bay horse colt;

of Caleb Grosvenor in Ashford, a brindle steer.

lost
by Isaiah Whipple of Norwich at the house of Mr. Benjamin Packer of Groton, a man's saddle.

found
by John Williams 3d on Groton shore, a leather double pocket book.

strayed
from Nathaniel Packard of Killingly, a dark bay mare; return to subscriber or to Comfort Wheaton in Providence.

taken up
by Samuel Richards in New London about a month ago, a blue sow.

new appointment
Gen. Gurdon Saltonstall is appointed Naval Officer for the Port of New London in the place of Jeremiah Miller, Esq., who has resigned.

Articles of Confederation
Articles of Confederation and Perpetual Union between the States have been published by Congress which we learn are sent to the several States for their approbation. Copies of said articles are now printing and next week will be sent to the several Towns in this State so that their opinion thereon may be known.

taxes and price fixing
We learn that Congress has recommended to the Legislature of the several states the calling in of 5 million dollars in tax. It is also said that they have proposed stating the prices of every necessary article of life.

****

From *The Gazette*, December 26, 1777

war news
Last Monday, part of Col. Webb's Regiment, which arrived here from Long Island, has marched for Peek's Kill.

American captured
Col. Webb, after being taken, was carried to Newport where, after remaining a few days, he was allowed to come out on parole and is gone to Wethersfield.

ships seized
A valuable prize ship from Scotland, bound for the West Indies, was taken by the Continental Brig *Resistance*, Capt. Chew of this port, New London, is safe arrived in Boston. The sterling cost of her invoice was about 70,000 pounds, chiefly in linens;

The privateer Brig *Fanny*, Captan Kendricks, has arrived at Nantes, in France, where she carried in a valuable ship, one of the Jamaica fleet.

sailors and marines needed
The Ship *Blaze Castle*, now lying in New London and commanded James Monro is in want of few good men - sailors and marines. The said ship is a fine vessel with 18 six pounders and 4 howitzers and will sail in a few days for a cruise of four months.

to be sold
to the highest bidder at the house of Benjmin Henshaw of Middletown, thirty or forty head of horned cattle, consisting of working oxen, milch cows, heifers and steers, some horses, kine; a house and one acre of land in Goshen, Litchfield County.

stolen
out of the house of Christopher Whipple of Woodstock by three soldiers, several coats.

strayed or stolen
from Rufus Darby of Canterbury, out of the pasture of Lt. Nathan Witter of Pomfret, a red cow; lately owned by Hez. Smith of Ashford.

hats for sale
beaver, beverett and felt hats to be sold by John Kinsman at his shop in Newent, Norwich for cash or country produce.

broke into the enclosure
of Jedidiah Higgins in East Haddam, a yearling heifer.

administration of estates
Notice by Ebenezer Spencer and Timothy Gates, Commissioners appointed by Court of Probate of East Haddam to receive and examine the claims against the estate of Joseph Sluman, Esq. late of East Haddam deceased and represented to be insolvent, to those obligated to it to settle up and to creditors to file claims; a meeting will be held at the house of Joseph Emmons.
N. B. Those who neglect to exhibit their account by dates specified will be excluded from receiving their demands.

settle up
Notice by Samuel Mather Jun. of Lyme to those who have accounts with him to settle up.

found
by Noah Beebe in Lyme, North Quarter, a good musket that was partially covered by brush and supposed to be stolen.

Thanksgiving collection
Last Thursday being public Thanksgiving, a collection was made in the North Parish of this town, New London, for the benefit of our soldiery in the Continental army consisting of 26 pounds of cash, 17 shirts, 14 pairs of stockings, 4 coats, 7 jackets, 3 pairs of breeches, 20 pair mittens, 1 trousers, 7 pair of shoes, 1 pair gloves, 2 felt hats, and 2 linen handkerchiefs.

****

1778

From *The Gazette*, January 2, 1778

ships on horizon
Last Wednesday morning, 16 sails of shipping of different sizes from the westward passed this harbor, supposed to be from New York and bound to Newport.

married
John Hallam to Miss Polly Harris, daughter of the late Capt. Peter Harris.

pay up
Samuel Mather Jun. of Lyme requests that all who owe him to settle accounts.

strayed
from by Rufus Darby of Pomfret, out of the pasture of Nathan Wister of Pomfret, a black mare.

lost
by Isaaih Whipple, a saddle near the house of Benejab Packer of Groton.

ferry for lease
the ferry at New London to be let; enquire of the Selectmen.
****

From *The Gazette*, January 9, 1778

taxes on States
The Continental Congress has recommended to the several states to call in 5 million dollars by quarterly taxes for the year 1778 in the following proportions:

New Hampshire: $200,000
Massachusetts Bay: $820,000
Rhode Island Providence Bay Plantations: $100,000
Connecticut: $600,000
New York: $200,000
New Jersey: $270,000
Pennsylvania: $620,000
Delaware: $60,000
Maryland: $520,000
Virgina: $300,000
North Carolina: $250,000
South Carolina: $500,0000
Georgia: $60,000

donations
Last Saturday there was a contribution of the several parishes of Norwich for the benefit of the non commissioned officers and soldiers in the Continental army of stockings, shoes, shirts, jackets, overalls, caps etc. as well as pork, cheese, wheat, Indian corn sugar etc.

to be sold
for cash only by Dudley and Samuel Woodbridge at their store in Norwich, Jamaica rum, sugar, rice etc.;

by William Terret of Stonington Long Point, good buckskin breeches and good strong leather breeches, suitable for use by army and laborers.

strayed
from William Underwood of Killingly, a mare colt.

****

From *The Gazette*, January 16, 1778

war news
Capt. Daniel Deshon, bound for the West Indies in a brig owned by this State (late the armed brig *Defense*) is taken and carried into Jamaica.

Last Sabbath, a flag of truce sailed from this port, New London, for New York with a number of English prisoners.

Sabbath evening, a brig from Providence bound for this port of New London was drove on Wickeposet reef by two British ships, who hulled her 16 times and fired a great number of shot through her rigging, but the brig soon after got off and got into Stonington.

ambush

on the 25th *ult*, Lt. David Barber of Groton, in company with another officer, walked out a few miles from our camp near the Sand Pit and, on their return, a party of Tories concealed rose and fired at them with buckshot. Lt. Barber was shot through the chest and died immediately. The character he sustained in the army as a bold and good officer renders his death as an essential loss. The murders robbed him of his money.

married

at Groton, the Rev Mr. Asher Rosseter of Preston to Mrs. Keia Perkins, widow of the late Luke Perkins, Esq.

died

Mrs. Temperance Bill, wife of Mr. David B. Bill of this Town, New London, and daughter of Capt. Joseph Harris.

administration of estates

John Richards, Samuel Latimer and Richard Dershon, Commissioners appointed by the Probate Court of New London for the estate of Major James Chapman, late of New London, deceased and represented insolvent, to the creditors to file claims and to those indebted to settle accounts;

Notice by Anne Clark, Administrator of the estate of Capt. Daniel Clark, late of Plainfield, deceased, to the creditors to file claims and to those indebted to settle accounts;

Notice by Temperance and Christopher Morgan, Administrators the estate of William Morgan, late of Groton, deceased to the creditors to file claims and to those indebted to settle accounts;

Notice by Ebenezer Way Jun. and Marvin Wait, Commissioners appointed by the Probate Court of New London of the estate of Capt. Edward Palmes, late of New London, deceased and represented insolvent, to the creditors to file claims and to those indebted to settle accounts. A meeting of creditors will be held at Wait's meeting office;

Notice by Zebelulon Stockin, Administrator of the estate of Elisha Stockin, late of Middletown, deceased, to the creditors to file claims and to those indebted to settle accounts; a meeting of creditors will be held at the house of Nathan Chaucery, Inn Holder in the North Society of Middletown;

Notice by Daniel and Sarah Howard, Administrators for the estate of Nathan Howard of New London, deceased, to the creditors to file claims and to those indebted to settle accounts.

settle accounts
Notice by Samuel Parsons, who is living outside the State, that those owing him in New London can pay Marvin Wait, Esq; in Windham, Hezekiah Bissel, and in Norwich and Preston and neighboring towns, Dudley Woodbridge, Esq.

for sale or exchange
by William Loring & Co. have for sale in their store at Norwich Landing, rum, sugar, coffee, chocolate etc.;

the ship *Amherst*, her sails, rigging etc. It is proposed for the benefit of the purchasers to sell the anchors, cables, sails in small lots, separate from the sale of the hull; enquire of Edward Hallam in New London; also mahogany and logwood for sale;

by Thomas Darral in Stonington, pewter plate, basins, prongers for cash

cash given for flax, linen yards spun at the rate of 4 or 5 runs to the pound at the Tape manufactory in Norwich;

Dilworth's spelling books to be sold by T. Green

moved his business
Stephen Miner informs his customers that he has removed from Stonington Point to Groton, Gales Ferry where he continues to sell all sorts of cloths.

exchange
the Committee charge with supplying the soldiers' families in the Town of New London hereby notify inhabitants that they have about 100 barels of good West India salt which they will exchange for corn, rye and pork at the store of Guy Richards.

farm for sale
in the North Parish of New London, now occupied by Mr. Joshua Fargo, 150 acres; enquire of Daniel Fox, Jun. living near the premises or the subscriber Alexander P. Adams in New London.

broke into the enclosure
of Daniel Tilden in Lebanon, a white yearling heifer;

of Francis Percival of East Haddam, a white faced heifer.

deserted
from Joshua Trffin's Company in Col. Henry Sherburne's Regiment, Nathan Martin about 40 years of age; 5 feet, 9 inches tall; dark complexion; notice by Ens. Ephraim Cary;

from Capt. Abijah Savage's Company in Col. Sherburne's Regiment, Henry Scott; 38 years of age; 5 feet, 10 inches tall; black hair and eyes; dark complexion;

from James Webb's Company in Col. Sherbune's Regiment, Thomas Blackwood; 19 years of age; 5 foot, 5 inches high; black hair; gray eyes.

****

From *The Gazette*, January 23, 1778

explosion
Last Friday, the powder mill in Windham blew up, by which accident the principal workman was so much hurt that his life is despaired of.

not responsible
Notice by James Freeman of Groton, that since his wife Elizabeth (daughter of James Niles of Charleston, South Carolina) has acted in a loose disorderly manner and left his bed and board and has refused to return and cohabit with him, that he is no longer responsible for her debts and forbids all person from trusting her on his account.

runaway
from Eleazer May of Haddam, a Negro man named London; about 34 years of age; six foot, 7 inches high.

lost
on the road between Norwich and New London, a castro hat almost new; enquire of Printer.

farm for sale
Notice by Richard Palmer of Stonington that to be sold at Wequequock Cove, about 20 acres of land, four acres of orchard, barn, pasture, dwelling house, crib, well fenced and well watered.

for sale
All the personal and real estate consisting of half a right of land in the Susquehanna Purchase of the estate of Samuel Tozer, Jun., late of Colchester, deceased and being represented insolvent sale, to be held at the house of John Tainter, Inn Holder in Colchester; notice by Elias Worthington, Jun. Commissioner.

****

From *The Gazette*, January 30, 1778

wanted to hire
a school master to teach reading writing and arithmetic; if he can teach Greek and Latin too, preference will be given; enquire of Joshua Babcock.

taxes due
Notice by Peter Strickland, Tax Collector for New London that taxes may be paid at the houses of Capt. Nathan Douglas, James Haughton, Dr. Seth Holmes, Jason Allen and Capt. Stephen Preston.

administration of estates
Notice by Nathaniel Clark of East Haddm, Administrator of the estate of Abel Clark, deceased and late of Pomfret, will receive and examine the claims; those obligated to it should settle up and creditors file claims.

Notice by Capt. Calvin Ely, East Haddm, Administrator of the estate of Calvin Ely, deceased and late of East Haddam, to receive and examine the claims, to those obligated to it to settle up and to creditors to file claims; a meeting will be held at the house of Aaron White, of East Haddam;

Notice by Hannah Banks, Administrator of the estate of William Banks, deceased and late of Middletown, will receive and examine the claims; those obligated to it should settle up and creditors file claims.

boat missing
Last Friday night, a small boat with seven people and two horses, sailed from hence to Long Island and, next morning, the two horses swam ashore about two miles west of this harbor. As the boat has not been since heard of, it is supposed that the people drowned.

died
in Marlborough in Colchester, Hez. Kneeland, second son of Dr. Hez. Kneeland in the 21st year of his life, after a tedious illness of the nervous kind.

dismissal from service
Congress having no further occasion for the services of Esek Hopkins Esq, who, on the 22nd of December 1775 was appointed commander in chief of the fleet by the Naval Committee. Resolved that the said Esex Hopkins be dismissed from the service of the United States.[27]
Charles Thomson, Secretary

adventurers wanted
None need to apply but good clever fellows, who are desirous of making their fortunes on board the privateer *American Revenue*, captained by Samuel Champlin; enlistments at house of John Owens in New London.

to be sold
by John Deshon at his store in New London, rum by the hogshead.

stolen
from Martin Welles at the door of Stephen Otis in Colchester, a bay mare.

settle accounts
Notice by David Belding to those indebted to him for papers, to pay up at houses of Capt. Abner, Amos Comstock, Lt. Abner Griffing or Col. Marshfield Parsons.

****

From *The Gazette,* February 6, 1778

lost boat returns
The boat, which has been supposed to be lost, as mentioned in our last, has returned from Long Island.

British ships nearby
Yesterday, two British ships from Eastward went up the Sound. One of them came almost within the Lighthouse.

threat
We have undoubted intelligence that our enemies in Newport are making preparations for an attack. If it is to be upon this place, we ought to be prepared in the best manner possible for their reception.

reduced size of newspaper
The printer is of necessity to issue half sheets of sundry news.

list of letters left at Post Office
Joshua Babcock - Stonington
Capt. Elijah Butler - New London
John Barber - Groton
Capt. Roger Billings - Pomfret
Thomas Hiscock - Stonington
Eliphalet Herbert - Stonington
Abraham Loper - Stonington
Sarah Langdon - New London
Thomas Page - Coventry
Thomas or Jonathan Penny - Middletown
John Phillipps - New London
James Tiller - Stonington
Ensign John Wylie - New London
Capt. John Wescote - New London
Hosea Wheeler - Stonington

Stonington lottery
All persons who subscribed for tickets to the Stonington Lottery are desired to make immediate payment to Nathaniel Minor, John Denison 3rd or Joseph Denison 2d.

farm to be let
in New Guilford, 180 acres, 50 or 60 of which is under good improvement; about 40 tons of good hay; two dwelling houses and a good saw mill on the premises; enquire of Daniel Packer in Groton.

administration of estates
Notice by Mary Brown, *Administratrix* of the estate of John Brown, deceased and late of Stonington, to those obligated to it to settle up and to creditors to file claims;

Notice by John Williams, Nathan Crary, Amos Geer, Commissioners appointed by the Probate Court of the District of Stonington for the estate of Peris Palmer, late of Stonington, deceased and represented to be insolvent to those obligated to it to settle up and to creditors to file claims; there will be a meeting of creditors at the house of Charles Thomson;

Notice by John Tainter, Joseph Isham, Daniel Fent, Commissioners appointed by the Probate Court of East Haddam, for the estate of Ebenezer Rogers, Jun., late of Colchester, deceased and represented to be insolvent, to those obligated to it to settle up and to creditors to file claims. A meeting of creditors will be held at the house of John Tainter of Colchester, Inn holder;

Notice by Elijah Baley, Executor of the estate of James Baley, deceased and late of Groton, to those obligated to it to settle up and to creditors to file claims;

notice by Hephzibah Strong and Elias Worthington Jun., Administrators of the estate of Jedediah Strong, deceased and late of Lebanon, to those obligated to it to settle up and to creditors to file claims.

permits needed
Whereas there appears to be general permits and others of ancient date to permit boats, persons and effects to pass and re-pass from Long Island (many of which we doubt not are forged and others used contrary to their meaning), this is to advise all officers and others empowered to inspect said premises that all such passes and permits granted before this date are hereby void and to be of no use.
John Hulbert, Obidiah Johnes and Thomas Dering.

musket left
at the shop of James Tripp in Stonington Harbor to be stocked; owner unknown but thought to be from the Connecticut River.

for sale
dwelling house at Gales Ferry in Groton; it is one story high with four rooms on the floor, a convenient work shop in the cellar, a small barn, shed and merchant' shop and has been used for several years as such; also a quarter acre garden; enquire of John Rogers of New London or Jonathan Rogers of Lyme.

****

From *The Gazette*, February 13, 1778

British foray
By a boat from the Vineyard, we learn that some armed vessels from Newport have been there and carried off forcibly in the night ten pilots, whom they promised to release after they had piloted the fleet from Newport to Boston, destined to take in Burgoyne' troops. They plundered the inhabitants of clothing and whatever they chose to carry off.

Tory lands to be confiscated
The Selectman of the several Towns in the County of New London are desired to give information to Benj. Huntington, State's Attorney, as to what lands and real estate of their Town belong to persons, not subjects or inhabitants of the United States, so that proper steps may be taken for their improvement for the benefit of this State, as the law requires.[28]

administration of estates
Notice by Ester Denison and Daniel Denison Administrators, of the estate of Capt. Daniel Denison, late of Stonington, deceased, to the creditors to file claims and to those indebted to settle accounts;

Notice by Samuel Chandler, Administrator of the estate of Isaac Fellows, late of Enfield, County of Hartford, deceased, to the creditors to file claims and to those indebted to settle accounts.

broke into the enclosure
of Lemuel Hungerford of East Haddam, a three year old steer.

to be sold
45 acres of land with a convenient house, shop almost new, excellent cellar and an excellent well of water; said land includes pasture, plow and wood land, the most part in fine order for wheat and an orchard standing thereon; situated in Middletown, on the road leading from Middletown to Hartford; apply to Thomas Rainey living on the premises.

lost
by Elisha Huntington at Mr. Waterman's Tavern in New London or between that place and Capt. Joseph Coit's Wharf, three $30 bills; please return to Printer, T. Greene or John Braddick in Norwich.

farm for sale
in Mansfield, First Society, lying about two miles north of the Meeting House; 60 acres half improved; dwelling house and barn thereon; enquire of Moses Phelps, living near the premises.

****

From *The Gazette*, February 20, 1778

prisoners in New York
We are assured that General Lee[29], on receiving the $500 which he drew in the New York lottery, immediately distributed some of it among the American prisoners in the city.
It is said that the American prisoners, since we now have a commissary in New York, are well served with good provisions, which are provided at the expense of the States and in general are very healthy.

British ships ashore
We learn that six sail of ships were drove ashore on Long Island the 6th instant, being part of a British Fleet from the east, bound to New York. One of them is a frigate of 36 guns.

smuggler seized
A boat from Long Island, bound for the Connecticut River with sundry articles of British manufacture, was a few days ago seized by a boat from the Ship *Trumbull*. It is hoped this may give check to a trade which already has been carried on with impunity and is very detrimental to the fair trade as well as contrary to the express laws of the States.

on parole
Colonel Enos and Ensign Mumford have come out of New York on their parole.

to be sold
Notice by Samuel Jones and Elizabeth Bloss, Administrators of the estate of James Bloss, late of Hebron, deceased, at public venue in Hebron, all the personal and real estate.

****

From *The Gazette,* February 27, 1778

more on the British ships ashore
from a person of this Town of New London, who was in the fleet which was cast away on Long Island, as reported in our last, five of the vessels ground belong to the British Government. The others were private property. Numbers of the people were drowned and, of those who were able to get ashore, several of them froze to death.

died
Thomas Harris of the Harbor's Mouth of this town New London, aged 57 years;

last week departed this life in Groton in a fit of the convulsive kind and on the day following was decently interred, Joseph Gallup in the 53rd year of his life; he has left a disconsolate widow and ten children.

farms for sale
in Woodstock, 110 acres; pleasantly situated within one quarter of a mile of a Meeting House; apply to Christopher Whipple;

110 acres, lying in Newent on the main road from Norwich to Boston, 8 miles from the Norwich state house; well proportioned for plowing, pasturing and mowing; good house, barn, small shop suitable for a tradesman or small trader; apply to Moses Porter living on the premises.

administration of estates
Notice by Martha Hyde, Administrator of the estate of Silas Hyde, late of Norwich, deceased, to the creditors to file claims and to those indebted to settle accounts.

settle accounts
Notice by Joseph Knight that those persons indebted to him in the town of Middletown for newspapers are desired to meet him at Mr. Feimo's Tavern; those in the upper house of the Town at Mr. Shauney's; those in Rocky Hill at Mr. Grimes'; those in Wethersfield at Capt. Wright's; those at Hartford at Mr. David Bull's.

wanted
Ship carpenters may fine good employ by applying to the Continental ship yard, Norwich River.
****
From *The Gazette*, March 6, 1778

storms at sea
Capt. Davisdson in a sloop from the port of New London, about five weeks since, sailed for North Carolina and, a few days after meeting with a gale of wind, lost his bowsprit upon which he put into the Vineyard and, after repairing his vessel, sailed again and met with another violent gale, where he lost mast and sails. Being thus disabled, he lay at he mercy of the seas for 14 days, when he was drove ashore on the south side of Long Island about the same time a 40 gun ship, a brig, a schooner and a sloop, all British, also

were wrecked on the back side of Long Island, the latter lay very close to each other.

ordination
Tuesday day the 22 of January last, was ordained to the work of the Christian Ministry at the Church and Society of Killingly, the Rev. Mr. Emerson Foster. The exercise was begun with singing. The Rev. Mr. Armstrong made the first prayer and the Rev. Mr. Isaac Foster of Stratford preached the Sermon and gave the Charge; the Rev. Mr. Williams made the Ordaining Prayer and the Rev. Mr. Cosswall prayed after the Charge and the Rev. Russell gave the Right Hand[30].

fire
On the night of the 24th of February, the house of Mr. Sherwood in New Milford took fire and was consumed. Eleven people were in the house and only three made their escape from it. Eight perished in the flames.

broke out of jail
Notice by Ephraim Miner, Goaler, that Thomas Rogers of New London, Great Neck; escaped the county goal in New London; he is pretty small; long black hair and dark eyes.

farms to be let
a hundred acres; pleasantly situated at Goshen in New London, Great Neck, with good dwelling house thereon; now in the occupation of Benjamin Jorom; the land is of the very best quality for mowing and plowing and has a good pasture thereon;
also a dwelling house and barn situated on White Beach at the mouth of New London Harbor; about 30 acres with a good orchard and a well of excellent water; enquire of Joseph Hurlbut in New London.

deserted
from Col. Johnson's Regiment in Providence, David Enos, a transient person; 5 foot, 6 inches high; light complexion; gray eyes; notice by Capt. Moses Branch.

to be sold
by Joshua Starr, liver oil by the barrel; Jamaica spirits; New England rum; split and slab whale bone by the hundred pound, Bohea tea and pins by the pack or paper.

****

From *The Gazette,* March 13, 1778

French ship in harbor
Last Saturday arrived here in New London from Port L' Orient in France, the ship *Lyon,* a three decker of about 1100 tons burthen, commanded by Captain Michael, having a defense commission and mounting 40 guns and having upwards of 200 men; deeply laden with European and India goods in a very large amount.

Benjamin Franklin assassinated?
The report of Dr. Franklin being assassinated appears to be without foundation, as he was well when the vessel sailed which brings intelligence about 20 days later than that we had before received. The following story is related to us as what probably happened to give rise to the report. A well dressed man came into the room where the Doctor was sitting in company with several gentlemen. The man enquired for Dr. Franklin and, being answered by the Doctor that he was that person, the man tells he would be glad to speak with him in private. The Doctor answered that none, but his friends, were present and he might tell his business. The man seeming to decline it, the Doctor stepped into a corner of the room and in a low voice asked him what his business was. Seeming much confused and at a loss for an answer, he asked the doctor if he wanted to buy a pair of stockings. The business being of such a frivolous nature gave rise to the suspicion that his design was bad and occasioned his being arrested. But we did not learn how the matter terminated.

war talk
A talk of war against England still continued when the ship left France and the Captain said it is expected that it will soon be declared.

to be sold
for cash, neat cattle or sheep.

to be let
and entered into immediately, several tracts or parcels of land, the property of the Rev. Eleazar Wheelock of Lebanon.

lotteries
drawing of Public Lottery by order of Congress; tickets available from David Trumbull of Lebanon;

tickets in the State lottery may be had of Samuel Gray in Windham or Mr. Andrew Huntington in Norwich and T. Green in New London, who also has a few tickets for sale in the Hartford Paper Mill Lottery.

for sale
Dilworth's Spelling Books to be sold at Green and Spooner in Norwich.

time to board
All those who have entered upon the Sloop *Beaver*, are directed to board immediately; a few more men are wanted.

ship arrival
Sunday arrived Capt. Theophilus Fitch in a schooner from North Carolina.

deserted
from Fort Trumbull in New London, John Dexter; about 5 foot, 8 inches tall; thick built; light complexion; walks lame.

broke out of goal
William Howard of New London; 32 years of age; 5 foot, 10 inches high; tawny complexion; dark eyes and hair; notice by Ephraim Miner, Goaler of New London.

farm for sale
180 acres lying in First Society in Groton, about a mile from the Ferry and near the Meeting House; well proportioned for mowing, pasturing and plowing; well watered; two good orchards; enquire of Benjamin Bill or Christopher Bill on the premises.

ran away
from George Sheffield of Stonington, an apprentice boy named David Saunders, Jun.; about 20 years old;

from Thomas Avery in Groton, Nathan Smith, well set and fair complexioned;

from James Sheffield of New London, an apprentice boy named Asa Crandal.

****

From *The Gazette*, March 20, 1778

sailors wanted
Notice by Thomas Allon, Captain of the private ship of War *Putnam,* carrying 20 carriage guns, seeks Gentlemen Volunteers for a six month cruise; they shall be put on daily pay from the time their clothes are on board until sailing.

administration of estates
Notice by John Devotion and Jonathan Layall, Executors of the estate of John Murdock, late of Saybrook, deceased, to the creditors to file claims and to those indebted to settle accounts;

Notice by Lucretia Jewett, Administratrix of the estate of Capt. Joseph Jewett, late of Lyme, deceased, to the creditors to file claims and to those indebted to settle accounts.

deserted
Notice by Lt. James Hall, Artillery, the following deserted in the march from Farmington to Fish kill from his detachment belonging to Col. John Crane's battalion:

Sgt. John Touse of Captain Perkins' Company; 26 years of age; 5 feet, 7 inches tall; long brown hair; blue eyes; dark complexion, a double upper lip; belonging to Long Island, a cordwainer by trade;

Corporal Benjamin Leach of Captain Perkins' Company; 25 years of age; 5 feet, 10 inches tall; curled black hair; blue eyes; a carpenter by trade, belonging to New England;

Jacob Evens, a matross in Capt. Sergeant's Company; 25 years of age; 5 feet, 10 inches tall; short black hair; dark eyes; dark complexion; belonging to Swansey in New England.

for sale
by Thomas Mumford of Groton at retail, for cash only, rum, sugar, coffee, cotton, wool, rice etc;

by Stephen Howell of East Haddam, a very likely sloop, about 60 tons, three years old.

farm for sale
a convenient dwelling house with a good cellar and garden; pleasantly situated at Stonington Harbor; enquire of Capt. Israel Lewis in Hopkinton or John Rathburn Jun. of Stonington.
****
From *The Gazette,* March 27, 1778

hospitals closed
Whereas the Hospital for inoculation for the small pox in the Town of Groton had been so crowded with patients from the neighboring towns that efficient care could not be taken to prevent the Disorder from spreading and is now in several parts of town. In consequence, of which the inoculation is now stopped in the Town.
The Civil Authority and the Selectmen of said town of Groton, having taken every precaution to prevent the spreading for the future from their own People, do hereby strictly forbid all those patients who might be returning from any of the hospitals in the

neighboring towns, through Groton, not to makes any stops in this town, either at a public or a private house, at their peril.

prisoners returned
Monday last, a flag returned from Newport with several Americans who had been prisoners in a Guard Ship.

prisoner dies
Mr. Michael Sage, son of Col. Sage of Middletown, died in a Guard ship in Newport.

broke out
notice by Ephraim Miner, Goaler of New London goal that escaped were:

James Holt, a smallish man; pretty much pox broken; light complexion and eyes;

James Davenport, short and well set, light complexion and eyes and dark hair.

runaway
from Joseph Stanton of Groton, Phebe Perkins, alias Morgan; 17 years; middling statute; has a down look; brown hair and dark eyes.

found
by Thomas Whipple, an ox chain on street in New London.

drug store moved
The apothecary business that has for a number of years been carried on by Messrs. Daniel and Joshua Lathrop is now carried on by Lathrop & Coit at their store in Norwich. They have lately received a fresh supply of drugs and medicines.

to Gentlemen Volunteers
who are desirous of serving their country and, at the same time, making their fortunes, an opportunity is now presented on board

Privateer Brig *Nancy*, Michael Melally, Commander; 16 carriage guns; a prime sailer; well fitted for a four month cruise and will sail in three weeks. The Commander may be found on board or at the house of Mr. Ichabod Powers, Jun. of New London.

pay up
Notice by Ebenezer Dutton of East Haddam to those indebted to him to settle accounts.

administration of estates
Notice by Thomas Starr, Administrator of the estate of James Starr Jun., late of Groton, deceased, to the creditors to file claims and to those indebted to settle accounts;

Notice to those obligated to John Denison iv, late of Stonington, to settle accounts.

Tories lands to be let
Notice by Jedidiah Elderkin, Attorney in Windham, that in the Towns of Killingly and Ashford there are tracts of land not belonging to any inhabitants of the United States which lands are to be let to the highest bidder for a term of not more than 3 years, according to the law of this state passed in October 1777. All business to be attended at the house of Isaac Perkins in Ashford and at the house of Jonathan Wilson, inn holder, in Killingly.

Benedict Arnold returns
The Honorable Major General Arnold is arrived at Middletown from Albany, but we hear he is not yet out of danger from his wound.[31]

ordination
Wednesday se'nnight, the Rev. Joseph Strong was ordained over the First Church and Congregation in Norwich to be a colleague with the Rev. Doctor Lord.

stolen
from the house of Joseph Waterman of New London, a large silver

spoon.

for sale
by Beriah Brown, Jun., Deputy Sheriff by order of the General Assembly, the property of George Thurston in Hopkinton in King's County.

****

From *The Gazette*, April 3, 1778

day of public fast
we learn that on the 22nd of April is recommended by Congress to be a day of public fast and His Excellency Governor Trumbull has issued a Proclamation appointing the same to be accordingly observed in this State.

ship ashore
Friday night last, the Continental ship *Columbus*, Capt. Hacker, in coming up the Providence River, was drove ashore on Point Judith by two of the enemy's ships. The *Columbus* was defended by her people with great bravery until her sails, rigging and provisions were secured. Soon after which, the enemy set her on fire.

to be sold
at the house of James Thomson of New London, a lot of excellent mowing land, about six acres adjoining the farm of Thomas Alice in New London, Great Neck; also several lots in Chapel's Hill, situated in New London, the whole under good improvement and well fenced.

passage boat
Notice by John Braddick of Braddick's Passage Boat to inform all persons, who may have the occasion to take passage or send freight, that I now ply between Norwich and New London as usual and at the price established by law .

to be let
a farm in Groton, containing 150 acres of good land adjoining the salt water; good for mowing, plowing and pasture; good orchard,

house and barn and good water; 2 and ½ miles from ferry and a half mile from the Meeting House; a half a mile also from a grist mill; enquire of Joseph Gallup living on the premises.

****

From *The Gazette*, April 10, 1778

news from New York

Last Sabbath, a flag of truce arrived here from City Island, near New York, which brought the master of a captured vessel who had been a prisoner in New York, but with Liberty of walking the City. By him, we learn that the Tories of New York City, despairing of the subjugation of America, were shipping their families and effects to England as fast as possible; that in a late storm, the shipping of New York suffered very great damage; that wharves where 325 sails of vessels lay were floated off and, with all the shipping, floated down the river upon Governors Island, where several of them were bilged; and that provisions have become extremely scarce in New York.

news from Newport

We also have accounts from Newport which make it probable that the enemy is dismantling their fortifications and embarking their heavy cannon, horses etc. and it is apprehended that they are quitting Rhode Island.

traitors convicted

At the Superior Court held last week in Norwich, Elisha Fox of the North Parish of New London was convicted of attempting to join the enemy, and for that purpose going to Long Island, and was sentenced to two years imprisonment and to pay a fine of 20 pounds. Benjamin Fitch, a lad, was also convicted of the same crime and was sentenced to two months imprisonment and a five pound fine.

taxes

Notice by Handly Bushnell, Tax Collector to the inhabitants of Saybroook who are obliged to pay taxes that they can make payment at the dates and times specified: at the houses of John

Buckingham, Danford Clark, Peter Stannard, Noah Platt and William Dudley.

runaway
from Samuel Summer of Pomfret, a mulatto wench about 16 years old named Ninah; thick and large.

wanted at Salisbury Furnace
a number of men cutting wood and making coal; will earn generous wage and be exempt from military service; also a number of good teams are wanted to purchase or be let through summer; a quantify of pork is also needed for which payment will be made in pig iron or cash; apply to Benjamin Henshaw or William Whiting, Managers.

to be sold
Notice by Adam Shapely that all the moveable estate of Dr. Thomas Moffat of New London, consisting of a valuable collection of books, some drugs and medicines, are for sale; also a farm of 100 acres in Lebanon, about a mile from Meeting House with a dwelling house, barn, orchard, well proportioned for mowing, pasturing and plowing; enquire of Ebenezer Gillit on premises;

46 acres of good land with convenient buildings thereon lying in the First Society in Groton about a half mile from the Ferry; well proportioned for mowing, pasturing and plowing; about 3/4 miles from Meeting House; enquire of Richard Starr, living on the farm;

dwelling house and barn situated at White Beach at the harbor's mouth of New London; 30 acres; good orchard and well of excellent water; enquire of Joseph Hurlbut in New London.

lottery tickets
tickets in the United States Lottery are being sold by Nicholas Cook, Jun. in Woodstock.

tape for sale
Andrew Perkins has broad and narrow tape of various colors for sale at his his Tape Factory in Norwich, opposite the house of Jabez Perkins; said Perkins has a number of farms in the Cohas country which he would sell, or exchange, for other lands nearer the sea shore.

taken up
by Edward Gillit in Lebanon, a brindle heifer.

wanted
by Benjamin Hanks of Windham, an apprentice boy to the watch making business.

****

From *The Gazette*, April 17, 1778

disaster at sea
Yesterday, Capt. Brunce arrived here in 13 days by whom we have some disagreeable intelligence.
The *Randolph*, Continental Frigate of 32 guns, commanded by Capt. Biddle, in company with a 20 gun ship and three armed brigs fell in with the *Yarmouth*, a British gun ship, to the windward of Barbados and engaged her for an hour, when the *Randolph* blew up and every soul on board perished, on which the remainder of the fleet made off and arrived in the West Indies.

another fight at sea
A letter from Lt. Leeds of the armed Brig *Resistance* from this port, dated in Martinico, gives an account that, on the 4th of March, the said brig fell in with a letter of marque ship of 20 guns with whom they had an engagement and, as they were preparing to board the ship, Captain Chew and three of his men were killed and 12 wounded. The brig, being disabled put into Martinico; and that, two days after the engagement, Mr. George Champlin of this Town, New London, one of the lieutenants, died of sickness.

prize taken
One day last week, a sloop from Halifax laden with coal, some coffee and other articles were taken by a boat with seven men and one swivel from Coaxet in Dartmouth.

American ships seized
Numbers of American vessels have been lately taken in the West Indies. The crews are mostly released in gaining port, owing to the scarcity of provisions.

help clothe our soldiers
The members of the Committee in New London to Purchase Clothing for the quota of soldiers of said Town earnestly ask the citizens to consider the necessity of immediately complying with so just and reasonable a request. Our friends and neighbors are at the present time venturing their lives against our common enemy and for the glorious cause of America. Can we do no less on our part than to fortify them with every necessity convenience in our power, so that a mutual happiness may exist between us?
Thomas Shaw, John Richards, William Douglass, Joseph Davis, Jabez Beebe, William Prince and John Hallam .

representatives chosen
at the Freeman Meeting on Monday last, the following were chosen members of the General Assembly:
New London: Nathaniel Shaw Jun., William Hillhouse
Stonington: John Williams, Peleg Chesebrough
Lyme: Col. Marshfield Parsons, Ezra Selden

libels filed
before Hon. Richard Law in New London County Court
in favor of Dudley Saltonstall; commander of the Ship *Trumbull* against unnamed vessel, Captain Casey, late master, and against a two masted boat, Joseph V, late master; their cargoes, boats, tackle, apparel and furniture, taken on the high seas;
in favor of Capt. John Kerr, commander of the armed schooner *Mifflin* against the sloop *Dory*, Capt Thomas Nye, the cargo, boats, tackle, apparel and furniture, as taken on the high seas;

notice by Wm. Saltonstall

administration of estates
Nathaniel Eaton and Gavin Eaton, Administrators of the estate of Ebenezer Eaton, late of Pomfret, deceased, to the creditors to file claims and to those indebted to settle accounts;

Notice by Anna Leeds, *Adminstratrix* of the estate of Jonathan Leeds, late of Groton, deceased, to the creditors to file claims and to those indebted to settle accounts;

Notice by Ezra Selden, Administrator of the estate of Capt. Dan Marvin, late of Lyme, deceased, to the creditors to file claims and to those indebted to settle accounts.

to be sold
a tract of unimproved land of 70 acres; by order of the Probate Court of New London, at the house of Edward Jeffrey Inn Holder in Groton; apply to Thomas Mumford at his store in Groton for more information.

moved
John Hudson has removed from Long Point in Stonington and now carries on the business of tanning and currying leather near the dwelling house of Col. Samuel Prentice in the North Parish of New London; he has a number of good heels for women shoes.

small farm for sale
Forty five acres, good orchard, fulling mill and cider mill and press; lying on the Post road through Groton and about a mile from the Mystic River; enquire of Stephen Avery.
****
From *The Gazette*, April 24, 1778

traitors
A certain Phineas Fairbanks, lately escaped from Harvard in Worcester county, and, for several days, lay secreted in Great Neck in this Town, but was afterwards assisted in his escape to

Long Island by a set of men in Great Neck whose constant practice it is to plague the public all that lays in their power. Fairbanks, with sundry others, was soon after taken on Long Island by the vigilance of a couple of Rangers under the command of Capt. Peter Griffing and the following papers were found with him:
(letter to Major Gen. Tryon, Governor and Commander in Chief of New York)
"that your Petitioner has been driven from his home and estate by the rebels can have no remittance and, of course, is destitute of the necessary means for his present support; that your petitioner has heard of a farm in Southhold in Suffolk county in Long Island, formerly belonging to Grover Glover, who is now in open rebellion. Your Petitioner humbly prays that Your Excellency in consideration of his present circumstances will be favorably pleased to grant him permission to take over the farm and building and utensils thereof in his possession and to occupy the same for his benefit and present support."

administration of estates
Notice by William Welch and James Bill, Commissioners appointed by the Probate Court of Middletown for the estate of James Johnson Jun., late of Chatham to the creditors to file claims and to those indebted to settle accounts; a hearing will be held at Deacon John Clark's, Inn Holder in Chatham;

Notice by Ebenezer Holt and John Crocker, Commissioners appointed by the Probate Court in New London for the estate of Nathaniel Holt, deceased and represented to be insolvent, to the creditors to file claims and to those indebted to settle accounts; a hearing will be held at Nathan Douglas' in New London.

wanted
by Palmer Carew in Norwich, an apprentice boy to blacksmith and edge tool business, a boy 14 or 15 years of age;

by John Culver in Norwich, an apprentice boy, between 13 and 15 years of age, to the tanning and shoemaking business.

United States Lottery
Tickets may be had from Andrew Huntington in Norwich and David Trumbull in Lebanon.

trusses and bandages for sale
Stephen Johnson of Ashford continues the business of making trusses and bandages to keep up the fallen parts of those troubled with the burst.

to be sold
ten acres on road from Norwich to New London, about a miles beyond Mr. Haughton's, situated upon a never failing stream and pleased by nature with waterworks, where a head of water sufficient for any purpose may be raised for a trifling cost; enquire of Aaron Cleveland of Norwich.

deserted
from Capt. Champion's Company of Col. Wyllis Regiment, William Foster; a native of Ireland, resident in Hebron Connecticut; about 46 years old; 5 foot, 9 inches high; light hair eyes and complexion;

from Capt. Jonathan Calkings in New London, Samuel Taber; middling size; light complexion; wears his own light brown hair; deliver him to Col. John Durkee.

****

From *The Gazette,* May 1, 1778

carriage for sale
a neat chaise to be sold. Enquire of Printer.

volunteers report on board
The Ship *Putnam*, Thomas Allon, Commander, is being fitted in the best manner. All gentlemen volunteers who have engaged for a cruise on such ship are desired immediately to report on board.

Notice by Simon Rhodes of Stonington regarding donations of soldiers' provisions.

lost
out of the pocket of Richard Chapman, between his house and the Court House New London.

farm for sale
by Elias Mason; 110 acres of choice land, located in the First Society in Woodstock; well proportioned between plowing, pasturing and mowing; well wooded; a large dwelling house, barn and tan yard on farm.

taxes in Lyme
Notice by Nathaniel Matson, Tax Collector in Lyme that taxes may be paid at the houses of Edward Champlin, Widow Mary Lee, Daniel Lord, Abner Griffing; Abner Comstock, and Wm. Brockway and Col. Marshfield Parsons.

salt for sale
by Stephen Knowlton Jun. in Chatham at the works at the head of the Niantic River in New London[32]; also a small quantity in East Haddam; also to be sold 200 to 300 cords of wood at the Cove above East Haddam.

taken up
off Goshen Reef, by Richard Spink, a battoe, sharp at both ends.

do not trust her
Whereas as Mary Soule has behaved in a very indecent manner refusing a virtuous compliance with the Apostle's injunction to wives, but, on the contrary, has made sundry attempts to take away my life, by stabbing me with knives and forks, beating me with the distaff tongs and hammer, scratching and beating me inhumanely and now has eloped from my bed and board and refuses to cohabit with me; this therefore is to forbid all persons from harboring her, or trusting her on my account for I will not pay.
          Jonathan Soule

taken up
by Samuel Booker, a sorrel horse in Killingly;

by Phineas Lester on the highway to Canterbury in suffering condition, a bay mare.

for sale
by Ebenezer Dayton, three large English swivel guns, a small anchor and cable, and a small quantity of old iron and rigging is left in the store of Nathaniel Shaw in New London.

at Joseph Trumbull's printing office in Norwich, near the Meeting House, Josephus' Works, a complete 4 volumes being the history of the rise, progress and final right of the Jewish nation; an entertaining and much esteemed work.

postponed
the sale of the late John Jeffrey's house in Groton is postponed until May 12.

to cover
The horse, Ranger, to stand stud. It has been owned by Col. Wyllys of Hartford and now by James Howard of Windham.

****

From *The Gazette,* May 8 , 1778

rich ship seized
Last Wednesday was sent into Boston by the *American Revenue,* Capt. Champlin and the *Revenge* by Capt. Conkling, both of this port, New London, the ship *Lovely Lass,* Capt. Wade, late master from London bound to New York with 255 bales of dry goods, hops, pepper, flour spirits, teas, and wine. The amount of her invoices in London are said to be 20,000 pounds sterling.

to cover
the famous horse Roe Buck will cover at stable of Zephaniah Rude in the First Society of Hebron.

road open
Notice by Timothy Tiffany that a road is now opened by subscriber's house to Lt. Timothy Tiffany's ferry in the North Quarter in Lyme

****

From The *Gazette*, May 15, 1778

prizes taken
Last Saturday, the *Mifflin*, armed schooner, Capt. Kerr returned home after a cruise and brought in as prizes coasting sloops and schooners laden with a variety of useful goods.

Saturday night, under the command of Capt. Dayton and Capt. Chester, with 24 men in both, went to Long Island and carrying one of the boats across a narrow part of the Island at South Hampton, they went about 60 miles down the south side of the island to Fire Island Inlet and took possession of five vessels which lay there laden with lumber, oysters, household furniture, some dry goods, provisions etc. The prizes are all safe arrived. More could have been carried off if they could have been manned. Among the prisoners is a British Sergeant.

prisoner exchange
Last Saturday, a flag with nine of the prisoners by Capt. Douglas sailed for Newport and on Monday returned with a like number of our people in exchange.

died
at Chatham of the small pox, Capt. Stephen Olmstead, aged 57.

stolen
from Thomas Kinyon, son of David Kinyon of Richmond, Rhode Island, a sorrel colored horse.

to stand stud
the horse Liberty at the stable of John Deming Colchester;

to stand stud at the stable of Jabez Tracy in the South Society of Preston, the horse Diamond, belonging to Col. Williams and bred on the farm of Elihu Chesebrough.

administration of estates
Notice by Sarah Harris, Executrix of the estate of Thomas Harris, New London, deceased, to the creditors to file claims and to those indebted to settle accounts;

Notice by John Christophers and Peter Christophers, Administrators to the estate of Richard Christophers, Merchant, late of East Haddam, deceased, to the creditors to file claims and to those indebted to settle accounts.

taken up
by Elisha Downer of Plainfield, a bay mare.

taxes
Notice by Joshua Hempsted, Tax Collector in New London, that taxes may be paid at the houses of James Haughton, Dr. Seth Holmes, Jason Allen Joseph Prentis, Clement Leech and Capt. Stephen Prentice.

****

From *The Gazette*, May 22, 1778

libels filed
before Hon. Richard Law in New London Court:
in favor of John Kerr and others against the Sloops *Speedwell*, James Hoit, late commander; *Betsy*, William Robins, late commander; *Polly and Hannah*, David Shadder, late commander; *Katherine*, John Rutgard, late commander; *Sea Flower* Isaac Seidmore, late commander and the *Schooner Industry*, Josiah Buffet late commander, their tackle, appurtenances and several cargos

Another libel has been filed in favor of Joseph Dodge and others against the sloops *Morning Star*, Pater Weglow, late commander; *Sea Flower*, George Webster, late commander their tackle, appurtenances and several cargos;

another libel has been filed in favor of Ebenezer Dayton and others against the Schooners *Peggy,* Charles Cameron, late commander; *Polly* George Hallock, late commander; sloop *George,* Samuel Tobet, late commander, the *Delancey,* Thomas Ming late commander; and the *Jacob,* James Smith, late commander;

another libel has been filed in favor of John Kerr, Ebenezer Dayton and Jason Chester against eight whale boats, their tackle, appurtenances and furnishings, all as taken on the high seas; notice by Wm. Saltonstall.

will cover
Elijah Willoughby's horse Diamond at his stable in Newent.

wife eloped
as Hannah, wife of the Subscriber, Daniel Culver, has deserted and refuse to cohabit with me, this is to forewarn all persons not to trust her on my account for I will pay no debt of her contracting, from the date hereof.

deserted
from Capt. Thomas Seymour's Company of Col. Elisha Sheldon's Regiment of Light Dragoons, John Cotteril, from Exeter, Rhode Island; 5 feet, 7 inches tall ; light complexion.

lost
Notice by Elisha Gallup of North Parish, New London, that lost in the horse shed of Mr. Henry, Inn holder in Paugwonck in Colchester, a striped linen gown.

taxes
John Crary, Tax Collector in Preston, advises that taxes may be paid at the houses of John Harkness and Dr. Joshua Downer.

strayed
from Elihu Ely of Lyme, a bay mare;

from Aaron Haskin of Bolton, a sorrel colt.

From *The Gazette*, May 29, 1778

a fraud
deserted from J. Michel, Captain of the French Ship *Lyon,* in New London Harbor one Labe Galand, who was under the character of a priest on board and has taken with him a quantity of gold, silver and paper currency, not his own; he is a short, thick, well set man; light complexion; large black eyes, short straight black hair; looks like a Jew; speaks very little English; can speak French, German and Latin; has a good notion of sleight of hand; rode a small black horse; had on when he went a brown coat, blue jacket and breeches and blue great coat; had a small gold watch with a small bell to the chain that he was very fond of showing. Whoever will apprehend such pretended priest and return him on said ship will have a reward of $200 paid by me.

for sale
choice hemp, thread, lately imported from France, by John Panevart at his house in New London.

found
near the Rope Walk in New London, a soldiers coat and jacket, almost new; apply to Printer's Office.

stolen
Notice by Jeremiah Harris of Norwich that stolen out of the Sloop *Brilliant* a silver watch with a China face. Watchmaker's name "Cabrier."

taken up
by John Dolbeare of New London, a brown bay horse;

by Abel Baker of New London, a dark bay mare;

taxes
Notice by Tax Collectors Nathan Bushnell Jun. and Caleb Knight, that they will be in the towns of Preston, Voluntown, Plainfield

and Canterbury for settlement of taxes and will be at the houses, on the dates indicated, of Robert Crary in Preston; John Harkness in the North Society; Deacon Gordon in Voluntown, Capt. Eaton in Plainfield and at Mr. Bingham, Inn Holder in Canterbury.

****

From *The Gazette,* June 5, 1778

remarkable
The following account of a weeks work done by an old lady in the North Parish of this Town, New London, aged 76, is thought worthy of remark -*viz,* she carded for a girl to spin 60 knots and carded and spun 30 knots of tow herself.[33]
N.B. She is a widow.

prizes captured
We hear that Capt. Champlin and Capt. Conkling of this port, New London, have taken a snow which they sent to the West Indies and that Capt. Conkling is arrived at Bedford.

broke out
broke out enclosure of Col. Sage of Middletown, a black horse with a white face.

to be sold
by Sam'l Mattocks, a convenient dwelling house and shop with about half an acre of land situated on the main street in Hartford, a little north of the Courthouse; said house is two stories high, 41 feet in front and 30 feet wide, with seven lower rooms, three chimneys and six fireplaces below and two above; well calculated to accommodate two families, with a good wall within ten feet of the back doors. The shop is 20 feet in front with a chimney. The house lot contains in front enough for another house of 40 feet; for further particulars, enquire of Daniel Goodwin, Merchant in Hartford.

one pair largest size potash kettles; enquire of Sylvanus Tinker, East Haddam.

strayed
from Jonathan Hartshorn of Preston North Society, eight sheep.

will cover
Brazen Buck at Zeb, Andrus Jun., in Norwich East Society. his sire is the famous English Horse Flying Buck; he is in size, strength, beauty and resolution, equal to any horse in this State of his age.

****

From *The Gazette,* June 12, 1778

prizes taken
On Monday, Capt. Ebenezer Dayton in an armed boat took three prizes (coasters) into New Haven which he took near Fire Island inlet on the south side of New England;

Last Sabbath, a schooner taken by Block island by two whale boats from the Connecticut River was sent in. He was from Jamaica laden with rum sugar and coffee and it is said belongs to Mr. Lopez late of Newport.

small pox at sea
The *American Revenue* and the *Revenge* American privateers from this port, New London, arrived in Bedford, their crews being taken down by the small pox.

sloop taken
Capt. Roland in a sloop from this port, New London, is taken and carried to Antigua.

execution postponed
The murderers of Joshua Spooner, who were to have been executed on the 4th inst, are reprieved to the 2 of July next.

for sale
sundry lots owned by a number of gentlemen in Plainfield and Preston lying in the town of New London, about one mile from the

Court House and suitable for plowing, mowing and pasturing; enquire of Dr. Joshua Downer of Preston.

strayed
from Stephen Olmsted of East Hampton in Chatham, a black mare.

notice of money owed
If one widow Ford, the mother of James Ford, who lately sailed out of Newbury port would apply to Spencer Bennet, she will be informed of a large sum of money to be paid to her.

broke out
of the stable of Roger Bulkley, four horses.

to be sold
a farm and dwelling house and barn in the First Society of Lyme; 60 acres, 12 of which is choice for plowing; the whole well proportioned for wood and pasture; new grist mill and fulling mill thereon; enquire of Edward and Matthew Dorr, living on the premises.

salt
to be sold by Amasa Allen at his salt works at he head of the Niantic River in New London

notice of meeting
to the Captains of Col. Latimer's Regiment of a meeting is to be held at his house in New London.

board immediately
All officers and seaman of the Brig *Resistance*, are notified to repair on board immediately.

taken up
by John Bolles in Norwich river, a chestnut canoe, foreign built.

escape
Notice by Ephraim Miner, Goaler, that escaped from the New London jail, a certain John Ames who was in goal upon an execution and for breach of peace; his abode for some times past was at the house of Broadhurst Bacon in Lyme; middling stature; very light colored eyes

runaway
from Elisha Lay in Lyme, Negro man named Tom; 23 years of age; 6 foot tall; well set; can read and write; took a fiddle.

****

From *The Gazette*, June 19, 1778

prizes taken
Thursday evening of last week, a schooner privateer, belonging to Newbury, Capt. Bentley, arrived here. The day before, off Montauk Point, he fell in and retook a French snow bound for Newport;

Sunday last, a boat bound from Block Island to Newport was taken and carried into Stonington by an armed whaleboat, She had on board 14 calves, 30 bushels of corn and some other article of provision for the comfort of the inhabitants of Newport;

Capt. Lathrop in a ship and Capt. Ripley in a brig, both of this port, New London, were lately taken on their passage to North Carolina and carried into the Delaware River;

The sloop *Friendship,* Capt. Crary out of Stonington, bound for North Carolina, was taken ten days after she sailed by a 10 gun sloop, fitted out of Bermuda.

died
in Martinico of the small pox, Capt. Theophilus Stanton of Norwich.

to be sold
in New London, eleven vessels from 23 tons burthen to 70 tons; well founded with sails, cables and all appurtenances.

sailors wanted
The sloop *Bever,* a prime sailer and mounting 12 guns, Capt. William Havens, is now in the harbor of New London and fitting out for a cruise; enquire of Capt. Nathan Douglas.

taken up
by Edward Smith in Middletown, Upper House, a brown stray mare;

by Jared Taylor in Killingly, near Capt. Felshaw's in Killingly, a black mare.

****

From *The Gazette*, June 26, 1778

wanted
Gentlemen Adventurers to sail aboard the Sloop *Revenge* Joseph Conkling, Commander, now in New London harbor.

board now
John Kerr directs all those who signed on the ship *Warren* in Boston to join him to go there and board the vessel

broke into the enclosure
of Stephen Clark in Windham, Second Society, a horse;

of Samuel Hart of Saybrook, a black mare

notice
Whereas my wife Abigail Bradford continues to behave herself in a very indecent manner, refusing to return to my family, notwithstanding the most earnest solicitations, this is to forbid all persons trusting her on my behalf.
William Bradford, Canterbury

to be sold
the cargo of the Brig *Neptune*, a retaken vessel from Teneriff, consisting of choice Teneriff wines. Enquire at Mr. Stoddard's, opposite the Printing Office in New London.

to be sold
schooner *True Love*, about 50 tons, three years old.
****

From *The Gazette,* July 3, 1778

pick up
The subscribers for *Buca's Family Physician* are expected to pick up their books at the Printer.

to be sold
by John Foster at Middletown, a prize sloop, about 30 tons with tackle and apparel;

schooner *Betsy,* 80 tons prime sailer almost new; well founded; apply to John M. Breed of Norwich Landing;

a quantity of blistered steel by Samuel Brand Jr. of Westerly, near Paucatuck bridge

the salt works on the land of Latham Avery in Groton

good refined bar iron for sale by Ebenezer Backus at his store in Windham;

a good mare and colt to be exchanged for a good saddle horse; enquire of the Printer.

strayed or stolen
from Paul Wheeler of Stonington, a sorrel mare.

prizes to be sold
three prize ships their rigging sale and apparel, guns, taken by Ebenezer Dayton and Company;

two sloops in New London about 40 tons, taken by Capt. Dodge; prime sailers

administration of estates
Notice by John Champlin, Administrator of the estate of Captain George Champlin of New London, deceased, to the creditors to file claims and to those indebted to settle accounts.

libels filed
before Hon. Richard Law in New London Court, in favor of Nathaniel Bentley, Commander of the armed schooner *Hornet* against a parcel of liquors and piece goods taken out of French snow, which was in the possession of British of the British Ship *Experiment*, Sir James Wallace Commander;
also in favor of Michael Melally, Commander of the armed brig *Nancy* against the snow *Dispenser*, William Pond, late Commander.

runaway
from the sloop *Revenge*, Capt. Conkling, two Negro men taken in a British prize; also a Negro owned by Capt. Bulkley of Wethersfield, named Sam; about 5 foot 10 inches;

also a Negro man named London owned by Picket Latimer in New London; 24 years of age; 5 foot, 8 or 10 inches tall.
****

From *The Gazette,* July 10, 1778

murderers executed
William Brooks, James Buchanan; Ezra Ross and Basheba Spooner were executed in Worcester for the murder of Johusa Spooner.

died
at Windham, Oliver Dyer, son of Eliphalet Dyer in the 23rd year of his life after a lingering distressing illness during which he behaved with exemplary fortitude and died in the hope of eternal life.

ship ready to sail
Gentlemen seamen and adventurers by the Sloop *Revenge*, Capt. Joseph Conkling to go on board.

to be sold
writing paper to be sold by the Printer.

wanted
Two or three journeymen saddlers may be assured of constant employment by applying to Ebenezer Wright of Wethersfield.

****

From *The Gazette,* July 17, 1778

Gentlemen Volunteers
sought by William Havens, Commander of the *Bever*, to sail on a cruise against the enemy.

subscriptions
for soldiers are being taken up Messrs Eliphalet Lyman of Lebanon; Mark Anthony Desolph of Chelsea in Norwich; Caleb Huntington of Norwich; Amamsa Desolph at Pomfret; Thomas Jones at Killingly.

for sale
American manufactured salt by Joseph Woodbridge at his home in Groton;

by Andrew Law of Cheshire Connecticut, a collection of psalm tunes and anthems;

by Edmond Darrow and Co. in Norwich, bar iron by the ton or hundred weight; wanted immediately two or three journeymen nailers; Primers to be sold by the gross, dozen or single by Green and Spooner of Norwich;

by Joshua Starr of New London, Jamaica spirits, by wholesale or retail turpentine and liver oil;

by William Stewart of New London, a good assortment of medicine;

by George Dennis, Jun. raisins, cinnamon, pepper, allspice at the store across from Zabdiel Rogers;

a likely Negro girl of 8 years old;

strayed or stolen
from Robert Fraser of New London, a cow; return to him or to Elisha Bliss of Norwich.

collect prize money
Notice by Thomas Mumford of Groton to the officers and crew of the Continental Frigate *Alfred,* under the command of Capt. Elisha Hinman, to come and receive their shares of the prize money.

libels filed
Notice by Wm. Saltonstall, Register, that a Libel is filed before and to be heard by the Hon. Richard Law, Judge of the Maritime Court for the County of New London in favor of the owners officers and men of the armed Sloop *Industrious Bee* and of the Boat *Revenge* against the sloop *Success*, John Fish, late commander, her cargo, tackle and apparel.

forgotten
Notice by Amos White that sometime past a quantity of flax was left at his store to a man belonging to the eastward, who was to call for it in few days, he being in a very poor state of health and has not been heard of since.

stolen
from James Hoard of Windham at the house of Mr. Levi Perkins in Norwich, a saddle.

deserted
from Capt. Whitney's Company in Col. McClellan' Regiment three soldiers:

Aaron Fish, belonging to Groton; 21 years old, something small; well built; light complexion; light hair and blue eyes, a tailor by trade and is somewhat crippled in his hand by a burn;

John Norman and Abner Geer, who belong to Preston; Norman is 17, small of stature, dark complexion and black eyes; Geer is about 16 years old, of small stature and light complexion and hair

administration of estates

Notice by Ebenezer Allen, Administrator of the estate of Jonathan Crosby of Mansfield, , deceased, to the creditors to file claims and to those indebted to settle accounts.

****

From *The Gazette,* July 24, 1778

prize money

Notice by Joseph Woodbridge, at the head of the Mystic River, to the crew belonging to the sloop *Revenge,* Joseph Conkling, Commander, to come to his house for their share of the prize money.

letters to the soldiers

Notice by Jonath Burnham, New London, to all those who have friends in General Huntington's and General Verum's Brigades that they can send them letters by leaving them with:

Captain Douglas, New London
Mr. Smith in Groton
Messrs. Stanton or Wheeler in Stonington
Dr. Downer or Mr. Harkness in Preston
Capt. Eaton in Plainfield
Messrs. Backus or Park in Canterbury
Mr. Flint in Scotland
Mr. Cary in Windham
Mrs. Alden in Lebanon
Mr. Lathrop in Norwich
Mr. Tainter in Colchester
Messrs. Olmstead, Emmons and Comstock in East Haddam
Col. Parsons, Messrs Lord and Griffing in Lyme
Messrs. Dudley and Stanuar in Saybrook
Capt. Buell in Killingsworth
Messrs. Graves and Tone in Guilford
Mr. Barber in Branford
Mr. Thomson in East Haven

Mr. Adam in New Haven Mr. Betts in Norwalk
Mr. Brian in Milford Mr. Webb in Stamford
Mr. Olcott's in Stratford
Mr. Penfield in Fairfield

broke into the enclosure
of Nathaniel Flint of Windham, Second Society, two mare colts.

taken up
by Elelazer McGhill in Killingly, a chestnut colored mare.

for sale
Notice by Nathaniel Thompson of a good assortment of European and India goods at the store in Groton of Joseph Woodbridge;

different types of cloths in East Haddam by John Nulbert and David Gelston;

at the store of Lyade M'Curdy in Lyme, a few hogsheads of sugar.

to the candid and impartial public
Whereas my husband, Mr. William Bradford of Canterbury has twice advertised me of being guilty of unreasonably departing from his family and refusing to return, notwithstanding his earnest solicitations thereto.
I now think myself duty bound for the vindicating of my own conduct to give short narratives of the reasons for my leaving.
As to my first withdrawal, which was in the month of April in 1776, I went Norwich on a visit to my children and other friends with a design to tarry about a week or ten days and then to return, but before the time expired I was surprised to see my name advertised in the *Connecticut Gazette* in as hard language as a master could have advertised a runaway Negro, not only forbidding anyone from trusting me, but forbidding all persons from harboring or entertaining me.
These matters and the cruel treatment I had before received from Mr. Bradford was fully heard and adjudicated by three gentlemen officially chosen to assist and advice us under our difficulties and,

after a full hearing, these gentlemen were convinced in the reasonableness of my complaints that they advised and ordered that Mr. Bradford should relinquish all interests which I had before my intermarriage with him and put it into the hands of my son for my sole use and benefit so that, if Mr. Bradford did not treat me with more kindness and respect than he had done before, I may take what was my own and fly upon it in a separate state, to which Mr. Bradford readily agreed and executed the proper writings accordingly and on his solemnly promising before these Gentlemen and others for the future to treat me with all possible kindness and never again to speak an angry or hard word against me, I consented to make another trial to live with him, resolving to do everything which in my power lay to please him and keep him in his present good humor, but I soon found myself an unwelcome guest in the family and that evil like spirit, which is so natural for Mr. Bradford began again to trouble him and I felt the sad horse whip

And that, in a very angry manner, he locked up every thing in the house from me, even those most common necessaries of life and, at length his pleasure was to sleep alone (which by the way was no mortification to me) and for more than a week before I left the house, I was every night belted up fast in my bedroom like a prisoner in a close goal and there obliged until Mr. Bradford or some other member of the family pleased to give me enlargement, which was generally late in the morning as to make my confinement very disagreeable. I, at length, one Sunday morning, made my escape from the bedroom window and went round to the kitchen door, but found it barred to me. I attempted to enter by a window but was pushed back by one of the family with such violence as I was much hurt by the means. I begged to get my clothes so as to go up to Meeting. I was denied and was obliged to go to a kind neighbor's for shelter. I suffered a second affront of the same kind and was determined to avoid a third. I went immediately to my son in Norwich and got him to send for my things which Mr. Bradford honestly delivered up according to the former Advice and Agreement and I have taken lodging with a kind friend where I live in peace and free from the cruel hands of tyranny. I hope my unhappy lot will be a warning to others and

excite the compassion of all candid Christian friend to whom I submit the case of their humble servant.
Abigail Bradford

deserted
Notice by Joshua Hempstd Jun. from the *Warren,* that Elnathan Mason, who belonged to either Stonington or Groton, has deserted;

administration of estates
Notice by Nathaniel and Sarah Millard, Administrators for the estate of Oliver Millard, late of Millington Society, East Haddam, deceased, to the creditors to file claims and to those indebted to settle accounts.

list of letters in New London Post Office

Jonathan Beebe - East Haddam	Abigail Martin - New London, North Parish
Mr. Waters - Killingsworth	Mr. Rouillard - New London
Benjamin Chillson - Killingsworth	Capt. Nathaniel Stanton - Groton
Nathaniel Cook - Norwich	Katherine Shelden - New London
Peter Fotor - New London	
John Hamilton - Norwich	Anna Smith - Norwich
Nathan Hodges - Mansfield	Jonathan Truman - New London
Samuel Avery - Stonington	
Capt. Samuel Leighton - Groton	Silvanus Wick - Groton

strayed or stolen
from John Miner of Lyme, a bay horse.

prisoner exchange
Yesterday, se'nnight in the afternoon, a flag of truce from the enemy with 24 American prisoners, arrived here in New London from New York.

****

From *The Gazette*, July 31, 1778

arrivals
Last Wednesday, Col. Clover's Brigade of Continental troops, arrived in Town from the Grand American Camp in White Plains and yesterday morning General Greene from the Grand Army passed through Town.

died
Yesterday se'nnight, died in Lebanon, Col. Joseph Trumbull, eldest son of his Excellency Governor Trumbull. He had been late Commissary General of the Continental Army after laboring for six months under severe bilious, paralytic and other complicated disorders and, after several partial recoveries, he sank into the arms of death at his father's house.

administration of estates
Notice from Isaac Stanton and Anne Stanton, Administrators, to the estate of Theophilus Stanton, late of Groton, deceased, to the creditors to file claims and to those indebted to settle accounts.

boat taken
last Tuesday, a schooner about 30 tons burden and mounting 8 swivel guns clandestinely took and carried away a whale boat, belonging to Elenathan Beebe on Plumb Island.

taken up
by Oliver Manwaring, a red cow.

for sale
genuine cannon and musket powder to be sold by Isaac Doolittle in New Haven wholesale or retail at moderate prices;

at East Haddam, two complete wagons with furniture and seven draw horses by Sylvanus Tinker;

at Nate Palmer's warehouse in Stonington the cargo of the sloop General Gage, sugar, rum, Jamaica spirits.

****

From *The Gazette*, August 7, 1778

drownings
Friday morning, a boy of about 2 years old, son of Elisha Perkins of Groton was found drowned in the Norwich River near his father's house;

Sunday towards evening, a canoe in which five boys were overset by a gust of wind at the mouth of Woter's cove and one of them, son of Christopher Greene, aged 9, was drowned and another had nearly shared the same fate.

lightning
Last Friday night, a large barn filled with grain and hay, belonging to Mr. Samuel Denison of Saybrook, took fire by lightning and was consumed. The same night four cattle were killed in Lyme by lightning.

died·
in Lyme, Isaac Hale of that Town.

broke into the enclosure
of Joseph Balcam in Mansfield, a bay horse.

for sale
a very good chaise, almost new, with a harness, an ox cart and yoke; enquire of John Hertell in New London;

by Solomon Lord in Saybrook, allspice, ginger, brimstone, hard soap, spectacles pins, thimbles, needles, coat buttons etc.

price hike
The exorbitant price to which country produce has risen obliges the publisher of this paper to raise the price thereof to 12 sh., for the half year, which is about half the price that most of the other papers in New England have been at for the past six months. Those who pay in country produce will have their paper at the old

price.

****

From *The Gazette,* August 14, 1778

ready to sail
All officers and Gentleman Volunteers going on cruise on the Brig New Broom , Israel Bishop, commander, should come on board

draft dodgers
Notice by John Riley of Windham, Recruiting Officer for the 5th Brigade that the following have all been properly ordered to join the army and have re fused to obey and have absented themselves:

from the Town of Killingly: Benjamin Farebanks; Isaac Atwood; Nathaniel Sunday; Ephraim Warrin; Nehemiah Lovejays; Thomas Wood; William Walton, Jun.; Peneul Cady; David Hascall; William Waitemour 3d; Henry Stone; Ebenezer Phimmer; Aaron Atgor; Barn. Tortocolom; Jesse Joslin; Henry Carpenter; William Straight; John Anderson; John Kee; Matthias Whitney and Elijah Young;

from the Town of Voluntown:; Jacob Patrick; Amos Gore; James Dixon Jun.,; Robert Thomson; Benomi Kinney; Abraham Harrington; Christopher Colegrove and Phineas Lawis,

from the Town of Plainfield: Elijah Cook;

from the town of Hebron: Zadock Man; Nehemiah Gilbert; Jeremiah Bolles; Asa Hutchinson; Ebenezer Haughton, Benjamin Archer;

from the Town of Lebanon Nathaniel Fitch and Edward Hawkins

from the Town of Woodstock: Richard Bolles; James Chasse, Jun.; John Willson; and John Bowers.

wanted
a Negro woman that understands house work; enquire of the Printer.

partnership to buy lottery tickets
Whereas Jonathan Darrow; John Wasseen; James Elwood ; Nehemiah Whitney; Andrew Thorp; Nathan Degget; John Alden; Simeon Spencer and John Lewis, entering on a cruise on the Brig *Defence,* Capt. Smedley, have bought twenty tickets to the U. S. Lottery, and expecting through the fortunes of war to be separated and dispersed before the drawing; they hereby notify the Public of their venture; notice by Marvin Wait.

to be sold
cheap for cash or country produce, a very new cane mill that will grind, with good attendance, seven or eight barrels a day;

store improved by Joseph Williams at Norwich Landing, a quantity of dry goods;

administration of estates
Notice by Bryan Parmalee and Stephen Olmsted, Jun., Administrators of the estate of Capt. Stephen Olmsted, late of Chatham deceased, to the creditors to file claims and to those indebted to settle accounts;

Notice by Bryan Parmalee and John Norton, Commissioners appointed by the Probate Court of Middletown for the estate of Capt. Thomas Doolittle, late of Chatham, deceased and represented insolvent, to the creditors to file claims and to those indebted to settle accounts. A hearing will be held at the house of Gideon Arnold, Inn holder, Chatham;

Notice by Elias Adams and Josiah Dewey, Commissioners appointed by the Probate Court of Plainfield for the estate of Samuel Faulknor, late of Canterbury, deceased and represented insolvent, to the creditors to file claims and to those indebted to settle accounts. A hearing will be held at the house of John Parks in said Canterbury.

runaway
from Abel Franklin of Groton, a Negro man named Timothy Titus; very light complexion; 24 or 25 years of age; 6 foot, 1 or 2 inches high; extremely well built; has a scar on his left hand, near his wrist;

from Joshua Bulkley of Colchester, a Negro man, named Guinea; 33 years of age; well built; 6 foot tall.

taken up
by Calvin Eaton of Ashford, a chestnut colored horse;

by Daniel Fox of New London near Millstone Point, a pine canoe; supposed to belong to Nathan Beckwith.

broke in the enclosure
of Benjamin Convers of Killingly, a lame mare;

of Asa Fuller of Colchester, a brown horse.

scheme of lottery
by the General Assembly of Connecticut to raise 3000 pounds to build a good bridge over the river Shetucket. The Managers are Christopher Leffingwell, Jacob DeWitt, Benjamin Coit, William Coit, Jeremiah Halsey and Roger Sterry.

cattle for sale
Notice by Jonathan Salmon that ten or eleven cattle, lately brought from Long Island, will be sold at public vendue at the house of the Rev. George Beckwith in Lyme, North Quarter.

lost
Notice by Levi Perkins that left at his house, a pack containing women's wearing apparel, by a woman, name unknown traveling to New London.

****

From *The Gazette,* August 21, 1778

storm
Thursday and Friday of last week, we had a severe gale of wind from the north east which blew down a considerable quantity of corn and trees. At Narragansett, a considerable number of boats were drove ashore.

to be sold
by Uriah Rogers, next door to Col Jabez Chapman in East Haddam, choice Jamaican spirits;

the Schooner *Mifflin*; enquire at Mr. Shaw's store in New London;

the hull of a sloop of 40 tons by Job Taber of New London;

by Thomas Allen in New London, a hay engine with its appurtenances.

strayed or stolen
Notice by Richard Hewitt of Stonington that strayed or stolen from the pasture of Capt. John Swan in Stonington, a sorrel mare.

****

From *The Gazette*, August 28, 1778

taxes due
Notice by Nathaniel Matson, Tax Collector, to the inhabitants of Lyme and those that live in the neighboring towns that taxes can be paid at the following places at the following time: at the houses of Daniel Lord, Captain Abner Comstock, Jesse Beckwith; the widow Mary Lee, Captain Marshfield Parsons, Edward Champlin and Abner Griffin.

strayed or stolen
from John Bulkley of Colchester a brown horse supposed to be rode towards Boston by a runaway Negro.

to be sold
nails of all sizes to be sold for cash or country produce by Charles Smith at his shop in Groton.

by Captain David Mumford in New London, two 12 lb. cannons, 4 large anchors, 1 1/8 inch cable and several tons of iron ballast.

****

From T*he Gazette,* September 4, 1778

fistfight leads to death
Tuesday se'nnight, as Mr. Samuel Holmes of Stonington was scuffling with another person at a house in that Town, Mr. Holmes was thrown with such force that he died a few hours after.

enemy sails by
Sabbath evening, about 70 sail of the enemy's shipping from New York went down the Sound, bound to Newport, and the next day a large frigate also went down in the Sound.

fighting in Rhode Island
On Saturday, there was a considerable action between the enemy and our troops on Rhode Island. in which we learn about 60 of our soldiers are killed and 120 wounded and 100 of the enemy were killed. We took about 300 prisoners.

accident
On the 3rd day of July last Deacon John Holbrook of Pomfret, riding in company with two others, having one of his children in his arms, coming off from descending ground onto a plain piece of way, the horses set out on a quick pace. A horned creature being in the road, one of the horses was suddenly diverted against, or under, the Deacon's mare upon which he was brought down. The Deacon fell as it is supposed with his head against a stone. The child was taken up seemingly dead but soon recovered. A physician was had soon, who let blood from the Deacon instantly and afterward repeatedly but, notwithstanding all means which could be used, he died in 2 ½ hours after his fall.[34]

to be sold
a tract of land in Lyme, situated about 2 or 3 miles northward from the Meeting House in the First Society; lately the estate of R. Marvin, an insolvent debtor, containing 286 acres. It consists of a variety of soils suitable to every purpose of husbandry, contains a large orchard and a great quantity of timber, a small part which is under a woman's dowry. Notice given by Abraham Bradley, Moses Seymour and Miles Beach of Litchfield.

****

From *The Gazette*, September 11, 1778

an enemy threat off the coast
The fleet of 53 sail of shipping which was mentioned in our last to have gone up the Sound yesterday se'nnight, continued their course to the westward for some hours with a fine northerly wind until they were nearly out of the sight of the harbor. The whole fleet, except 5 or 6 which is supposed proceeded to New York, suddenly came about and stood to the eastward and, by 1 or 2 o'clock, had returned to offshore this harbor, where they continued to wait until near sunset with the apparent design of coming immediately up the harbor. For this they were prevented from doing by the wind and tide against them. By sunset, the whole anchored fleet lay about a mile and a half southwest of the lighthouse, in a line east and west as the shore runs and having their boats out as if they designed immediately to land their troops, they having a large number on board. This alarmed the inhabitants of the Town who were immediately called to arms. Expresses were sent to the neighboring towns for assistance and, by Friday evening, about 4,000 troops, well equipped, had arrived in New London and Groton and the roads were crowded with others who continued to march from towns more remote until they were countermanded. The fleet continued in the above situation until between 4 and 5 o'clock Friday afternoon, when they came to sail and stood out into the Sound in the evening and the next morning were out of sight.

Great praises due to the militia of the neighboring towns who on this occasion so generally and with such alacrity came to our assistance. Major General Huntington was so sensible of this that, on Saturday, the several regimens being drawn up received his thanks and general orders.

The above fleet on Thursday drove ashore near the lighthouse a sloop from Connecticut River laden with provisions and bound for this port, New London. The people cut away her sails and some riggings which they brought off and some others afterwards took several barrels of bread, but the enemy took out the remainder of the cargo before scuttling her and sending her adrift.

representatives chosen
General Gurdon Saltonstall and Nathaniel Shaw are chosen to represent the town of New London in the General Assembly.

shortened paper
So much of our time having been taken by this late alarm that we have not been able to publish more than a half sheet this week.

taken up
Notice by David Richards, Jun. of New London that a black mare was taken up by him near the Meeting House.

administration of estates
Notice by Joseph Morgan, Administrator of the Estate of Deacon William Morgan, late of Stonington, deceased, to creditors to file claims and to those indebted to settle accounts. A meeting will be held at the house of Daniel Eldridge in Groton.

to be sold
Good liver oil to be sold by William Howard in the Canada Society of Wyndham at $6 per gallon.

A few casks of choice Tennerief wines to be sold. Enquire of John Stoddard, opposite the Printing Office in New London.

****

From *The Gazette*, September 18, 1778

troops ordered to New London
Since the last alarm at this place, two regiments of militia are ordered here for the security of the Town and Harbor.

raid
Beginning of last week, Major Ebenezer Gray with a party of men from Colonel Amiegs, went to Huntington on Long Island and brought off 16 prisoners. Three others were killed in the skirmish and two others made their escape. They were all disaffected persons who had gone over to the enemy from this State.

died
at Norwich, Mr. Daniel Leffingwell, age 27;

at Newent in Norwich this morning, died Lt. Simon Perkins in the 42nd year of his age. He was taken ill in Brooklyn after our troops landed there.

hospital open
A hospital to innoculate for the smallpox is now opened in Saybrook under the direction of the Public's humble servant, John Ely.

To all Gentlemen Volunteers
The noted Brig *Nancy*, Sylvanus Pinkham, Commander, is being fitted out for a cruise. Articles of Agreement may be seen at Mr. Icabod Powers Jr. in New London.

to be sold
at the store of the Messers. Ledyard in Groton, a large assortment of dry good and cutlery ware which goods were taken and brought into this port by the Schooner *Hornet*, Captain Nathaniel Bently.

the privateer sloop *Betsy* lying in New London, about 30 tons.

lost
Notice from Christopher Leffingwell that he lost between New London and Norwich Landing, a leather pocketbook.

found
in the street near the Courthouse in New London by Frederick Niles, a large silver teaspoon.

taken up
by Thomas Daniels in East Haddam, a stray horse with a white strip in his face.

administration of estates
Notice by Eliashid Adams and Josiah Dewey, Commissioners appointed by the Probate Court of Plainfield to the estate of Samuel Faulkoner, late of Canterbury, deceased and represented insolvent, to creditors to file claims and to those indebted to settle accounts. A meeting will be held at the house of John Parke in Canterbury.

strayed or stolen
from Enoch Freeman in Mansfield, a black mare;

from Allen Campbel of Voluntown, a dark bay mare.

****

From *The Gazette*, September 25, 1778

privateer returns safely
Yesterday se'night the privateer sloop *Revenge* returned into port from a cruise, being chased by several British cruisers. They were obliged to throw over part of their guns.

prisoner exchange
All the American prisoners are nearly all sent out of New York, but there are 615 French prisoners still there.

to be sold,
a genteel curricle with a stand of excellent horses or a chaise with one horse by Benjamin Henshaw, Middletown.

by Thomas Allen, the furniture, etc. in his house, as heretofore advertised.

broke into the enclosure
of Elisha Lewis, Jr. of Stonington, a white mare;

of John Green of Stonington, a black bull.

return weapons
In the late alarm in New London, many people were supplied with ammunition and muskets and all have not returned them. They may depend upon it that they shall not only be advertised in next week's paper, but proper methods taken to recover them.

wanted
Good encouragement will be given to a man that is suitable for a hosteller at a tavern and can be well recommended by Nathan Douglass in New London.

administration of estates
Notice by Sarah Stanton, Administrator of the Estate of Andrew Stanton, late of Stonington, deceased to creditors to file claims and to those indebted to settle accounts. A meeting will be held at the house of Colonel Joseph Champlain of Stonington.

list of Tory prisoners
taken by a party under the command of Major Gray who landed on Long Island:
boatmen: John Baker, Aaron Olmsted and Thomas Smith of Middletown; Chapman Judson and Lemeul Bradley of New Haven ; Joel Murray of Preston; Hez. Wheeler of Fairfield and Daniel Smith of New Milford,

landsmen: Joseph Olmsted, Billious Ward, William Nichols, A. Camp of New Haven and Howell, supposedly from New Haven, Abid Hull from Stratford; William and Hezekiah Chandler escaped.
killed: Isaac Coffin of Woodbury, Peter Lyon of Reading; and Nathaniel Mall at New Milford.
They burnt one brig and two sloops.

deserted
from Capt. Goodwin on their march from Boston to New London

	William Price
Thomas Gray	Robert Moss
William McKeever	William Grant
Henry Thomas	Dominick Harberson
Samuel Killey	Joseph Rustin
James Rosecarry	James Johnson
James Tier	William Ward
Thomas Parker	Michael Knox
John Moss	Thomas Fortune
John Cilles	Alexander Hellen
Marham Wilson	William Noble
Alexander McCloud	Seal Chandler
John Blomer	James Camby
James Downy	James Sandler
William Taylor	William Eton
Griffith Roberts	Edward Christin
Samuel Otberltbrow	
John Smith	

libels filed
Notice by Wm. Saltonstall, Register, that a Libel is filed before, and to be heard by, the Hon. Richard Law, Judge of the Maritime Court for the County of New London:
in favor of the sloop *Lydia*, her owners and all associated, Jabez Lord, Commander against sloop *York,* her appurtenances etc ;

in favor of the sloop *Two Brothers*, her owners and all associated, Thomas Chester, Jun. Commander and in favor of sloop *Betsy*, Nathan Moore, Commander against another vessel, unnamed, brought into New London.

****

From *The Gazette*, October 2, 1778

list of letters in New London post office

Joab Alden - Norwich
Joshua Babcock - Stonington
Elizabeth Barry - New London
Jonathan Beebe - East Haddam
John Brown - Groton
Jesse Billings - Colchester
James Davenport - Norwich
Charles Eldridge - Groton
Capt. James Eldridge - Stonington
Jaspar Griffin, Jun. - New London
Christian Gosner - New London
Phoebe Gardner - Norwich
Purnel Houston - New London
George Horner - Stonington
Samuel Ivery - Stonington
Capt. Thomas Kennedy - New London
John Longworthy - Stonington
Jacob Moags - New London
Samuel Plumb - Stonington
Capt. John Rathbun - Stonington
Oliver Smith - Stonington
Thomas Swan - Stonington
Edward Tinker - New London

deerskins
a quantity of deer skins on hand to be sold by Howland and Coit at Norwich Landing.

to be sold
for want of employment, a likely Negro man, 27 years of age;

a grist mill in Windham, the lower end of that Town near the line between Windham and Norwich and Lebanon. Enquire of Eliphalet Dyer or in his absence to Thomas Dyer in Windham.

administration of estates
Notice by James Allyn and Ephraim Allyn, Executors for the estate of James Allyn Sen, late of Groton, deceased to creditors to file claims and to those indebted to settle accounts.

Notice by Hezekiah Manning, John Perkins and Jonathan Rudd, Commissioners appointed by the Probate Court of Windham for the estate of Abner Flint, Windham, deceased and represented to be insolvent, to creditors to file claims and to those indebted to settle accounts.

strayed or stolen
from Joshua Elderkin in Groton, a black horse;

from Elijah Weston in Tolland, a horse;

from Asa Edgerton in Mansfield, a brown horse.

****

From *The Gazette*, October 9, 1778

come and get paid
Jabez Perkins at his store at Norwich Landing is ready to settle with the crew of the armed Ship *Oliver Cromwell*, commanded by Timothy Parker, regarding the two prize ships *Admiral Keppel* and *Cyrus*.

taxes in Preston
Notice by John Crary, Tax Collector of Preston, that taxes may be paid at the houses of Capt. Roger Billings, Capt. Moses Tyler, John Harkness, Robert Crary and Dr. Joshua Downer.

western lands
Notice by John Hempsted, Justice of the Peace for New London County, regarding a meeting of the Proprietors and owners of the Township of Lincoln in New Hampshire at the house of Jeremiah Clement in Norwich to chose a clerk and agent of said propriety;

Notice by James Avery regarding a meeting of the Proprietors and owners of the same for the Town of Landaf, New Hampshire to meet at the house of Jeremiah Clement in Norwich to chose a clerk in room of Dr. Amos Mead who has resigned.

price regulation
Notice to all who work in the clothing business to meet at James Leavens Tavern in Mansfield in order to regulate the prices of their goods so as to do justice to themselves.

to be sold
by John Stoddard, near the Printing Office in New London, wines rum, sugar, Bohea tea and coffee.

strayed or stolen
from Roger Gibson of New London, a horse;

from Lemuel Geer in Preston, a horse.
****
From *The Gazette*, October 16, 1778

British prisoners arrive in Town
Last Friday arrived here between 200 and 300 British prisoners from Boston under guard. They were taken in the *Senegal* sloop of war, captured by Count D'Estaing and are to remain in Town until an equal number of French prisoners are sent from New York in exchange.

found
on board Nathaniel Dyre's sloop, coming from Norwich Landing, a walking stick.

come and receive pay
Notice by Capt. Jonathan Calkings to the non commissioned officers and soldiers in his Militia Company that can receive pay at his house in New London.

taken up
by Samuel Rogers in New London, a suckling colt.

****

From *The Gazette,* October 23, 1778

lost
by James Turner on Norwich Plain, a black leather pocketbook; return to Matthew Turner of New London, North Parish for a reward.

strayed or stolen
from Ebenezer Evetts in Salisbury, a mare; return to Jonathan Evett in East Guilford.

broke into the enclosure
of John Green of Stonington, a mare;

of Elijah Lewis, Jun. of Stonington, a white mare;

of Elijah Hatch, New London, sorrel mare.

house sale postponed
Notice by Thomas Allen to the public that the postponement of the sale of household furniture etc. at his house was occasioned by sickness in his family, but will be held on November 3.

to be sold
at the dwelling house of Hez. Kneeland, Administrator of the estate of Hez. Kneeland, Jun., so much of said estate as to pay his debts.

****

From *The Gazette,* October 30, 1778

deserted
from Capt. Goodwin on their march from Boston to New London, the following persons, *viz*:

Thomas Gray   William McKeever

Henry Thomas
Samuel Killey
James Tier
Thomas Parker
John Moss
Alexander Mc Cloud
M. McClean
John Bloomer
James Downey
William Taylor
Gifford, Roberts
Samuel Orberltbrew
William Price
Robert Moss
William Grant

Dominic Henderson
Joseph Rustin
James Johnson
William Ward
Michael Knox
Thomas Fortune
William Noble
Anthony Ross
Seal Chandler
James Cambry
James Sanders
William Eton
Edward Christin

strayed or stolen
from of Thomas Green of Stonington, a bull;

from Eber Evetts of Salisbury, a bay mare; if found return to Jonathan Evetts of East Guilford for reward.

broke into the enclosure
of Elisha Lewis, Jun. of Stonington, a white mare;

Elijah Hatch of New London a sorrel mare.

for sale
by Benjamin Henshaw of Middletown, a genteel curricle with a span of excellent horses or a chaise with one horse;

The public are informed that the postponement of the sale of furniture from Thomas Allen's house was occasioned by sickness in his family but will be held on November 3.

lost
by James Turner out of his pocket on Norwich Plain, black pocket book; if found return to Matthew Turner of New London North Parish for a ten dollar reward

****

From *The Gazette*, November 6, 1778

died
of Pomfret Lt. George Summer, in the 48th year of his life. He left a father, wife and two children to mourn him.

libels filed
Notice by Wm. Saltonstall, Register, that Libels are filed before, and to be heard, by the Hon. Richard Law, Judge of the Maritime Court for the County of New London:
in favor of Timothy Lock, Commander of the whale boat *Jolly Robbins;* Elijah Champlin, Jun., Commander of the whale boat *Revenge;* Jonathan Salisbury, Commander of the whale boat *Industry* and their associates against the brig *Venus,* Samuel Dunn late Commander;
in favor of Joseph Morse, Commander of the schooner *Weasel*, his associates and the fitters of such scheme against sloop *Dispatch*, Capt. William Gill;
in favor of Capt. Silas Talbot and associates on board sloop *Hawk* against the sloop *Pigeon* Capt. Dunlap;
in favor of Jonathan Salmon, Captain of the armed boat *Refugee* against 18 head of cattle.

tape
Notice by Andrew Perkins of Norwich of his tape manufactory in that Town.

deserted
Notice by Capt. Abner Robinson of Col. M'Clellan's Regiment that deserted from there Timothy Winter; 23 year old; thick set; dark complexion, light colored eyes; 5 feet, 9 inches tall.

broke into the enclosure of
Ebenezer Hovey of Windham, a bull.

taken up
by Joseph Cresea of Pomfret, a sorrel horse.

lottery
tickets in the second of the United States Lottery to be sold by T. Green.

****

From *The Gazette,* November 13, 1778

ships taken
Capt. Oliver Goodrich in a privateer schooner of 4 carriage guns sailed from this port last Friday and, on the same day, was taken by a privateer of 8 guns from Newport;

The privateer Brig *New Broom* from this port, New London, Capt. Bisbee is taken and carried into New York.

storm
Last Wednesday, we had a violent storm from the southeast, but happily very little damage was done to the shipping in this harbor.

new war ship
A very fine ship called the *Confederacy*, belonging to the State, to mount 36 gun, is being built in the Norwich River.

school meeting
The Proprietors of Union School in New London are desired to meet at the school house this evening at sunset precisely.

to be sold
by Jonathan Brooks in New London, a good oak frame, 26 feet by 16, suitable for a store or dwelling house.

wanted
a quantity of well seasoned sheep skins, for which a generous price will be given by John Richards at his shop in Norwich, near Christopher Leffingwell's.

strayed or stolen
from William Wheeler in New London, a sorrel horse.

pay ready
Notice by Col. Oliver Smith in Stonington to the Captains who were in his Regiment in the late expedition to Rhode Island that he has their pay to distribute.

certification of military service
from Capt. Samuel Robinson, Clerk of the Court of Inquiry, that Mr. Samuel Ely, the Preacher, who was in the two bloody battles at Bennington and behaved with the greatest honor, valor and courage in both actions and, on all other accounts, did, when desired, appear before this Court of Inquiry and made a handsome defense relative to the charge of plunder he had taken, which, as he said, was taken at the point of a sword as a volunteer for his groaning, bleeding country and he further said he has supported himself and lived upon his own money and was at no charge to his country.
And the Court, being fully satisfied as to what he said and what he did, they never ordered Mr. Ely to be advertised, nor stigmatized, to my certain knowledge as I was both a Member and Clerk of that Court.

choice shoe leather
to be sold by Thomas Jones at his shop opposite the church in New London.

the Norwich packet
being a double decked boat, built in Providence and fitted in the most convenient manner for passengers, with a large commodious cabin; will ply between Norwich and New London; for freight or passage, apply to Stephen Culver, at the Sign of the Stage Boat,

near the store of Jabez Perkins at Norwich Landing and, in New London, at Mr. Miner's Tavern, next door to the Court House. N.B. All letters and small packages go *gratis*.

administration of estates
Notice by Mary Williams, Executrix of the estate of John Williams, late of Killingworth, deceased, to creditors to file claims and to those indebted to settle accounts.

settle up
Notice by Joseph Smith of New London to those indebted to him to settle accounts.

a few volunteers
for the new ship Governor Trumbull, Henry Billings, Commander, now lying in New London, are still wanted to sail on a cruise against the enemies of America.

taken up
by Joshua Holt, Jun. of Windham, a steer.

****

From *The Gazette,* November 20, 1778

ship wreck
Last Friday night, Capt. John Crocker in a coasting sloop was drove by a gale of wind onto Pine Island, near the mouth of the river, where the vessel was beat to pieces.

prices ease in Boston
We have good advice from Boston that since D'Estaign's fleet has sailed from thence and, after the Continental troops marched off from the State, the price of provisions have fallen fifty per cent in Boston. This must shortly have a salutary effect on the price of provisions in this State.

for sale
by Noble Hinman a ley, benches and a complete set of turner's tools.

strayed or stolen
from Phineas Leffingwell of Norwich, a bright bay horse.
****

From *The Gazette*, November 27, 1778

farm for sale
lying in the First Society in the Town of Lyme , about 80 acres of good land, with a larger dwelling house, barn and orchard thereon; also three-eights of a new sawmill; apply to Matthew Marvin, living on the premises.

wanted
Gentlemen Volunteers for Brig *Middletown* to sail on a cruise of six months, a prime sailer, fourteen pound and two 6 pounders guns; Capt. Nathan Sage Commander.

broke into the enclosure
of Rufus Randall of Colchester, a black steer.

runaway
from John Williams and Elihu Champlin of Stonington, two Negroes, one named Cyrus; 23 years of age; about six feet high; well set and stoops; has a large scar on left cheek and another named John; 5 foot, 6 inches high; thick set; straight built; has lost one eye.

pay up
Ebenezer Hovey of Windham, Second Society, desires all persons indebted to him for newspapers to make payment at the times specified: at the houses of Asa Bishop in Woodstock; of Nathan Child and Ephraim Ingals in Pomfret; of Doctor Howe in Ashford; of Maj. Clark; James Leaven and Dan Storrs in Mansfield.

died
Mrs Lydia Hubbard, age 37, the amiable consort of William Hibbard, Merchant. She was a lady who earned the esteem of all who knew her.

a bon mot
A British officer in New York, being in company with a lady whose sentiments were favorable to the cause of liberty, was making some severe remarks upon the American troops.

"However, Madam" said he, "I think you have a Howe and a Clinton in your Army[35]."

"We have, Sir," replied the Lady, "but you have not a Washington in yours."

notice
from William Bigland, linen stamper, Middletown that he will be leaving Middletown soon and, if any one has any clothes not fetched, they should make immediate arrangements.

strayed or stolen
from Israel Loomis in Colchester, a yearling red heifer;

from Joseph Burnham of Lyme, a dark brown horse.

taken up
by Nathan Ackly of Millington, a black yearling heifer.

****

From *The Gazette,* December 4, 1778

prisoner exchange
Last Sunday, a flag from Boston bound for New York put in here for a harbor and sailed the next day. The flag had been in Newport and delivered part of her prisoners. Capt. Burke, late commander of the *Resistance,* was on board, his parole being nearly expired.

new war ship ready
Monday, the *Confederacy* frigate came down the river.

enemy deserters arrive in Town
Monday evening five green coats arrived here from Long Island, having deserted from the enemy.

ship seized
Last week, a very neat and valuable coasting sloop belonging to Mr Ebenezer Hayden of Saybrook was taken in the Sound near Stratford by a schooner in the service of the enemy.

come receive prize money

Notice by Joseph Conkling to the crew of the sloop *Revenge* that they are desired to call at Joseph Woodbridge's in Groton to receive their balance from the prize ship *Lovely Lass*.

salt works for sale
Notice by William Griswold and John Graham that a large and very valuable salt work is for sale, situated in the western part of the Town of New London, near the head of the Niantic river. The works are in complete order for the business of making salt, including a pump carrying the proper amount of water from the operation into the furnace; ten large pans and 8 pot ash kettles are well set in the furnace; also to be sold about 30 acres of woodland about one mile from the works.

boarding house
Notice by Thomas Wilson that he has a genteel boarding house (in the house lately improved by Mr. Noble Hinman for a tavern) being for the reception and entertainment of gentlemen and travelers.
N.B. good keeping for horses.

broke into the enclosure
of Benajah Bushnell, Jun. of Norwich; a 2 year old heifer.

liver oil
to be sold by Ebenezer Spalding of Canterbury.

good farm for sale
about three miles west of New London; about 50 acres with a large house and barn, also a good orchard; well proportioned for plowing and pasture; about a mile from a good grist mill; enquire of Ezekiel Beebe on premises.

taken up
by the mouth of the Connecticut River by Jeremiah King of Lyme, a Moses boat.

Gentlemen Volunteers wanted
aboard the privateer sloop *Revenge*, Nathan Post, Commander.

deserted
from Capt. Lee Lay's Company in Col. M'Clellan's Regiment, a soldier named Philip Minard; 17 years old; 5 feet, 8 inches tall; dark complexion; dark short hair; black eyes.

pay up
David Belden desires that his customers in East Haddam meet him at Joseph Emmons' Tavern to settle accounts.

****

From *The Gazette*, December 11, 1778

day of thanksgiving
Congress has recommended to the Authority in each state to appoint Wednesday the 30th instant to be observed as a day of public Thanksgiving, with which recommendation, the Governor and Council of Safety of this State has concurred and his Excellency the Governor has issued a Proclamation appointing the same to be observed with dignity.

births and deaths
Last Saturday, the wife of Richard Wait, Jun. in Lyme was safety delivered of three living sons. The children are since dead. The mother is in a fair way of recovery.

price rise
The price of the *Connecticut Gazette* for the present half year will be the same as formerly paid in country produce at the old price. Otherwise it is expected an equivalent will be paid in money. The present quarter is 13 sh.

to be sold
by Joseph Winthrop at the store of William Stewart in New London, different items of clothing;

by Prosper Wetmore that the sloop *Dispatch* will be sold at public auction in New London;

turnips
to be sold at 12 sh. per barrel at Nathan's cellar in New London.

privateer to sail
the privateer slop *American Revenue*, William Leeds, Commander, will sail on a cruise on the 18th instant. All those who have engaged must be on board by that time or their places will be supplied by others.

lottery
tickets for the State lottery are to be sold by John Porter of Lebanon and David Trumbull.

lost or stolen
by Joshua Babcock in New London on the road from there to the North Parish, a pocketbook.

by Solomon Dart, near Edward Hallam's store in New London, nine and one half yards of brown bear skin.

administration of estates
Notice by Elisha Prior, Administrator of the estate of Jonathan Chester, deceased, late of Groton are desired t bring their in their accounts immediately.

deserted
Notice by Phineas Beckwith, Sergeant, by order of Col John Durkee the following soldiers have deserted:
Isaac Basset of Canterbury; 22 years of age; a stout well built fellow; 5 feet, 8 inches tall; light complexion and short brown hair;
Comfort Chappel, belonging to New London; a well built fellow; middling stature; dark complexion with shorter dark hair; about 20 years old;
John Miller of Lyme; small of stature; light complexion; has short brown hair; and is a very sprightly and active soldier;
the well known Allen Pratt from Middletown, lately an apprentice at Lebanon, a small, dirty soldier, about 18 years of age, but has the countenance of 30 years; a dark smutty, insignificant countenance; noted for being lousy and having an unsoldier like appearance, yet to the first appearance, he is possessed of such a good nature and has distinguish himself in the duty of soldier;
Ely Wigger of Stonington, a stout, well built fellow; middling stature; dark complexion and short dark hair.

not responsible
Whereas Mary, the wife of the subscriber, has behaved in a very indecent manner and wholly refuses to bed and board with me, therefore, this is to warn all persons not to trust her on my account as I will not pay any debt of her contracting after this date.
Alexander Phelpes of Lyme

broke into the enclosures
of Timothy Swan of Groton, a white boar hog;

of David Nichols of Killlingly, nine sheep.

****

From *The Gazette,* December 18, 1778

prison ship victims
Last Monday, a flag arrived here from New York with seventy of our countrymen, sent from their horrible prison ships; thirty of them are in a very sickly condition; two have died since they arrived.

salvage
Yesterday was brought into New London by the sloop *American Revenue,* a parcel of the rigging etc. It took, together with the ship *Governor Trumbull,* from the wreck of the ship *Marquis of Rockingham.*

ship wrecked
A transport from Newport, bound to New York with hay, was set ashore last Sunday on Gardiner's Island. Out of 22 persons on board, only five were saved; the others were either froze to death or drowned.

married
Mr. Park Avery of Groton to Miss Grace Denison of this Town, New London.

to be sold
at the store of Nathaniel Shaw in New London, a quantity of ermine, saddle trim, spars and rigging, taken from the wreck of a ship.

homes needed
Several likely boys and girls, from four to eight years of age, being poor Children, are to be bound out; enquire of the Printer.

administration of estates
Notice by Paul Woodbridge, Executor to the estate of Capt. Paul Woodbridge, late of Groton, deceased, to creditors to file claims and to those indebted to settle accounts;

Notice by George Palmer of Stonington, Administrator of the estate of John Rockwell, late of Stonington, deceased, to creditors to file claims and to those indebted to settle accounts;

Notice by Desiree Beebe, Administratrix of the estate of Samuel Beebe, late of of Stonington, deceased, to creditors to file claims and to those indebted to settle accounts. A hearing is to be held at Administratrix's dwelling house in Stonington on Long Point (so called).

to be sold
a farm containing about 140 acres of good land, lying about five miles of the Town plat of New London; well wooded and watered with a house, barn and orchard thereon; enquire of William Moor living on the premises;

at Nathaniel Shaw's Wharf in New London, the prize schooner *Juno*, lately captured by the *American Revenue*.

broke out of the enclosure
of Jehiel Rogers of New London, North Parish, a two year old steer.

****

From *The Gazette*, December 25, 1778

ill prisoners of war returned
Last Friday, a cartel arrived here from New York with 132 prisoners and the next day they were landed in this Town (New London) and Groton. The greatest part of them are in sickly and most deplorable conditions, owing chiefly to all outrages in the prison ships where numbers of them of them had their feet and legs froze.
We have secured a list of most of them who are in the hospitals in Groton and here insert for the information of our friends.
Three of their number, whose names we could not learn (one of them an elderly man, the other a tall man who had been a boatswain and one other, have died since they were landed.)

James Woodbury -   Thomas Chappel - Old York
Nantucket   Jonathan Banks –

Solomon Morgan - Cape Ann
Jeremiah Darry - Boston
Alexander M'Douglall - New York
John Darby - Salem
Thomas Vendiero – Frenchman
John Hart -
Silvanus Jinks - Providence
Daniel Pinkham - Nantucket
Benjamin Simonds - Salem
Benjamin Richer – Plymouth
Ned Derry - Negro
Timothy Brown - Providence
James Kennedy - Boston
James Adams - Vineyard
Elijah Carpenter - Providence
William Robbins - Wethersfield
Richard Steelwood - Egg Harbor
Isaac Mitchel – Maryland
Zedrick Holston - Maryland
Ebenenzer Ward – Boston
Nathaniel Silber - Salem
William Stanis - Marblehead
John Nutting - Marblehead
Jame Adshed - Baltimore
William Allen - New Haven
John Shaw – Egg Harbor
Thomas Pemberton - Egg Harbor
Abel Lynes - New Haven
William Teefry - Marblehead
John Peatman - Lancaster
Nicholas Scull - Philadelphia
Charles Farmer - Baltimore
Josiah Webb - Beverly
Robert M'Danielson
Edward Sears - Yarmouth
Dominico Levine – France
John Joyce - Warwick
John Smith - Eustatia
Nicholas Trayer - Plymouth
Daniel Smith - Eustatia harbor
Matthias Pinyard - Philadelphia
John Martin
Tomas Webb - Norfolk
Ezekiel Hudmel - Virginia
Daniel Belden - Wethersfield
P. Loomis - Fairfield, Virginia
Phineas Woolsey - New Jersey
John Scull - New Weymouth New Jersey
Thomas Grunman - Salem, New Jersey
Silas Collins - Wethersfield
John Fairbanks - Providence
Stephen Stewart - Egg Harbor
Henry Hacker - New York
John Turner of the armed schooner *Plymouth*
Elisha Doane - Massachusetts
Peter Potter
Gabriel Miller - Charleston, South Carolina
Henry Coffin - Nantucket
Richard Herrick - Cape Ann

drowning
Last Saturday, one Hatch of Milford, on his passage from Nantucket, was knocked overboard by the vessel's boom and was drowned.

to be sold
by Thomas Guion on board the ship *Judith*, lying at Capt Deshon's Wharf in New London, a quantity of choice rock salt.

lost
a quantity of woolen yarn was left on Board John Braddick's Passage Boat.

broke our of goal
Notice by Ephraim Miner, Goaler for New London County, that broke out of goal Noble Hinman, confined for passing counterfeit money; of fresh complexion; pitted with small pox; a long chin.

please settle accounts
Notice by Barnard Phillips to those indebted to him for newspaper delivery to make payment.

taken up
by Amos Lester at the harbors mouth of New London a battoe with a bottom like a Moses Boat, supposed to come from the Norwich River.

come for payment
Notice from Thomas Dering of Middltown to those who transported families and effects from Long island to Connecticut in 1776 to come for reimbursement.

grievance day
The Assessor for the Town of New London and those persons who feel aggrieved are desired to meet at the Court House.[36]

broke out of the enclosure
of Samuel Hovey of Canterbury, a milch cow
****

1779

From *The Gazette,* January 1, 1779

body found
One day last week, the body of Captain William Morgan of this Town was found dead in the road back of this Town.

prisoners die
Sixteen of the prisoners who arrived here in the cartel on the 18th of July have died since and a great number of the others still remain sick.
Last week, another cartel arrived here from New York with 200 more prisoners, chiefly French. Fifteen died in the vessel in passage and most of the others are sick. Provisions, clothing, fuel, and other necessaries are greatly needed for their subsistence.

privateers seek sailors and marines
The sloop *American Revenue,* Capt. William Leeds, is ready to sail having got her bread and everything on board. A few more hands are needed.

All Gentlemen Officers and Men, entered upon privateer brig *Middletown,* Nathan Sage, Commander, should be on board; others interested may apply at John Owen's.

deserted
from the brig *Venus,* Samuel Davis, after receiving their first month's wages and signed the Portage Bill[37];

Elisha Reynolds; a native of Greenwich New Town in Rhode Island; said to have family there; about 30 - 32 years of age; 5 feet, 8 inches tall; thin faced; very dark skin; dark hair; very talkative;

Benjamin Blogget a native of Stonington; son of the late Dr. Bloggett; also signed the Portage Bill; 30 years of age; 5 feet, 6 inches high; dark hair and skin; somewhat slim.

lost
Paul Swain of Nantucket, a prisoner now in Groton, sick, had his chest landed in New London. The chest is small and the key is in the hands of Major Ledyard.

****

From *The Gazette*, January 8, 1779

ill prisoners and care givers
The mortality of the prisoners lately arrived from New York still continues, 17 or 18 of them have died since our last. It is unhappy for the inhabitant of this town, New London, that a number of them, through an anxiety to relieve the distress suffered by their fellow creatures, have taken their distempers, which added to the extreme scarcity of the necessities of life to render their case most distressing.

come and collect prize money
Nathaniel Thompson in Groton notifies all those for whom he was agent in the sloop *Revenge* Samuel Champlin, to call on him at Mr. Daniel Eldridge's in Groton to receive their prize money.

broke into the enclosure
of Ester Miner at the head of the Niantic River, Lyme, a one year old bull without marks.

deserted
Notice by Paine Converse that deserted from his company in Col. McCullogh's Regiment, Jacob White; tall fellow; about 18 years old; light complexion.

tax notice
by Joshua Hempsted, Tax Collector for New London that at the dates and times specified, he will receive payments at the houses of James Haughton, John Raymond Jun., Jason Allen, Jun, Joseph Prentis; Clement Leech and Capt. Stephen Prentice.

record depository
Notice by G. Hurlbut that the Affairs and Letters of the Town of New London for 1778 will be deposited at the house of Nathan Douglas of New London.

to be sold
by Reuben Goodwell, a dwelling place in Norwich ;two stories high, four rooms a floor and a small barn.

administration of estates
Notice by Moses Park, Administrator to the estate of Zebulon Park, late of Preston , deceased to creditors to file claims and to those indebted to settle accounts;

Notice by Mary Allen, Adminstratrix to the estate of Ebenezer Allen, late of Norwich, deceased to creditors to file claims and to those indebted to settle accounts.

****

From *The Gazette*, January 15, 1779

cave in
On the 18th ult., the following happened in Killingly, as a young man about 18 years of age was digging the ground after a fox, the ground caved in by which means he lost his life.

died
Mrs. Manwaring, wife of William Manwaring.

died of fever
Capt. John Rogers; Mrs. Smith, wife of David Smith, and Daniel Latham of Groton, the three dying with a putrid fever communicated by prisoners lately brought here.

broke into the enclosure
of James Underwood of Plainfield, a heifer.

taken up
by Ebenezer Avery in Groton, a hog.

out of the business
Caleb Knight has stopped his business of delivering papers and wants to settle accounts at the houses of Rev. Carey, John Harkness, Moses Robbins or Joseph Eaton.

****

From *The Gazette*, January, 22, 1779

accident
Last Tuesday, two Negro boys of this Town, New London, were at play with a loaded musket. The musket went off and shot one of them in the head.

died
Mrs. Samuel Champlin; Mrs. Bashseba Waterman, wife of Joseph Waterman; Mrs. Eunice Sethsbel and William Moor.

false alarms
Whereas some disorderly person or persons, lost to all sense of good order, was guilty of firing alarm guns on the 2nd instant at 10 pm at night on board an armed vessel lying in the harbor which much alarmed the citizens of both New London and Groton, therefore, in order to prevent any such conduct in the future, this is to give public notice that any person or persons guilty of such disorderly conduct may depend on being treated according to the nature of their crime.

lottery
The Manager of the Shetucket Bridge Lottery advises the Public that there are a few tickets remaining on hand.

wanted
a small farm with good land and a dwelling house thereon; well situated and convenient for a tanner; not more than twenty or less the three miles from New London, enquire of the Printer.

administration of estates
Notice by Samuel Shipman, John Shipman, Jun. and Samuel Tally, Commissioners appointed by the Probate Court of Guilford for the estate of Moses Dudley, late of Saybrook, deceased and represented to be insolvent, to creditors to file claims and to those indebted to settle accounts. A meeting will be held at the dwelling house of William Dudley, Inn Holder in Saybrook.

broke into the enclosure
of Elijah Humfree in Killingly, a dark brown mare.
****

From *The Gazette,* January 29, 1779

small pox
The Public may be assured that the utmost care is being taken to prevent the spreading of small pox int this town New London, that inoculations are not allowed (despite a report in the country to the contrary) but that when a person breaks out with the distemper, they are immediately removed to a different part of Town.
The only houses that are infected with the distemper are Jeremiah Chapman and Mr. Asa Manwaring at the back of the Town, Mr. Joseph Lewis near the Harbor's mouth and Mr. John Rogers at Quaker Hill, at each of which houses a white flag is put up and the roads turned.

warning
The inhabitants of the Town are cautioned not to buy any of the clothing of the French prisoners or any old clothing of anyone by which the fever and the small pox are communicated.

died
Joseph Lewis, Samuel Lamb, Miss Zeporrah Bolles, daughter of Joseph Bolles, Miss Elizabeth Beckwith, a child of George Hazzara and a child of William Rogers;

at Groton, the widow Coit, relict of the late Daniel Coit;

at Hoebuck [Hoboken, NJ] Capt. James Denison, late of New London;

for sale
by Jedidiah Leeds of Groton, choice Virginia tobacco by the hogshead, hundred or single pound;

a small shop in New London opposite the church, belonging to Capt. Debow.

wanted
Gentlemen Adventurers on board the sloop *Beaver*, Capt. William Havens.

broke out of the enclosure
of Benjamin Tallman of Norwich, a brown heifer.

****

From *The Gazette*, February 5, 1779

ship snatched
Last Sunday, the *Ranger*, a privateer brig of 12 guns in the employ of the enemy, which, it is said, has been cruising in the Sound for some time past, was brought into this port of New London by the brig *Middletown*, Capt. Sage, the *Beaver*, Capt Havens and the sloop *Eagle,* Capt. Conkling. She was taken from a wharf in Sag Harbor, Long Island after a short resistance. Five of her people were taken, the rest ran off.

farms for sale
in the North Parish of New London, near Jason Allen's, 150 acres, 80 improved; a dwelling house barn. Enquire of Alex P. Adams in New London;

In Colchester, 100 acres; well proportioned for pasture, plowing and mowing; well fenced; with dwelling house, corn house and two orchards. Enquire of George Fox on premises.

deserted
notice by Lt. David Dorrance that deserted from Col. Starr's Battalion: Corporal Judah West; 5 foot 11 inches high; 22 years of age; black eyes; dark hair; he is a resident of Goshen in Lebanon;

Ephraim Cox; fifer, 5 foot, 10 inches tall; 20 years of age; light complexion and hair;

Joseph Billings of Stonington; 5 foot, 11 inches high; 22 years of age; light hair and complexion and dark eyes.

for sale
by Henry Treman at his shop near Court House in New London, blue, green, black and dove colored broad cloths, black serge, linen etc.;

lampblack and linseed oil to be sold by the Printer.

broke into the enclosure
of Benjamin Tallman of Norwich, a heifer.
****
From *The Gazette*, February 12, 1779

administration of estates
Notice by Gilbert Fanning, Elnathan Rosseter and Thomas Randal, Commissioners appointed by the Probate Court of Stonington for the estate of John Denison of Stonington, deceased and represented to be insolvent, to creditors to file claims and to those indebted to settle accounts. A meeting will be held at the dwelling house of Elisha Denison in Stonington.

tax meeting
Notice by George Hurlbut, Clerk to the Assessors and Listers of the Town of New London for 1778 to meet at the house of Capt. Nathan Douglas of New London.

to be sold
for cash or new land in Norwich, East Society at a village called Poquattanuk, a large elegant dwelling house, three stories in the front with a small barn about 200 rods of land, very good well that never fails of water, 60 rods from a grist mill and saw mills; enquire of Ezra Chapman, living on the premises.

libels filed
Notice by Wm. Saltonstall, Register, that Libels are filed before, and to be heard by, the Hon. Richard Law, Judge of the Maritime Court for the County of New London:
in favor of the Brig *Middletown*, Master Nathan Sage; *Beaver*, Capt. William Havens; *Eagle*, Edward Conklin; sloop *Hunter*, Asa Dansly, Commander; *Lady Trumbull*, Capt. Eliphalet Buddington and their associates against the Brig *Ranger*, the Brig *Peter* of Workington, Joseph Browne, late Master, and the brig *Thomas and William* of Scarborough, James Smith late master their tackle, apparel, furniture, boat and cargo;
also in favor of, John Shipman 2d, Commander of the Boat *Revenge* its associates and fitters of the vessel against sundry goods, merchandise and monies, taken on Long Island.

****

From *The Gazette*, February 19, 1779

reinforcements
A detachment of troops from the Continental Army arrived here at New London last week from the westward under the command of Col. Dearborn for the protection of this Town and Harbor. They are an excellent body of men, well clothed, healthy and in high spirits and are abundantly sufficient, in conjunction with the militia stationed here, to answer the purpose for which they came. On Saturday last, Brig. Gen. Parsons arrived in Town to take charge of this Department.

prisoners released
by Capt McNeil, who arrived in this port from Port L'Orient, France, we learn that John Welch, Peter Richards and Charles Buckley, all of this Town, late officers of the Continental Ship *Alfred* and since prisoners in England are exchanged and arrived in Port L'Orient before Capt. McNeil sailed.

small pox
A report prevails in the neighboring towns that the people with small pox in this town are so situated so as to endanger people who may come into Town, which may prevent the usual supplies from the countryside.
We do hereby certify that the houses of Asa Manawarring and Jeremiah Chapman, situated at a safe distance in the back of the Town and Joseph Lewis at the Harbor's mouth are the only infected houses, except those licensed for inoculation, all of which are situated in the interior part of Town, the nearest of them being two miles distant from the town plat, none of them on public roads and a white flag is in front of each.
Marvin Wait, Thomas Shaw and Timothy Green

runaway
from Dan Throop of Lebanon, a Negro boy named Newport; 17 years of age; small stature; well set; straight limbed; one of his eyes is much less than the other.

deserted from Col Sherbune's Regiment
Nathan Stoddard, Corporal; 5 feet, 8 inches high; black eyes; dark complexion; brown hair; 23 years of age; was a resident of Goshen;

Elisha Fox; 5 foot, 6 inches tall; dark hair, dark eyes and complexion; 22 years old; was a resident of Lyme.
****

From *The Gazette*, February 26, 1779

Capt. Hinman acquitted
At a General Court martial held on board the Continental Frigate *Providence* for the trial of Elisha Hinman, late Commander of the Continental Frigate *Alfred,* the Court, having duly and maturely considered all the evidence presented it on the part of Thomas Thompson Esq. Prosecutor and on the part of Elisha Hinman, prisoner, are fully and clearly of the opinion that the aforesaid Elisha Hinman of the three charges preferred against him by Thomas Thompson, charging the aforesaid Elisha Hinman of refusing to follow orders, neglect of duty and unprecedented conduct on the 9th of March 1778, when commanding the Continental Frigate *Alfred* in company with the Continental Sloop *Raleigh,* then in the command of Thomas Thompson, from all of which charges and evert part of the same do acquit the aforesaid Elisha Hinman and, with the highest honor, approve the whole his conduct, he having behaved himself in accord with the strictest rules of naval discipline and agreeable in all respects to the 27th article of the Rules and Regulations of the Continental Navy.[38] Abraham Whipple, President by William Story.

ship ashore
Last week, a privateer belonging to the enemy was drove ashore near Sachem's Head by a gale of wind. She had a few days before taken Capt. Giles Sage in a sloop bound for this port from the West Indies with a valuable cargo on board. The privateer on taking Capt. Sage took him and the people on board, who by this occasion have got their liberty.

sloop taken
The whale boat *Revenge,* Captain Champlin, has taken off Port Judith and brought into Stonington, a sloop from Sag Harbor, bound for Newport, laden with wood and provision.

Benedict Arnold
The *Pennsylvania Gazette* of the 10th instant contain some charge against General Arnold of mal-administration, published by the

Council of that State, but, for want of room, we omit them for the present.[39]

died
in Groton, Mrs. Ledyard, consort of Ebenezer Ledyard.

wanted to hire
a man used to work on a farm for six or twelve months. The pay shall be made to the satisfaction of the person inclining to engage; enquire of John Bolles.

for sale
by Amos White, a quantity of fax at East Haddam Landing.

lots of land in New London for sale
at public vendue by Robinson Mumford on Thursday March 25 next, at the house of Thomas Wilson of New London, sundry lots including:
South lot number 1 - 4 rods by 5 rods, opposite Capt Melally;
North lot number 2- 4 rods by 5, adjoining the blacksmith shop;
lot number 3 - 8 rods by 6 rods, west of Mr. Adam Shapely's house;
lot number 4 - 4 rods by 6 rods, west of Fortune's house;
lot number 5 - 3 acres adjoining D. Richards;
lot number 6 - two 5 1/4 acre lots adjoining with young orchard of grafted fruit;
lot number 7 - 3 acres, near Asa Manawarring, called More's;
lot number 8 - 2 and 1/2 acres adjoining westward;
lot number 9 - 2 and ½ acres adjoining westward;
lot number 10 - 3 and ½ acres adjoining westward;
lot number 11 - 3 and ½ acres adjoining westward;
Lots 5 through 11 are well watered and about a quarter of a mile from the Meeting House;
lot number 12 - large double storied, well finished, good wharf and good depth of water;
lot number 13 - house, lot and wharf adjoining;
lot number 14 - a large dwelling house, well finished with a barn garden etc., now in tenure of Stephen Holt;

lot number 15 - two acres of salt marsh on Goshen Point;
lot number16 - a farm containing 250 acres, well fenced with a large dwelling house and barn, well wooded, two miles from the Meeting House, lately belonging to Joseph Stubbins;
lot number17 - a farm containing about 200 acres with a good dwelling house with convenient out houses, large barn 50 feet by 24, cyder house, well finished with a store room above it; a large and valuable cedar swamp with three good orchards, well wooded and watered and well fenced;
also a number of farming utensils, corn plows, trucks and household furniture; one large scale beam, scales and weights etc. Any person inclining it view any of the premises, apply to said Mumford at Cedar Hill.

escaped
from the main guard in Providence, a certain William Crossing, who says he is of Captain in Whitman's Corp of Tory Refugees and Joseph Caswell of said Crossing's Company, who were captured at Seconnet. Crossing is about 30 years of age; 5 foot, 9 inches tall; light complexion; light blue eyes; short brown hair; is marked with the smallpox and is a man of great activity;
Cawell is about 40 years old; 5 foot, 7 inches high; full faced; remarkable black bushy beard, wears his hair short;
published by Order of Maj. Gen. Sullivan by William Peck, Adj. Gen.

stolen
from John Williams 3rd of Groton one piece of saddle leather and two of new leather, not finished.

retirement
The Subscriber Nathan Bushnel, Jun. Norwich, informs his customers that he shall discontinue the business of riding Post after this week, having served many of them upwards of 15 years in that capacity. In consequence of his long continuance in said business; he has a number of debts due him and requests a speedy settlement of same. He takes this opportunity to return his hearty thanks to his kind customers from whom he acknowledges the

receipt of many favors; And he would inform them that they may still be supplied with the *Connecticut Gazette* by Aston Bushnell of Norwich and Aaron Bushnell of Lebanon who will continue to deliver the papers afer the present week.

broke into enclosure of
James Smith 2d of Groton, a black bull.

****

From *The Gazette*, March 5, 1779

prisoners taken and confined
In our last, we mentioned that a British Privateer was drove ashore at Sachem's Head, from which the Captain, Samuel Rogers of Norwalk, and the crew, amounting to 36, were brought here to New London and confined.

Last Wednesday was brought into Stonington, a schooner privateer named the *Refugee* from Bedford, laden with lumber and wheat. On board were two brothers, Thomas Gilbert Jun. and Bradford Gilbert, sons of Col. Gilbert, a noted Tory. On Friday, they were brought to this Town, New London, and committed to goal. It is said that the younger Gilbert lately piloted a party from Newport to Warren.

American prisoners exchanged
Last week, a flag arrived here from New York which returned with 36 American prisoners in return for some sent lately. What is very remarkable is that they are all in good health. From the prisoners, we learn that the principal inhabitants of New York were about to return to Great Britain, despairing of complete conquest of the country this summer. The Tories are disgusted with their King's luke warm speech which breathes neither peace nor war.

died
Monday night last, died here, Mrs. Abigail Green, relict of the late deceased Timothy Green.

broke into the enclosure
of Caleb Lomis Colchester, a steer.

administration of estates
Notice from Mary Comstock, Executrix of the estate of Benjamin Comstock, late of New London, deceased, to creditors to file claims and to those indebted to settle accounts.

for sale
40 acres in Westchester Parish, Colchester on the Post Road between New London and Hartford, near the Meeting House; with a good dwelling house, mechanic's shop, barn; two orchards; well fenced and under good improvement; enquire Timothy Dutton on premises.

strayed or stolen
by Samuel Minard of New London, Great Neck, a horse

deserted
from Capt. Reuben Mayton's Company of Col. William Shepard's Regiment in Providence, John Clark, an Irishman; dark colored hair, large eyes; a malicious look and is much marked by small pox;

from Capt. Henry Williams Company of Col. Sherburne's Regiment, Nathan Stoddard; 5 foot, 8 inches tall; black eyes; dark hair and dark complexion;

from Capt. Henry Williams' Company of Col. Sherburne's Regiment, Elisha Fox; 22 years of age, 5 foot, 6 inches high; brown eyes; dark hair and complexion.
****
From *The Gazette*, March 12, 1779

lottery top prize
the ticket Number 84, 653 drew $20,000 in the State lottery.

died
in Southhold in Long Island of advanced age, Robert Hempsted formerly of New London;

in Lyme, Capt. Elisha Miller in his 62nd year; he has left a sorrowful widow but no children. He left a sizeable estate, much of which he directed for public use. He was a teacher for upwards of 20 years; was kind and charitable to the Poor and, we trust, has gone to reap the benefit of his labors.

for sale
a dwelling house on a half acre of land on the Main Street in New London, opposite Capt. Joseph Hurlbut.

farm for sale
in Ashford, about two miles from the Meeting House, with a good house, large barn and potash works; it has been a noted tavern for many years, being on the great Hartford road; formerly improved by Mr. Holmes and presently improved by Mr. Grosvenor; enquire of William Russel, North Parish Woodstock.

administration of estates
Notice by James Rhodes Elna Rossiter John Denison 4th, Commissioners appointed by the Probate Court of Stonington for the estate of Samuel Beebe of Long Point Stonington, deceased and represented to be insolvent, to creditors to file claims and to those indebted to settle accounts.

to be leased to the highest bidder
four lots of land in Colchester left by the worthy Lieutenant David Day for the maintenance of the ministry and schools in Westchester parish. The auction will be at the house of Solomon Lomiss in said Westchester; for further particulars enquire of John Bliss, Nehemiah Gates. Adonijah Foot, Stephen Brainerd and Aaron Foot.

found
by Samuel Bicknell in Ashford, near the country road of that town, three guns.

****

From *The Gazette*, March 19, 1779

prisoners escape
Last Thursday night being very dark, three prisoner stole a sloop from a wharf in this town, New London, and made their escape undiscovered.

died
Mrs. Samuel Bill of New London.

get on board
Notice by Samuel Barker, Commander of the *Oliver Cromwell* to Gentlemen Adventurers, who are a mind to make their fortunes in a cruise against the enemies, that they are desire to board immediately;

Notice by Seth Harding, Commander of the Ship *Confederacy* that a few able seamen and landsmen are needed for a cruise against the enemy.

passage boats
the sloop *Norwich Packet*, Capt. Stephen Culver, having excellent accommodations, plies daily between Norwich and New London; enquire of said Culver at his house at Norwich Landing or Mr. Ephraim Miner, or on board the sloop, which may be known by a blue flag and a white ball;
Braddick's Passage boat between Norwich and New London; enquire of Mr. Braddick at his house in Norwich and in New London at Capt. Douglass' tavern.

for sale
by Thomas Jones at his house in New London superfine blue broad cloth, beaver hats, linen handkerchiefs, shoe bindings of various colors, black ribbons, silks etc

stolen
seven yards of white cloth from Moses Warren of Lyme.

to stand stud
the horse Yorkshire owned by Samuel Brewster of Preston.

From *The Gazette,* March 26, 1779

enemy off shore!
Last Tuesday evening, intelligence was received by a vessel that was sent up the Sound to makes discoveries as to the movements of the enemy, that about 20 transports of sail had come through Hellsgate[40], with a number of flat bottom boats, several row galleys and sloops of war; that one ship of 64 guns and another of 50 had sailed from Sandy Hook to come up the south side of Long Island to the Sound;
that General Clinton was at Southampton with 2500 troops and that this force was to make an attack here and the harbor. The same day, two ships and several transports, all of which, except the largest ship of 50 guns, went into Gardiner's Bay. The *Renown,* about sunset, anchored off the mouth of this harbor, distant 5 or 6 miles where she remains at this publication.
Expresses with this intelligence were sent off into the country the same night and we doubt not that a force will seasonably be collected and, in conjunction with our troops now here, will be abundantly sufficient to repel the enemy if they think it proper to pursue their plan.

shipwreck on Gardiner's Island
We learn that 25 of the vessels are in or near Sag Harbor and 12 or 14 of them were driven ashore on Gardiner's Island in the gale of wind Monday last.

died
here since our last, Asa Manawarring, a bachelor, aged 66 years, of small pox;
John Harris;
Daniel Shapely;

cloud on title
Whereas Robinson Mumford of New London had advertised sundry lots for sale in New London; notice is therefore given by Joseph Hurlbut and Amos Chesebrough that Mumford cannot give title.

to be sold
near Brooklyn Meeting House in Pomfret by Gilbert and Miles, a good assortment of hollow ware, nail rods, rum, sugar, clean cotton and linen rages, taken in by them.

****

From *The Gazette*, April 1, 1779

to be sold
at Public venue at James Harris' wharf in New London, the sloop *Rachael,* 50 tons, her tackle and apparel.

ready to sail
The ship *Oliver Cromwell*, Capt. Timothy Parker, is ready for a cruise against the enemies of the United Independent States, all Gentlemen Adventurers, who want to make their fortune, should repair on board.

burglary
Notice by John Champlin that there was a burglary at his goldsmith store and much jewelry taken.

clockmaker
Benjamin Hanks, clock and watch maker in Windham, advises the Public that he still carries on his business in New London.

sale postponed
sale of Robinson Mumford's lands and farming utensils, postponed because of the severity of the weather, has been rescheduled for April 6.

broke into the enclosure
of Elisha Gallup in New London, North Parish, a red sided cow.

for sale
a farm 60 acres, a house, two orchards, well fenced with stone wall and equally divided between pasturing, mowing and plowing land;

a large house and barn on an acre of land, pleasantly situated near Jordan Brook; well fenced, good well of water; on Post Road to Rope Ferry; enquire of Freeman Crocker living on the premises.
lost
Notice by Basheba Smith that she lost between her house at the back of the Court House New London, and Elisha Richards', a green pocket book with $30 in it.

trusses
Stephen Johnson of Ashford continues the business of making trusses or bandages to keep up the fallen parts of those trouble with burst.

please settle up
Notice by Amos Main to those to whom he has delivered *The Gazette* and who have not settled accounts, that he will be at John Denison's, Inn Holder, at Stonington Point next Wednesday to settle accounts

****

From *The Gazette*, April 8, 1779

wreck in Plumb Island
Last Wednesday se'nninght, Capt. Richard McCary sailed from this Port of New London in a sloop for the West Indies, having six people on board, but was cast away in a snow storm on Plumb Island. Some articles of clothing were found on the quarter deck, but, as no person was aboard and as the boat was not found, it is supposed got off in her and were lost.

update on enemy movements
The British ship *Renown*, which lay off this harbor when our last was published, came to sail on Thursday and anchored near Gardiner's Island with a brig and a sloop and, since that time, they have been cruising the Sound.
The gathering of ships and soldiers in Southampton had so alarmed this town last week and occasioned the inhabitant to move their possessions for more security. Meantime, the militia was ordered to hold themselves in readiness and those in the country ordered in.

counterfeiters arrested
Monday last, one Amos Smith of this town, New London, was taken into custody on suspicion of counterfeiting the continental currency. and, the next day, his brother was taken into custody for the same offense.

half page this week
Having thought it necessary to remove most of our type in the last alarm, our readers will forgive our publishing a half page of news this week.

more fortifications being built
The Militia, which has lately arrived from the country, are employed in erecting some works on an eminence for the better protection of this Town and Harbor in case of an attack from our unnatural enemy.

deserted
from the Regiment of Lt. Colonel Dearborn, William Berry, belonging to the 8th Connecticut Battalion; 5 foot, 9 inches tall; about 24 years of age; red complexion; short brown hair; dark gray eyes; something pitted with the small pox;

William Benson, Indian, from the 3rd Connecticut Battalion; 30 years old; 5 foot, 11 inches tall; a stout, well set fellow; lame in his right leg, occasioned by being shot in the hip; notice by Capt. Samuel Comstock.

settle accounts
John Bolles, 2d, as he is moving from New London, would like to settle his accounts.

unfinished ship for sale
the greater part of the plank and timber 55 feet, now on the stock on the Mystic River; enquire of Col. Samuel Aborn of Warwick, Rhode Island or Capt. Daniel Packer of Mystic.

to be sold
a pair of choice combs, very cheaply; enquire of the Printer;

at the shop of Edward Hallam of New London, a quantity of rigging, some old iron, anchor and a large long boat;

at the house of Martin Lee in Lyme, a piece of woodland containing about 15 acres; formerly belonging to Nicodemus Miller, lying on the road about one and one half miles from the head of the Niantic river;
also 14 acres of cleared land, formerly the property of Elisha Beckwith; about 1 mile west of the head of the river.

notice
by Win. Saltonstall Clerk to those tavern owners who were selected to be licensed by the selectmen, that they must apply to the full Court.

libels filed
Notice by Win. Saltonstall, Register, that Libels are filed before, and to be heard by, the Hon. Richard Law, Judge of the Maritime Court for the County of New London:
in favor of Edward Conklin Commander and Associates of the sloop *Eagle* against a brig of unknown name, full of salt;
in favor of William Dennis and Associates of the ship *General Sullivan* against the sloop *Refugee,* Capt. Gilbert, Jun., late Commander;

in favor of Elijah Champlin and Associates of the whale boat *Revenge* against the sloop *Polly*, Joseph Warren, late Commandeer;
in favor of William Leeds and Associates on board sloop *American Revenue* against the schooner *Polly*, Samuel Price, late Commander.

runaway
from William Brockway in Lyme, a Negro man, Perow; 30 years of age; speaks broken English; seemingly good natured.

escaped
Notice by Moses Cleveland[41] that broke out of the goal in Norwich, one Forsythe, convicted of horse stealing and sentenced to Newgate Prison in Simsbury.

****

From *The Gazette*, April 15, 1779

day of fast and prayer
Congress has recommended to the several States to appoint the last Thursday of May next to be a day of fasting, humiliation and prayer to the Almighty.[42]

British prisoner recaptured
Saturday morning, was brought into port by the *Beaver* and *Hancock*, privateers, a privateer sloop of six carriage guns, Capt. Charles Letelier, belonging to New York; she was captured near Block Island. On board this privateer was one John Oliver, Lieutenant. The same person was taken about two months ago in Capt. Rogers' privateer, which was cast away at Guilford. He was soon thereafter brought to this Town with the rest of Roger's crew, but, with a few others, found a sloop from a wharf in this Town and made his escape to Newport. This is but one of many evils that might be said to have arisen to the Public for the want of a Commissary for prisoners of this Town.

representatives selected
Nathaniel Shaw and William Hillhouse are chosen representatives for this Town in the General Assembly and in Groton, Thomas Mumford and Col. Nathan Gallup.

runaway
from Obidiah Wheeler of Woodbury, a Negro man named Pomp; 23 years of age; 5 feet, 9 or 10 inches tall; well built; very black; small round head; flat nose; talks good English and is a pitted on the nose with small pox.

taxes in Lyme
Notice by Nathan Matson, Tax Collector in Lyme, that those obliged to pay taxes may make payment at the houses of Edward Champlin, Widow Mary Lee, Jesse Beckwith, Abner Griffings, Nathaniel Pick, and Abner Comstock.

American prisoner escapes
Just as this paper was put to press, Mr. Mortimore, late mate of the schooner *Spy*, Robert Niles, Master, arrived here from New York from which place he had made his escape a few days before.
****
From *The Gazette,* April 22, 1779

for sale
the prize privateer sloop *Game Cock*; 30 tons, six carriage guns and sundry military stores.

strayed or stolen
from Thomas Brown of New London, black horse.

libel filed
Notice by Wm. Saltonstall, Register, that a Libel is filed before, and is to be heard by, the Hon. Richard Law, Judge of the Maritime Court for the County of New London in favor of William Havens and Associates of the *Beaver* against the ship *Carlotta,* Charles Wheeler, late Master.

burglary
reported by Joseph Smith, clothier New London, North Parish of sundry cloths.

farm for sale
Twenty acres in Groton on road from New London ferry to Preston, about 4 miles from the ferry; near a grist mill; good house, orchard and barn thereon; well fenced with stone walls; equal pasturing, plowing and mowing; well watered with a stream that never fails; good for a tanner.

American ship seized
We hear theat the private Ship *Governor Trumbull* was seized in the West Indies by the Ship *Bunker Hill,* owned by Massachusetts but taken by the enemy.

****

From *The Gazette*, April 29, 1779

married
Marvin Wait of this town to Miss Patty Jones;

at Groton, Mr. Peter Richards to Miss Catherine Mumford, daughter of Thomas Mumford.

warning
Ordered by the Selectmen of the Town that a true account under oath of the number of people in each family in New London and all the wheat, grain, Indian corn, rye, meal, flour that the citizens have in their possession and, if they refuse, to forfeit the same and pay double its worth.

Marvin Wait	John Raymend
Thomas Shaw	Griswold Avery
Timothy Green	

ran away
from James Culver on Jordan Plain in New London, an apprentice boy Daniel McCollum; 15 years of age, small for his age; has black hair and eyes.

deserted
Notice by Capt. D. Allen in New London that deserted from the Continental Detachment under Col. Johnson four soldiers: Mills Woolman; Ebenezer Allen; H. Lee and Asher Bull.

to be let
a convenient dwelling house in Norwich Landing; enquire of Abel Brewster in said Norwich.

notice
by Gen. Samuel H. Parsons to all officers and soldiers on furlough to join their respective Regiments

for sale
a number of marble mortars, suitable for privateers, now on sale at the Printer's office;

an excellent five guinea watch, enquire of T. Green.

list of letters at New London Post Office
Joseph Blackwell - Worthington
John Blanch - New London
Joshua Babcock - Stonington
Elizabeth Barry - New London
James Bradford - Plainfield
William Brooks - New London
Christopher Crandle - Westerly
William Colbert - New London
Nathan Clark - Westerly
John Chapman - New London
Nathan Cooper - New London
Samuel Copp - Stonington
Frederick Calkins - Norwich
Moses Cobb - Tolland
Caleb Dyer - New London
James Davenport - Norwich
John Elderkin - Groton
James Gray - New London
Christian Gosner - New London
Mons. Restais du Graces - Norwich
Nathaniel Hempsted - New London
Joseph Holt - New London:
Israel Hewie - Stonington
Hobart, Eliphalet - Stonington
Simon Ingram - Voluntown
Joshua Munro - New London
Levi Munson - New London
Beriah Norton - New London
Joseph Noyce - Westerly

Mercy Prentice- New London
Thomas Palmer - New London
Mrs. Potter - New London
Jedidiah Pratt - Saybrook
Joseph Rogers - Stonington
P. Picot - New London
Josiah Smith - New London
Samuel Smedley - New London
Andrew Stockholm - New London
William Stone - Col. Swift's battalion
James Totton - New London
George Thayer - Groton
–Tester, - Norwich
Charles Thompson - Stonington
Oliver Warner - Middletown
William Weaver - New London
Thomas Willson- New London
Alex. Whaley - New London. North Parish

****

From *The Gazette*, May 6, 1779

lost or strayed from Crown
Thirteen colonies, situated in America with all the territories appendages thereto; a most valuable and well established commerce, worth at least two million per annum; about 16,000 good, well disciplined soldiers; our national consequences on the politics of Europe; the honesty of our ministers; the Liberty of our subjects
and the virtues of Justice and Prudence of the Sovereign. Whoever may be able to restore or to point out how to restore all or either of the above articles to the proper owners may, by applying, to either of His Majesty's lost or strayed officers will receive a promise of being handsomely rewarded for their service or services.

epigram
The common soldier, who has broke
the bands of military yoke,
in plain blunt language has deserted
is seized and home comes broken hearted.
Five hundred lashes he receives,
each one of which a furrow leaves,

yet he survives it, drinks his cup,
determined to depart again;
but Brtiania tender preserved,
for a worse spectacle reserved,
a spectacle before unseen --
oh, could we draw a veil between --
while fate unfolds her secret types,
she now bleeds to death from thirteen stripes.

runaways
from Jeffrey Champlin of Exeter, Rhode Island, a Negro man named Prince; about 6 feet tall; pretends to be a very religious man and a great exhorter;

from Nathaniel Pearse of Pomfret, a Negro Man named Warwick; 5 foot, 10 inches high; about 25 years of age; very talkative; slim built; very active .

to stand stud
Apollo will cover at stable of Ebenezer Grosvenor in Pomfret;

Young Ranger will cover at stable of James Howard in Windham;

Liberty will cover at stable of Jonathan Deming in Colchester.

to be sold.
The taken sloops *Polly* and *Refugee* at John Denison's wharf in New London.

wanted
a few good shipping horses by William Stewart in New London.

found
by John Tilley of New London, two aprons, four handkerchiefs on the road between Mr. Horton's and Norwich.

strayed or stolen
from Asa Edgerton of Mansfield, a large a cow.

From *The Gazette*, May 13, 1779

to stand stud
Ranger will cover at the stables of Eliphalet Bulkley in Colchester;

Harlequin, a beautiful Arabian horse, will cover at the stables of Joseph Tyler of Newent Society in Norwich.

taken up
a wrecked sloop of about 35 tons burthen, brought into Mystic River by an armed whale boat, commanded by Thomas Parks of Groton.

administration of estates
Notice by Elna Rosseter, Amos Chesebrough and John Hillard, Commissioners appointed by the Probate Court of Stonington for the estate of Andrew Stanton, late of Stonington, deceased and represented to be insolvent, to all those indebted to the estate to settle up and creditors to file claims. A meeting will be held at Lt. Robert Stanton's, Inn Holder in Stonington;

Notice by Joseph Hurlbut and Marvin Wait, Commissioners appointed by the Probate Court of New London for the estate of Joseph Waterman, late of New London, deceased and represented to be insolvent, to all those indebted to the estate to settle up and creditors to file claims. A meeting will be held at Wait's Writing Room in New London;

Notice by Samuel Belden and Marvin Wait, Commissioners appointed by the Probate Court of New London for the estate of Capt. Samuel Champlin, late of New London, deceased and represented to be insolvent, to all those indebted to the estate to settle up and creditors to file claims. A meeting will be held at Wait's Writing Room in New London.

****

From *The Gazette*, May 20, 1779

to stand stud
Sterling will cover at the stables of John C. Hillhouse New London, North Parish;

Brazen Buck at the stables of Zebadiah Andrus, Jun., Norwich East Society.

to be sold
dwelling house in Groton, adjoining the Mystic River; one acre, having a living spring thereon that never fails; convenient for tanner or fisherman; one and one half stories tall; two good rooms a floor; enquire of Solomon Perkins in Groton.

administration of estates
Notice by Roger Gibson and George Gibson, Executors, to those with demands on estate of Asa Manawaring of New London to bring them in, properly stated for settlement.

runaway
from Pierpont Bacon of Colchester, an apprentice boy, William Marson; 14 years old.

elections
The following have been elected representatives for their respective towns to the General Assembly:

in New London County
for New London: Nathan Shaw and Maj. William Hillhouse;
for Norwich: Nathan Niles and Aaron Cleveland;
for Groton: Thomas Mumford and Nathaniel Gallup;
for Lyme: William Noyes and Samuel Ely;
for Saybrook: Capt. Edward Shipman and Col. William Worthington;
for Killingsworth: Hez. Lane and Capt. Samuel Crane;
for Preston: Col. Samuel Mott and Timothy Lester;
for Stonington: Jonathan Palmer, Jun. and Col. Oliver Smith

in Windham County
for Windham: Col. Hez. Bissell and Capt. Nathaniel Wales;
for Coventry: Capt. Ebenezer Kingsberry and Col. Jesse Roor;
for Woodstock: Capt. Elisha Childs and Charles C. Chandler;
for Mansfield: Capt. Exp. Storrs and Daniel Dunham;
for Ashford: Capt Simeon Smith and Maj. John Keyes;
for Lebanon; Jacob Eliot and Elkanah Tisdel;
for Voluntown: Joseph Shepard and Elisha Perkins;
for Pomfret: Capt. Samuel Cras and Col. Joseph Abbot;
for Killingly: O. Claugh and Samuel Danielson, Jun.

libels filed
Notice by Win. Saltonstall, Register, that Libels are filed before, and to be heard by, the Hon. Richard Law, Judge of the Maritime Court for the County of New London:
in favor of Edward Conkling, now deceased, of the *Eagle* and Associates against the schooner *Hero,* John Leake, late commander;
in favor of William Havens of the *Beaver* and Associates and Elisha Hinman of the *Hancock* and Associates against the schooner *Mulberry,* Philip Ashner, late commander, and armed sloop *Hunter,* Robert M'Larty, late commander;
in favor of Nathaniel Saltonstall of the *Putnam* and Associates against the sloops *Hunter,* F. Sullivan, late commander, and *Polly* John Pergine, late commander;
in favor of Charles Jenks of two masted *Hornet* and Israel Stoddard of armed whaleboat *Prudence,* against sloop *Defiance,* Christopher Allen, late commander and the *Adventurer,* John Doe, late commander and *Dispatch,* William Hingston, late commander;
in favor of Edward Conkling of the *Eagle* and Associates against *Phebe,* John Tilton, late commander and *Three Friends*
****
From *The Gazette,* May 27, 1779

trick works
The brig *Venus,* Captain Dunn, is arrived in Plymouth from Cape Francois. She was captured by a British privateer, but previous to

their coming on board, Capt. Dunn desired several of the passengers to repair below and conceal themselves, supposing, he added, it probable that the enemy would send but a few men on board the brig. His conjectures were right and, as the privateer soon discovered and pursued another vessel, the persons below rushed upon the deck recovered possession of the brig and conducted her safe to the above port.

deserted
Notice by Timothy Parker, Captain of the Ship *Oliver,* that deserted from his ship were: Solomon Dunham, David Butler, Allen Bidwell, Cuss Chesebrough, Paul Dunn, Alexander Lowrey, Joseph Walker, Jabez Kings and Peter Granger. In Captain Parker's absence, contact Nathaniel Shaw.

runaway
from John Dorrance of Voluntown, a Negro man named Si; 24 years of age; 5 foot, 7 or 8 inches tall; well built.

administration of estates
Jacob B. Gurley Mansfield of Windham appointed Administrator estate of Charles Apthrop, late of New York. All persons having any demands upon the estate are to submit them to Constant Sothworth and Capt. Amariah Williams of Mansfield who are appointed Commissioners.

sales at auction
the following vessels, captured by the *Beaver* and *Hancock:*
Bellona, burthen 160 tons well fitted as a privateer and pierced for 16 guns;
schooner *Mulberry* - 70 tons;
schooner *Hunter* - 90 tons;
sloop *Charlotte* - 60 tons;
privateer sloop *Lady Erskine* - 60 tons;
an unnamed vessel captured by the sloop *American Revenue;*
schooner *Sally* - 50 tons
sloop *Dispatch* - 50 tons;
sloop *Polly* 40 tons;

sloop *Three Friends* - 90 tons,
sloop *Phebe* - 45 tons;
sloop *John* - 30 tons;

confiscated estates
Ezra Selden, John Griffing, Harris Colt have been appointed Commissioners by the Court in Norwich to examine the confiscated estate of William John Brown, late of Salem, Massachusetts. A meeting will be held at the house of Abner Griffing in Lyme;

John Salter has been appointed Commissioner by the District Court in Windham, of the estates of Mr. Thomas Fucker and Isaac Winslow late of Boston, which estates have by the County Court of Windham ordered forfeited to, and for the use of, the State as the estates of persons inimical to the Independence and Liberties of the United States

settle up
Notice by Elijah Parsons that all persons owing him for the delivery of the *Connecticut Gazette* should make settlement.

****

From *The Gazette*, June 2, 1779

drowning
James Tompson was bathing himself in the river near Norwich Landing and was unfortunately drowned., his body was taken up and he was decently interred the next day. Born in Ireland in the village of Antirim, he was a weaver by trade.

ship explodes
We have certain advice by several persons in New York that the sloop *Eagle*, lately commanded by the brave, but unfortunate Capt. Conkling, was lately blown up in New York by means of the snapping a pistol among some powder which communicated to the magazine. It is said that a number of persons were on board at the time, including infamous Murphy who murdered Capt. Conkling.

naval appointments
Capt. Dudley Saltonstall is appointed to be Commander of the *Warren* Frigate and Elishsa Hinman of the *Trumbull* Frigate.

for sale
by Dudley and Samuel Woodbridge at their store in Norwich, Madeira wine, brown sugar and raisins;

by Joseph Tilley in New London, a few hogsheads of stone limes.

wanted
forty or fifty 50 barrels of salted alewives.

farms for sale
about 3,000 acres of choice land lying near Pomfret, being the best and greatest part of the famous Malbone's Farm; mansion house; with gardens, well walled and stocked with suitable fruit trees and suitable barns; there are also several houses upon the property; enquire of John Taylor on the premises or Joseph Palmer or Joseph Pearse Palmer in Germantown, near Boston;

choice piece of property of 38 acres in Norwich West Farms; well watered and equal proportions for pasture, plowing and mowing; on the road from Lebanon to Norwich; also a piece of land lying in Lebanon, about a mile from the Meeting House; 25 acres good dwelling house and barn; enquire of Daniel and Benjamin Hyde, living in Lebanon.

court adjourned
Notice by Edward Hallam, Clerk, that the Probate Court for New London is adjourned until the 4th Tuesday in June.

postage requirements
Those gentlemen who send letters from the post office in New London are desired to send the money ready changed or their letters will be detained.

please settle accounts
Notice by Bernard Phillips of Pomfret, Post Rider, to those who are indebted to him for newspapers delivered, to settle accounts.

house of entertainment opened
by Ephraim Miner in New London at the elegant house lately improved by Capt. Thomas Allen, near the Courthouse.
****
From *The Gazette*, June 9, 1779

died
of small pox, John Hempsted, who over the years, had held a number of positions in this Town, all of which he discharged with great fidelity.

taken up
by Elias Rouse, Blacksmith in Voluntown, a sorrel mare;

by John Henry of Colchester, a mare.

lost
by Isaac Turner of Windsor, a pocketbook between John Moor's and Samuel Taber's, at the head of the Niantic River.

to be sold
at Stonington Point by Capts. Jenks and Stoddard, an unnamed prize sloop taken by them;

by Alexander Merril on Winthrop's Neck, New London, a new six oared barge, 24 feet long; also a new Moses Boat, 16 feet long;

aboard the sloop *Shemburg*, lying at Capt. Mumford's wharf in New London or at John M. Breed's, at Norwich Landing, a large quantity of limes, by the thousand or the hundred, and pineapples by the dozen.

strayed or stolen
from Roger Bulkley of Colchester, two horses.

****

From *The Gazette*, June 16, 1779

prisoners recaptured
Saturday, four prisoners, who had made their escape from Providence, were retaken in Long Island by Capt. Peter Griffing and brought to this town, New London. They were fired upon before they surrendered and one man was shot through the knee.

died
at Preston, Dr. Jedidiah Tracy, in the 87th year of his age in a sudden and surprising manner. He fell from his horse, while riding to a mill about 3 miles from his house and seemed not to breathe by the people, who got to him about three minutes from when he fell. He had served as a deacon in the First Church in Preston for near 50 years. He was also a Justice of the Peace for several years and was a Representative of his Town to the General Assembly, all of which offices he discharged with integrity and fidelity and used his mental powers and abilities remarkably to the end.
He had two wives, both of which died before him. He has left numerous offspring, children, grand children and great grandchildren to the number of 137 still living to mourn the life of their worthy predecessor. His funeral was attended by a considerable concourse of people and a sermon preached suitable for the occasion from Hebrews chap 24, verse 44 "Therefore, be Ye also ready."

pick up prize money
Notices to the officers and privates of the privateer *Hancock*, Capt. Elisha Hinman and the *American Revenue*, Capt. William Leeds, to go to Thomas Mumford of Groton to receive their shares of the prizes.

wanted
an active young man to attend at a tavern; enquire of Nathan Douglass at the Golden Ball in New London.

strayed or stolen

from Samuel Alvord of Bolton, a mare.

****

From *The Gazette,* June 23, 1779

for sale
at public auction by John M. Breed at his store at Norwich, Virginia tobacco, turpentine; also the good Schooner *Proteus,* burthen 80 tons, Virginia built.

ships for sale
private schooner *Eagle,* ten carriage guns and ten swivel guns; also at the wharf of Christopher Leffingwell in Norwich, the hull of the ship *Amherst.*

stolen
from William Stewart's store at the Old Coffee House Wharf, a 7 by 9 foot box of glass.

administration of estates
Notice by Elijah Dyar, Executor of the estate of Col. John Dyar, late of Canterbury, to all those indebted to the estate to settle up and creditors to file claims.

deserted
Notice by Joshua Hemsted, Jun. that deserted from the ship *Warren,* one Thomas Douglass; 5 feet, 6 inches tall; dark brown hair; ruddy complexion; straight and well made; stole a watch and silver buckles from Alexander Hamilton of that ship.

taken up
by John Williams the 3d, of Groton, a mare.

receive pay
Notice by Col. Oliver Smith of Stonington to officers of his former Regiment that money is now available to pay them and to come to his house in Stonington to collect same.

****

From *The Gazette*, July 1, 1779

alarm

On Friday last, at 12 o'clock meridian, we were informed of a fleet off Point Judith by the firing of alarm guns in Stonington. Directly afterwards, the alarms guns were fired at Forts Trumbull and Griswold and kept up the whole afternoon. Several expresses sent into the country, directing the militia to be ready to march on a moment's notice, at which time orders were sent to the four Scarlet Regiments to march in immediately. We have the pleasure of informing the public that the militia of the several towns (where possible) turned out at this alarm with greater cheerfulness and alacrity than ever. Within hours of when the alarms first sounded, numbers appeared at this post. At 7 o'clock, the fleet consisting of upwards of fifty sail, seven ships, the rest brigs, schooners, sloops and two row galleys, appeared off Fisher Island Point, standing to westward. In the evening, the necessary care was taken to observe the motion of the fleet. At 11 o'clock, the whole of them anchored opposite Plumb Island and at, 4 a.m., weighted anchor and continued their course to the westward, at which time counter orders were sent into the country to prevent any more militia from coming in. At 11 o'clock, Brigadier Major Gen. Tyler's brigade that had gone upon the ground were paraded and dismissed with the General's thanks for their alertness and spirited behavior on the occasion.

Putnam returns

On the 25th of June arrived at Boston, the Ship *Putnam* from this port of New London, Capt. Nathaniel Saltonstall, returning from a three month cruise, at which time she took six prizes, two of which have arrived at this port, two at Boston. One of the prizes is the snow *Clinton* from Glasgow, mounting ten 12 pounders and eight 6 pounders, having a hundred barrels of provisions and dry goods to a value of 16,000 pounds; another is a brig from Cork not yet arrived. The sixth they gave to prisoners - 238 in all - and bought 60 of them to Boston, which was the most they could take without confining them to the hold. She spoke with the *Rural Felicity,* which was an old prison boat from New York. They gave them a tierce of bread etc. and allowed them to proceed to England.

administration of estates
Notice by Ephraim Powers that the Probate Court for the District of Guilford for the estate of Nathaniel Martson, late of the City of New York, which estate has been ordered forfeited to, and for the use of, the State as the estates of persons inimical to the Independence and Liberties of the United States, has appointed Edmund Rogers and John Parmels, Commissioners, to conduct a hearing at the house of Farrington Harrington, Inn Holder in Branford.

to be sold
at private sale, the sloop *Sally*, (formerly the *Wooster* privateer out of New Haven) about 80 tons; enquire at General Saltonstall's or with the Printer.

moved
Notice by Joseph Persons of Norwich that he has moved from Deacon Simon Huntington's to Elisha Leffingwell's and Jonathan Starr's adjoining the Paper Mill in Norwich, where he carries on the clothier business in all its branches. He also wants a journeyman clothier and two apprentice boys, 14 or 15 years of age, to learn the weaving and clothing business.

newspaper delivery
Daniel Carew notifies the people of Norwich and vicinity that he has undertaken the business of delivering the *Connecticut Gazette*.

pay up
Nathan Bushnell, late post rider, want those indebted to him to settle accounts.

fighting monopoly
At a town meeting in New London, it was approved that we agree with the rising spirit in Philadelphia against the enormous growth

of monopoly and oppression and that we will cooperate with other Towns in this State in every measure to remedy that growing evil, VOTED that a committee of three persons be appointed to communicate with other Towns in this county on that subject and desire a meeting with such other towns. Accordingly, Winthrop Saltonstall, William Hillhouse and John Deshon were appointed to be that Committee.

volunteers wanted
by the Brig *Saratoga*, Commander James Monro, a prime sailer of sixteen 6 pounder which preparing to sail on a cruise against the enemy of the United States. Those with an intention to take a cruise should repair on board and apply to Lt. Champlin.

strayed or stolen
from Samuel Latimer in New London, a sorrel horse.

ran away
from Samuel Fox Jun. of New London, North Parish, an apprentice girl named Lydia Preston; about 14 years old; born in this Town, New London.

****

From *The Gazette*, July 8, 1779

Fourth of July celebrations
Sunday last, being the Anniversary of the Independence of America, was on Monday, the day following, observed as a day of festivity on the heights of Groton, where a very large number of the respectable inhabitants from the surrounding towns were very elegantly entertained at dinner and, after dinner, thirteen patriotic toasts were drunk, under the discharge of field pieces. The whole was concluded with the great festivity and satisfaction.

for sale
a quantity of logwood and mahogany at Mr. Shaw's store;

the prize sloop *Nautilus*; 90 tons, Bermuda built.

Gentlemen Adventurers wanted
by William Havens, Commander of the *Beaver*.

clothes needed
Notice by Chauncey Whittlesley of Middletown, Purchaser of Clothing for the several Towns of the State, to all to forward the clothing, required by the late Act of the Assembly, as soon as possible. The clothes are very much needed, especially the shirts. Clothing can be received by Andrew Huntington of Norwich; Joshua Elderkin of Windham; Newton Whittlesley of New Haven; Abel Hine of New Milford; and Dr. Reuben Smith of Litchfield.

escape
from Nathan Baley, Jun., goaler of New London, Thomas Douglas; 26 years of age; 5 foot, 6 inches high; short brown hair; ruddy complexion; straight and well made; committed for theft and deserting from the Ship *Warren*.

receive wages
Notice by Captain David Miller in Colchester to the soldiers belonging in his Company to meet him at Roger Fuller's in Hebron to receive their pay.

taken up
by John Kimball of Pomfret, a horse.

command
Notice by Capt. B. Shipman to non commissioned officers and soldiers of the Second Connecticut Brigade to march to join their Regiment at Fishkill or be deemed deserters.

runaway
from William Williams in Colchester, a Negro man name Quam 30 years old; straight built; 5 feet, 8 inches tall; very black; speaks quick.

****

From *The Gazette,* July 14, 1779

for sale
by Frederick Tracy of Norwich, Madeira wine;

the brig *Nancy,* 100 tons burthen at Norwich Landing; enquire of Levi Huntington and Joseph Williams.

strayed or stolen
from Samuel Belden of New London, a horse;

from John M Curdy of Lyme, a mare.
****

From *The Gazette,* July 21, 1779

garrison
Since our last a large body of Militia under the command of Gen. Tyler arrived in New London and Groton. They are a corp of well disciplined troops, consisting of substantial yeomanry of the State, who appear to be determined to put a stop at every hazard to the recent insolvence and savage conduct of the British incendiaries. The troops now here are employed in strengthening the works erected in defense of the Town and Harbor.

arson and theft
Last Thursday, some people landed in Fisher's Island from the shipping lying off this (New London) harbor and placing some combustible material in the cellar of the house, lately improved by Mr. Brown, they blew up the middle of the house and then putting fire on the westward end of it, consumed the whole. They also set fires to the outbuildings and consumed them too and also a quantity of hay and corn on the Island.

married
at Preston, by the Rev. Mr. Hart, John Cady of Plainfield to Miss Issana Pemberton, late of Newport, Rhode Island.

to be sold
at private sale at Norwich Landing, the ship *Otter*, burthen about 200 pounds, the sloop *Lord Howe*, a pilot boat, about 30 tons and a quantity of goods of different assortments.

come collect prize money
The officers and crew entitled to share in the prizes in *American Revenue,* Capt. William Leeds, are directed to go to his house.

Notice by John Gelston of Norwich, Agent, to the officers and crew entitled to share in the prizes of the sloops *Revenge* and *Washington and Gates* to meet at Norwich landing for their divisions of the prize *Otter*.

administration of estates
Notice by Charles Church Chandler and Amos Paine, Commissioners appointed by the Probate Court of Pomfret for the estate of Jonathan Skinner, late of Woodstock, deceased and represented to be insolvent, to all those indebted to the estate to settle up and creditors to file claims. A meeting will be held at the house of Paul Tew, Inn Holder in Woodstock.

strayed or stolen
from Nathaniel Dike of Killingly, a dark brown mare

not responsible
Notice by Nathan Burrows of Groton that his wife Anna has eloped from his bed and board and refuses to return and perform her duties.
He is not responsible for any debts she incurs.

****

From *The Gazette*, July 28, 1779

sail by
Last Thursday, the town New London was alarmed by the sight of 20 sail coming down the sound and two three appearing from the eastward at the same time. Those from the westward passed our harbor and joined the others and sailed off to Newport.

shark attack in River!
Last Friday, three of the militia belonging to Captain Raynsford from Canterbury, *viz.* William Baldwin, John Bates and Jeremiah Mott, having been fishing near the Light house at the mouth of the harbor in a small canoe, on their return to shore, in about four feet of water, they discovered a large shark (which afterwards proved to be nine and ½ feet long) making towards them with great fury and struck the canoe with such force as to throw Mott into the water. The other two seeing their companion in danger of being devoured, leaped into the water and one of them seized the shark by the tail and the other plied the paddle to the head so effectively that after a considerable struggle they killed it and afterwards brought it into town. The curiosity drew together a number of spectators.

American Revenue privateer taken
We hear that Capt. Champlin in the privateer *American Revenue* was taken by the *Unicorn* and that the sloop *Hancock*, Capt. Bowdwich Champlin, chased by the same ship, had to throw her guns overboard and made it to Boston.

meeting of the inhabitants of the town of Windham on inflation
At this meeting, taking into consideration the rapid deterioration of our currency, occasioned by the enormous prices of every article necessary to the comfort and convenience of life, therefore destroying the scale and balance of justice, corrupting the morals of people, reducing the innocent and helpless to poverty, weakening and lessening our abilities to support the unavoidable necessities of the war and forgiving the greatest encouragement to the enemy to continue the war, it was
VOTED: It is our opinion that the people of these States ought to take the most effectual measures to put a final stop to any further rise in the price of necessities and conveniences of life and to prevent any further depreciation of the currency and that we are ready to yield our utmost efforts and assistance therein and to unite in every salutary measure to restore an equal balance among the people;
VOTED: that a Committee be created to communicate the sentiments of this Town as above expressed especially to the other towns of this County and others with in this or other States in the

United States as they may think proper and further to correspond with them on this interesting subject and the measures therein to be taken.
Members of the Committee: Eliphalet Dyer; Ebenezer Mosely, Sandford Kingsbury, Nathaniel Wales Jr. and Hezekiah Bissel. Samuel Gray, Town Clerk.

broke into the enclosure
of Hobart Mackall of Lebanon, a bay mare

libels filed
Notice by Wm. Saltonstall, Register, that libels are filed before, and to be heard by, the Hon. Richard Law, Judge of the Maritime Court for the County of New London:
in favor of Nathaniel Post of the *Revenge* against the Brig *Neptune*. Joseph Dorcen, late captain;
in favor of Isaac Freeburn, commander of the *General Sullivan* against the schooner, *Charlotte*, late commander William Spence;
in favor of Thomas Harding against sundry goods found and seized in New London by lawful authority in connection with illegal; trade.

New London taxes
Notice by Joshua Hempsted, Tax Collector, to all those inhabitants who are obliged to pay taxes, that payment may be made at the houses of James Haughton, John Raymond, Jason Allen, Capt. Nicholas Bishop, Clement Leech and Stephen Prentis.

come and collect pay
Notice from Capt. Timothy Percival to the solders and officers, who served in his Company in the expedition to Rhode Island, that he will meet those belonging to New London and Lyme at the Widow Lee's in Lyme and those in East Haddam at Landlord Ransom's in Colchester, to settle their wages.

administration of estate
Notice by Justus Buck and John Buckingham, Commissioner appointed by the Probate Court of Guilford for estate of Dr. Appleton Wolcos Rosseter of Saybrook, deceased and represented to be insolvent, to all those indebted to the estate to settle up and

creditors to file claims. A meeting will be held at John Buckingham, Inn Holder in Chester, Saybrook.

strayed or stolen
from Allen Matteson of Coventry, a bay mare that broke out of the pasture of James Delop in Canterbury, return to subscriber or to Richard Waterman of Coventry.

from Jonathan Brewster of Poquatanuck in Norwich, a black cow.
****

From *The Gazette*, August 4, 1779

prisoners exchanged
Friday, a flag arrived here from New York in which came Lt. John Chapman of the Ship *Oliver Cromwell*, William Reed and several other prisoners.

wanted immediately
by Dudley and Samuel Woodbridge black oak hogsheads stays and a quantity of hoops for which payment will be in rum, sugar, molasses, rock salt or cash.

to be leased
for three years, the ferry between New London and Groton with the buildings and lot of land on the Groton side.

strayed or stolen
from Sarah Woodward, Widow of Niantic in New London, a black cow three years old.

to be sold for continental money
twenty five acres with a large new house, barn and horse shed, pleasantly situated in Norwich West Farms. Enquire of Nathan Stedman of East Haddam.
****

From *The Gazette*, August 11, 1779

burglary thwarted
We hear from Saybrook that a vessel, lately returned to the Connecticut River from Long Island where she had been on an illicit trade, was stopped by the Fort at Saybrook when a quantity of goods were taken out of the boat and lodged on the custody of one Mr. Tully, an officer of the Fort, who stored them in his dwelling house and that, on Saturday night last, eight men broke into the house with a view toward carrying off the goods; on which the officer fired on them, killed two at the first shot and wounded another with his bayonet. On this the others made off, carrying the wounded man with them.

clothes for army
Notice by Chauncey Whittlesey, in Middletown, Purchasing Clothier to the several Towns in this state, that prices for good shoes cannot exceed $15 per pair; stockings from $10 to $12, depending on the quality and brown tow cloth, $6.[43]

confiscated estates
Notice by Jacob DeWitt; John M. Breed and Jonathan Brewster, Commissioners for the confiscated estate of Ebenezer Punderton, now joined with the enemies of the United States and the estates of William Byard and Charles Ward Apthorp of New York that they will hear claims against same at the house of Jonathan Brewster of Poquatanuck in Norwich.

libels filed
Notice by Wm. Saltonstall, Register, that libels are filed before, and to be heard by, the Hon. Richard Law, Judge of the Maritime Court for the County of New London:
in favor of Samuel Brooks, Commander of the sloop *Harlequin*, against the schooner *William*, William Reid, late commander;
in favor of Nathan Post of the sloop *Revenge* and Silas Talbot of sloop *Argo* against Brig *King George*; Lt. Hazzard, late captain and against the sloop *Mosquito*, Neil McNeil, late captain.

supplies for soldiers needed
Notice by Benjamin Payne, Clerk, that at a meeting of the Governor and the Council of Safety that the Selectmen of the several Towns are directed to furnish for the protection of this state, one tent, one iron pot or kettle, and two wooden bowls for every six men, officers included, raised in their respective towns.

died
in Windham, of a consumptive disease,[44] Jabez Dyer, son of the Hon. Eliphalet Dyer, in the 22nd year of his age. He survived a brother by a year, who died of the same disorder.

eloped
Notice by Silas Champlin of Stonington that his wife has left his bed and board and refuses to live with him. This is to advise the Public that he is no longer responsible for her debts and will not pay same.

broke into the enclosure
of Shubael Child of West Society Woodstock, a black mare.

runaway
from John Howard of Windham, a Negro man named Derry; about 5 feet, 7 inches high; well built; a large scar on both his shins; speaks broken English.

to be sold
at Poquatuck River in Westerly at Thompson's Wharf, schooners *Carolina* and *Stellar* and their cargoes, appurtenances, boats etc.

in New London North Parish, three little horses suitable for saddle, draught or shipping; enquire of William Prince.

by Samuel Wheat and Daniel Rodman at their store in Norwich, opposite the store of Col. Zabdiel Rogers and adjoining Wheat's dwelling house New London, wood, rolled iron, white and red lead etc.

strayed or stolen
from the door of Dr. Downer in Preston, a mare; notice by Joshua Grant.

****

From *The Gazette,* August 18, 1779

prisoners exchanged
Wednesday returned here to New London from New York, a flag that had been detained several weeks. It brought in 31 prisoners among them Capt. Samuel Champlin, late commander of the *American Revenue* and Capt. Wm. Leeds, late of the Brig *Nancy,* which vessels were taken by the *Greyhound* Frigate. It seems from the prisoners that the *Greyhound* was one of a fleet of seven ships which had sailed from Sandy Hook to Penobscot about the third instant.

counterfeit currency
Sunday, a man was detected in Town with a quantity of counterfeit Continental bills printed on blue paper and not signed or numbered.

safe arrival
Captains Jabez Starr, Hez. Perkins and Jabez Lore, who sailed from this port, New London, have arrived safely in Boston from the West Indies.

collect prize money
Notice to those who served under Captains Elisha Hinman and Peter Richards on the *Hancock* to go to agent in Groton and collect their share of prize money.

administration of estates
Notice by Hez. Bissel and Jesse Everit, Commissioners appointed by the Probate Court of Windham, for the estate of John Rouse of Windham, deceased and represented to be insolvent, to all those indebted to the estate to settle up and creditors to file claims.

to all Gentlemen sailors
and other who have a mind to make their fortunes, the schooner *Experiment*, lying at Rocky Hill, under the command of Capt. Nathan Sage of Middletown, on a cruise against the enemies of our country.

broke in the enclosure
of Jesse Brown of Groton, a two year old heifer.
****

From *The Gazette*, August 25, 1779

condition of prisoners improves
Last Sabbath, a Flag arrived here from New York with forty one prisoners, among whom were Capt. Parker, late of the *Oliver Cromwell*, and Mr. Angel and Mr. Prentis, late officers of the *American Revenue*. Although taken from the Prison Ship *Good Hope*, it may be, for once, acknowledged that all were healthy. They inform us that only 150 prisoners remain on the ship when they left, who, it is thought, will all be let off on the arrival of an exchange ship from Boston with 300 prisoners. We learn there are a number of grave faces in New York because of our late successes.

administration of estates
Notice by Eliashid Adams and David Erost, Commissioners appointed by the Probate Court of Plainfield, for the estate of Nehemiah Parish of Canterbury, deceased and represented to be insolvent, to all those indebted to the estate to settle up and creditors to file claims.

Notice by Desiree Beebe, Adminstratrix of the estate of Samuel Beebe of Stonington of the sale of the assets of the estate, subject to the encumbrance of the widow's dower.

to be sold
at East Haddam the Brig *Neptune,* 120 tons burthen.

strayed or stolen
from Samuel Cleveland of New London, a bay horse;

from Robert Gibson of New London, a sorrel mare.

come and collect pay
Notice by Capt. William Whitney to those who served under him in 1778, that their wages and bounty are ready and he will deliver them as specified at the houses of Lt. Nehemiah Smith of Groton, Jesse Swan in Stonington and Dr. Joshua Downer in Preston.

lost
by John Chapman Jun. of New London between Benjamin Gordon's and William Douglas', a pocketbook containing about 50 and 60 dollars.

stolen
from the store of Jabez Fitch Jun. in Windham different types of clothing.

****

From *The Gazette*, September 1, 1779

deserted
Notice by John Bulkley, that deserted from Conductor Oliver Olmsted's Company of Teamsters in the Continental service: Benjamin Robinson, formerly of East Haddam; middling stature; dark complexion; about 20 years of age; and Abraham Bailey of Canaan; a tall slim fellow, light complexion.

come and collect wages
Notice from Lt. Ezra Kinne to all the officers and enlisted men who served in his company at Fort Griswold that he will meet with them in Groton and Stonington at John Denison' at the head of the Mystic and at John Harkness' in Preston to pay wages.

broke in the enclosure
of Jeremiah Main of Stonington, three sheep.

prize taken
A schooner with 110 puncheons of rum was taken by the *Washington* and the *Gamecock* and was sent into the Connecticut River last Tuesday.

volunteers wanted
The *Hancock* will again go on a short cruise in five days. Some good sailors once more have their opportunity to make their fortunes; apply to Captain Champlin at his house or aboard said sloop and at Mr. Mumford's Wharf in Groton.

found
at Capt. Jabez Perkins' Wharf in Norwich Landing, some time back, a Hadley Quadrant.

strayed or stolen
from Major Joseph Harris in New London, a chestnut colored mare; apply to him or to Joseph Hale in Coventry;

from Lot Dimock of Mansfield, a mare.

lost
by Joseph Champlin of New London between David Latimer's and James Penniman's, a pocket book, half worn and of a moldy cast.
****
From *The Gazette*, September 8, 1779

submit bills and return tools
Notice by Guy Richards Jun. of New London to those who have bills for services rendered to, or for, the public works that they be submitted immediately, properly vouched, for settlement.
Note: He has information on the embezzlement or concealment of sundry tools and implements, used at the public works in New London and belonging to the State, and he would advise all persons, who have them in their custody, that in case they return them to him immediately, there shall be no questions asked; otherwise, they may depend on the most rigorous steps of the law to recover them.

volunteers needed
by sloop *Beaver*, Capt. William Havens, to make their fortune on a cruise against the enemy; apply on board the ship, sitting in New London harbor, or at Capt. Nathan Douglas' in New London.

broke into the enclosure
of Joseph Davis Jun. of Mansfield, a black mare.

strayed or stolen
from Benjamin Randal of Colchester, a brown mare.
****

From *The Gazette*, September 15, 1779

inflation measures studied
Yesterday, the Freemen of this Town New London, having convened to choose their Representatives, a letter was handed to the meeting by the Committee of Correspondence of this Town, which having been read, they unanimously agreed to have a meeting of the County of New London to be held in the Town of New London and made choice of a Committee to meet the Committees of the other Towns to take into considerations the actions of the County of Windham and to adopt such measures against such inflation as shall appear expedient. The members of the Committee chosen were William Hillhouse, General Saltonstall, Nathaniel Shaw and John Deshon.

libels filed
Notice by Wm. Saltonstall, Register, that libels are filed before, and to be heard by, the Hon. Richard Law, Judge of the Maritime Court for the County of New London:
in favor of the sloop *Hannah,* Commander Ludwick Champlin and all concerned against the schooner *Little William*, Samuel Darrel late master from Bermuda and brig *Strumpet,* John Ayeea of Jamaica;
in favor of the sloop *Argo,* commander Silas Talbot and the sloop *Revenge*, Nathaniel Post, Commander, against the sloop *Adventurer*, Thomas Jackson, late commander from Tobago and the Brig *Elliot,* Francis Squires, late commander, from London;

in favor of the sloop *Retaliation*, Azihiah Whittlesey, Commander, against the brig *Walpole*, William Robertson, late commander from Cork;
in favor of the sloop *Young Cromwell*, William Wattles, Commander, against the sloop *Peggy*, lately commanded by Herman Kenny from Halifax, and against the Brig *Endeavor*, George May, from Boston, all taken on the high seas.
also in favor of John Shipman against sundry goods found and seized in Saybrook.

administration of estates
Notice by Aephia Boynton, Administratrix for the estate of Samuel Boynton of Coventry, deceased, to all those indebted to the estate to settle up and creditors to file claims;

Notice by Martha Rogers, Administratrix for the estate of Joseph Rogers of Lyme, deceased, to all those indebted to the estate to settle up and creditors to file claims.
****

From *The Gazette*, September 22, 1779

young men flee Long Island
Friday last, 35 young men came to Saybrook from Long Island. They left their homes on account of their being ordered to work on the fortifications at the west end of the Island, apprehending that they would be ordered from thence to garrison at some fort in the West Indies.

married
Captain Robert Hallam to Miss Lydia Adams;

Lt. Samuel Hempsted of the Navy to Lucretia Stoddard.

died
Mrs. Lucy Lester of Saybrook, wife of Eliphalet Lester and daughter of William Manawaring of New London.

wanted
a school master to teach reading, writing and arithmetic, who can be well recommended; apply to John Williams 3d, near the Ferry in Groton.

administration of estates
Notice by Nathan Gallup and Stephen Billings, Commissioners appointed by the Probate Court of Stonington for the estate of Roger Fanning, late Groton, deceased and represented to be insolvent, to all those indebted to the estate to settle up and creditors to file claims. A meeting will be held at dwelling house of John Morgan, Inn Holder of Groton.

broke out of the enclosure
of Christopher Greene of New London, a mare.

receive pay that is due
Notice by Capt. John Williams 3d to those who served in his Company at Fort Griswold to meet him at Charles Wheeler's in Stonington; Dr. Downer's in Preston or Samuel Andrus of Groton to receive their pay.

deserters
Notice by quartermaster William Whittlesey of Col. Angel's Regiment that the following deserted:
Covel Lark, Ensign; belonging to Hopkinton, Rhode Island; 22 years of age, 5 feet, 2 inches tall; dark complexion; black hair; has a scar on his right jaw;
Thomas Sarls, belonging to Stonington; 18 years old, 5 feet, 5 inches high; fresh complexion; well built; dark brown hair; has a mole on his left breast;
Joseph Congden of Hopkinton; 17 years of age; 5 feet, 8 inches tall; dark brown hair; light complexion.
A reward for the capture of any deserter to be paid by Lt. Commander Jeremiah Olney;

Notice by Lt. Simeon Drake of Capt. Cone's Company of Col. Jonathan Walls Regiment, that deserted a soldier named James

Allen; dark complexion; short black hair; has an impediment in his speech.

beware the fraud
For the benefit of the public, notice is hereby given that Capt. Abraham Remsen of Westerly, Rhode Island, is a public cheat and, as such, it is Subscriber's Samuel Delivan's duty to let the Public know. He bought a horse from the Subscriber in Norwich, for which he gave an order for 110 gallons of rum of Major Hart of Saybrook and John Foster of East Haddam which was entirely false. The Subscriber pursued him to South Kingston and got his horse back. He later went from John Denison's Tavern in Stonington, where he stayed three days and left without paying his bill. He did the same thing at Capt. Douglas' in New London and also to Ephraim Miner of New London and Azariah Lathrop of Norwich; he is 5 feet, 10 inches high; well set; 40 years old; cross eyed and near sighted; brown complexion; well dressed; writes a good hand and has the appearance of a gentleman; talks smooth and a little of the Dutch.

****

From *The Gazette,* September 29, 1779

privateers arrive in port with prizes
Last Saturday and Sunday, the *Hancock, Bever, Gates* and *Young Cromwell* returned from a cruise, during the course of which the *Young Cromwell* took a sloop from Newfoundland headed for New York, laden with fish and a few casks of wine and the *Bever* took a brig from New York, bound for Quebec and laden with salt. Both prizes have arrived.

exchange prisoners arrive
A flag of truce brought from New York 117 prisoners, belonging to different parts of New England and last Thursday landed the same at the western part of Town.

privateers wrecked
On the 8th instant, Capt. Champlin on the *Hancock* and Capt. Welden of the *Venus* and Capt. Fosdick of the *Eagle* fell in with

a letter of marquee ship of 20 carriage and a three decker which they engaged for three glasses but, her force being so much superior to them, they were forced to leave her. The *Hancock* lost three men Joseph Starkweather, Palsey Baker and Jonathan Brown and four wounded and was much disable in her rigging and spars. The *Venus* had two men wounded. A few days after the action the *Venus* and *Eagle* were drove on shore in Egg Harbor by the British Ship *Daphne* and three of her cruisers. The vessels were lost, but rigging etc. saved.

salt regulations
At a meeting of the Government and Council of Safety of Windham, this board taking into consideration that the inhabitants of this State may be entitled to obtain sufficient quantities of that useful valuable article, salt, for their own consumption, do hereby grant, order and permit any inhabitant of this State to export from this State to any neighboring State any of their own produce and manufacture, as shall be necessary for their respective use for the coming season.
John Porter, Clerk

wanted to purchase
a Negro wench, 18 to 25 years of age, who understands house work and can be well recommended. Enquire of the Printer.

taken up
on the highway near the church in Groton by Henry Morgan, a black mare.

deserted
from the Company of John Wood of Col. Jonathan Wales' detachment of militia, stationed in New London, one Elisha Allen of Hartford West Division; he is about 34 years old; 5 feet, 10 inches tall; well built; light hair and light complexion; somewhat marked with small pox.

wanted immediately
by Edmond Darrow in Norwich, two or three journeymen nail makers; he has for sale iron, Jersey nail rods, and bloomery.

prize to be sold
Notice that the Brig *Strumpe*t, prize of the *Hancock*, will be sold together with all her stores. she now lies in Poqutanuck Cove. Enquire of Thomas Mumford of Groton.

stolen
from the house of Daniel Lathrop of Norwich, various articles of jewelry and clothing.

****

From *The Gazette,* October 6, 1779

prizes taken
Last Thursday, a schooner with upwards of 90 hogsheads of rum and other articles was sent into port, a prize of the *Shelah*, Capt. Ezek Hopkins;

The *Washington* last week sent two sloops into safe ports, loaded with oysters taken at Blue Point;

raid on Long Island
Last Monday, the sloop *Revenge*, Capt. Parker, the Brig *Defiance,* Capt. King, the *Retaliation,* Capt. Whittlsey; the sloop *Sally,* Capt. Warner and the schooner, *Experiment,* Capt. Sage, went into Oyster Bay on the north shore of Long Island and captured a Guard brig pierced for 14 guns, but only had ten mounted, commanded by Samuel Rogers (who has been thrice taken and brought to the Town since March last) three other sloops and a schooner, taken from under a two gun battery. Three of the prizes are laden with wood and one a large well built Bermudian sloop with ballast. The prizes are all landed in safe ports.

****

From *The Gazette,* October 13, 1779

enemy transport taken
Monday last, Capt. King of the Brig *Defiance* arrived here New London from a cruise. Last Saturday off Blue Point on the south side of Long Island, he fell in with and took the transport ship *Badger,* commanded by Edward Flynn, under jury masts, having on board 122 troops, but she was met the next morning by a British cruiser and retaken. Capt. King took out of the vessel four Hessian officers and nine soldiers and twelve British soldiers belonging to the 44th Regiment, the Captain, mate and nine seaman from the *Badger* and also a parcel of small arms. We learn the *Badger* sailed from New York in company with 11 other transports, bound for Quebec with the two regiments of Hessians and 44th British Regiment, but met with a violent gale.

new President of Congress
We learn that the Hon. Samuel Huntington, a delegate to Congress from this State, has been chosen President of Congress. The late President John Jay is to shortly embark for Europe.

deserted
from Windham, the place of rendezvous, the following soldiers, drafted and New London enlisted:
James Griffey, Abraham Hartington, Ichabod Randal and David Perkins, all of Voluntown; Jonathan Angel and Benjamin Farr of Lebanon, the latter lately lived in a new settlement near the Connecticut River in the Bay State and is supposed to have gone there; William Hall of Canterbury and John Frederick, a Frenchman of Coventry; John Robinson and John Johnson, said to be of Manchester in the State of Vermont; said Robinson is about 40 years old, dark hair and dark complexion, a thick well set man, about 5 feet, ten inches high; said Johnson is about 30 years old; light hair; light complexion; a well built fellow; about 5 feet, 8 or 10 inches high;
notice given by John Ripley, Recruiting Officer for the Fifth Brigade in the State of Connecticut

for sale
Freebetter's Almanac for the Year 1780, wholesale or retail, by Tim. Green on the most reasonable terms.

for no fault of her own but want of employ, a likely, lively Negro girl, 14 years old for a term of 7 years; enquire of the Printer; note the purchaser will be obligated not to keep her upon the completion of her term.

at Capt. Richard's Wharf in New London, the brig *Walpole*; the brig *Endeavor* and the sloop *Fly*.

taken up
by Henry Morgan of Groton, a mare;

by Benjamin Greene of New London, a gray horse.

broke in the enclosure
of Gurdun Watrous of New London, North Parish, a steer.

runaway
from headquarters, an unnamed likely, dark mulatto man; 5 foot, 6 inches tall; 18 years of age; smooth face; is very artful and speaks good English; notice James Browne, S. G. M. H. W. D.

administration of estates
Notice by Samuel Latimer and Jed Beckwith, Administrators for the estate of Absalom Thomas, a Mulatto, late of New London, deceased, to all those indebted to the estate to settle up and creditors to file claims.

****

From *The Gazette*, October 20, 1779

privateers captured
The sloop *Harlequin* of 10 guns, Capt. Hurd and the Schooner *Eagle* of 12 guns, Capt. Brooks, both of this State, were taken by the enemy and brought into New York.

enemy leaving Newport?
From various accounts from Rhode Island, we have undoubted intelligence that the enemy is preparing with the utmost expedition to leave Newport.

mother kills children
The following tragic affair happened in the North Parish of Killingsworth on Wednesday last, *viz,* the wife of Mr. Higgins of that Parish, being disordered in her reasoning and being left in the house with her three children, she called her son of seven years old to her, telling him she wanted to pin his collar and immediately cut his throat; she then cut the throat of her daughter 5 years old and her infant which lay on a bed.. Mr. Higgins, upon soon coming into the house, found her on her knees, cutting her own throat with a dull knife which he wrestled away from her, but she had wounded herself to that degree that she soon died afterwards.

U. S. lottery tickets for sale
by John Porter of Lebanon at Gov. Trumbull's office.

come collect prize money
to the officers and crew of the late Privateer *American Revenue* in her cruise under Capt. Samuel Champlin are desired to come to house of Thomas Mumford, their agent in Groton, to receive their shares of the prize money.

strayed or stolen
from Ellis Bliss of Hebron, three red steers;

from Amos Prentice of Groton, a mare;

from Elisha Child of Woodstock, a horse;

from Moses Bicknell and Stephen Bicknell of Mansfield, a yoke of oxen.

found
on the beach, near Four Mile River, by Peter Vivee of Lyme, a swivel gun.

died
at Danbury this past Thursday, Col. Giles Russel of the Continental Army. He was the son of the late Rev. David Russel of Wethersford, deceased and an inhabitant of the Town of Stonington for the past 16 years. He received an early and liberal education at Yale College.

acquittal
Mr. Green:
There having been sundry items in the Boston newspapers with respect to the lost of the Continental Ship *Alfred,* and my trial consequent thereon, you are desired to print in your newspaper the

record of the proceedings of the Marine Committee of Congress Elisha Hinman
"The Committee having considered the proceeding of the court martial held in Boston from January 28 to February 12 in the case of Elisha Hinman whereas the court has honorably acquitted Capt. Hinman of all and any of the charges alleged against him touching the loss of the Continental ship *Alfred.*"

libels filed
Notice by Wm. Saltonstall, Register, that Libels are filed before, and to be heard by, the Hon. Richard Law, Judge of the Maritime Court for the County of New London:
in favor of the sloop *Hannah,* Commander Ludwick Champlin and all concerned against the schooner *Little William,* Samuel Darrel late master from Bermuda and brig *Strumpet,* John Ayeea of Jamaica;
in favor of the sloop *Argo,* commander Silas Talbot and the sloop *Revenge,* Nathaniel Post, Commander, against the sloop *Adventurer,* Thomas Jackson, late commander from Tobago and the Brig *Elliot,* Francis Squires, late commander, from London;

in favor of Nathan Sage, Schooner *Experiment*, Esek Hopkins, Jun, the schooner *Lively* against the *Argyle*, Thomas Page, late commander and the schooner Charming *Sally*, Robert Clark, late commander and schooner *Dolphin*, John Stanton, late commander; in favor of Seth Warner of sloop *Sally* against the brig *Union*, William Haynes, late commander.

to be sold at public vendue
by permission of the General Assembly at the store of General Saltonstall in New London, six hogshead and ten barrels of white sugar.

country seat for sale
by Benjamin Thurber, hundred acres of land, lying in the most delightsome part of the town of Pomfret, a large and convenient dwelling house, completely finished; a barn 30 feet by 60 and other outbuildings.

wanted
full employ and good wages will be given a clothier by Joseph Parsons in Norwich.

administration of estates
Notice by Mary Palmer, Executrix of the estate of William Parker, late of Stonington, deceased, to all those indebted to the estate to settle up and creditors to file claims.

to be let on reasonable terms
a dwelling house lying on about 20 acres of choice land, suitable for tanning at the head of the Mystic River in Stonington; owned by the heirs of the estate of Paul Woodbridge; enquire of Sarah Woodbridge at the premises.

all weavers to meet
Notice to all gentlemen weavers in Norwich and neighboring Towns that there will be a meeting at Jacob Witter's dwelling house to agree on prices that will do them and their customers justice.

confession
Notice by Ebenezer Pelton, Jun. of Groton that, as a soldier in Col. Starr's Company in General Huntington;'s brigade, he did, by the temptation of the Devil, steal a large brown mare from Dr. Peter Hays of Danbury, for which sin he begs the forgiveness of God and the Public. He wishes that this be published in the New London papers as the Public may be informed of his villainy
Witnessed by: John Morgan, Benjamin Hickok, and Mary Fanning

****

From *The Gazette*, October 27, 1779

taxes assessed
We learn that Congress has ordered an assessment of 15 million dollars a month on the inhabitants of the United States. The first payment is to be made the first day of February next and will continue to October following. This State's proportion of said tax is $1,700,000 per month.

body discovered
Yesterday se'nnight was found about 4 miles from Hartford Ferry on the Boston Road about 30 rods from the road, the bones of a man who was supposed to have been murdered some five months ago. His saddlebags, boots and several articles of clothing were found near him. A pistol which had been discharged was also found near him. A horse was found about five months ago near the place and supposed to be his. Although advertised, no one came for it.

fleet leaves Newport
Yesterday morning about daybreak, the grand fleet from Newport passed this harbor and stood up the Sound. They consisted of about 90 sail of vessels of different kinds and have doubtless brought off the garrison.

died
Alexander Merrel of this town, New London;

in Pomfret, departed this life in the comfortable hope of entering a better one, Nathan Frink, Attorney at Law. He endured a consumptive illness with exemplary patience, resignation and becoming fortitude.

stolen
Notice by Louis Tousson tin New London that two French men had stolen from them, while at Chappel's in New London, gold and silver; supposed to be taken by one John Allen; 30 years old; 6 foot; dark complexion; black eyes, one ankle thicker than the other; pitted with small pox.

administration of estates
Notice by Ephraim Root and Caleb Stanley, Jun., Commissioners appointed by the Probate Court of Windham, for the estate of Samuel Boynton, late of Coventry, deceased and represented to be insolvent, to all those indebted to the estate to settle up with Administratrix Aephia Boynton and creditors to file claims. A meeting will be held at dwelling house of Elijah Grosvenor, Inn Holder.

broke into the enclosure
of George Martin 3d of Windham, a black horse;

of Richard Chapman of New London, a mare.

found
by James Rogers in New London (near Mammocock), two or three miles on the Norwich road, a pocket book with a small amount of Continental bills.

strayed or stolen
from John Robinson in New London, a horse.
****

From *The Gazette,* November 3, 1779

evacuation of Newport
The enemy left in Newport large quantities of wood, hay and salt.

murder victim identified
The person who was mentioned in our last as being murdered near East Hartford is said to have been a gentlemen who belonged to Philadelphia and was traveling to that place from the state of Rhode Island.

libels filed
Notice by Wm. Saltonstall, Register, that libels are filed before, and to be heard by, the Hon. Richard Law, Judge of the Maritime Court for the County of New London:
in favor of Esek Hopkins Jun. of the schooner *Lively* and all against the schooner *Chance*, Adam Ladle late commanded, her cargo, appurtenances, tackle, boats etc.

to be sold
a quantify of powder; enquire of the printer;

a likely Negro wench; about 20 years old, who understands house work; enquire of William Williams of Stonington.

runaway
from Joshua Powers in Lyme, a Negro man named Wooder; 42 years of age; this country born; 5 feet, 8 inches tall; thick lips; somewhat long favored; has a scar on the back of his hands occasioned by having been burnt when a child; when he stoops down, the small of his back sticks up, as if it were broke.

come and collect prize money
Notice by John Celston of East Haddam, agent for those officers and crew of the *Washington & Gates* involved in the taking of the prize *Otter;* also the crew of the sloop *Revenge* to come and claim their prize money.

****

From *The Gazette*, November 10, 1779

married
John Thomson to Miss Polly Goddard, daughter of Ebenezer Goddard;

Harris Rogers to Miss Fanny Packwood, daughter of Capt. William Packwood.

died
William Manawaring

lost
by William Harris of New London, a black leather pocketbook.

for sale
Notice by John Phelps, Manager of the Stafford Furnace, that the furnace is now in blast and will be for several months and will make all kinds of hollow ware.

by Samuel P. Lord of East Haddam Landing, liver oil of the first quality by the barrel or by retail.
****

From *The Gazette,* November 17, 1779

clothier
Notice by John Smith of New Concord in Norwich that he is now conducting the clothier business at the fulling mill, lately occupied by Rufus Perkins, near the Meeting House in the New Concord Society of Norwich.

letters left in the New London Post Office

Abigail Bill, New London
Joshua Bradley, New London Mr. Baldan, New London
Galas Bissel, New London
Daniel Billings, Stonington
William Avery, Groton;
James Bradford, Plainfield
David Basker, Windham
Josiah Crane, New London
Nathan Cooper, New London
Elizabeth Cornwall, New London
Samuel Copp, Stonington
Marston Cabot, Woodstock
William Eyman, New London
William Engs, New London
William Foster, New London
Timothy Forsythe, New London
Gilbert Fanning, Stonington
Christian Gosner, New

250

London
Francis Green, New, London
Samuel Graves, Stonington
Griffin Green, Coventry
Roger Huntington, New London
Nicholas Hyman, New London
Guidon Hamilton, New London
John Hillard, Stonington
James Johnson, New London
Samuel Ingrahm, Voluntown
William A. Livingston, New London
Joshua Munroe, New London Robert May, New London
Bariah Norton, New London
David M'Ninch, New London Mons. Noel, New London
James Noyes, Stonington
Thomas Palmer, New London
Benomi Pierce, New London
James Penniman, New London
David Phipps, New London
Jonathamn Palmer, Jr., Stonington
Darkis Pompe, Groton
M. Parker, Voluntown
Capt. Pricott, New London
William Robinson, Plainfield
Josiah Smith, New London
Remembrance Smith, New London
William Stone, New London
Capt. Henry Tew, New London
William Vance, New London
Marvin Wait, New London
William Weaver, New London
Ebenezer Wood, New London
Anthony Wells, New London
Thomas Whipple, New London

deserted
Notice by Lt. Richard Chapman that deserted from Adam Shapely's Company at Fort Trumbull, Thomas Buck; 17 years old; 5 feet, 4 or 5 inches tall.

collect pay
Notice by Capt. Richard Wait, Jun. to those who were in his Company in Col. Mason's Regiment in New London that he will be at Wait's Waiting office and will pay those who attend.

****

From *The Gazette,* November 24, 1779

drownings
Mr. John Holly Newman, son of Dr. John Newman of Stonington, and Mr. Cooper of that Town, in attempting passage from Newport to Stonington, were on Monday the 8th of November last unfortunately drowned. The body of Mr. Newman, found on Narranganset Beach, was from there brought to Stonington and, on last Saturday, his remains were decently interred, attended by a large and respectable body of people. Circumstances particularly distressing have attended the doctor's family. About two years past, his eldest son, engaged in the service of his country, was instantly killed by shot from the enemy in the siege of the Red Bank fort[45]; a promising and agreeable youth, upon whom the family's expectations were great. His youngest and only remaining son was made prisoner about one year past and still remains in captivity in the West Indies.

died
at Stonington in the past October, Capt. Simeon Miner, aged 74. His superior abilities in Church and State earned him the esteem of all his acquaintances. Early, he was appointed Justice of the Peace and, for a long succession of years, was a representative of the Town of Stonington to the General Assembly.

to be sold
at Capt. Guy Richard's store in New London, a quantity of damaged sugar and coffee and also a quantity of coffee, not damaged;

The best rock salt for cash or exchange for wheat, rye and corn by Rodman and Woodbridge of Norwich.

broke into the enclosure
of Samuel Stickland of New London, a heifer.

come collect pay
Notice by Griswold Avery to the officers and men in his Company in Lt. Parsons Detachment at New London to meet at Clement Leech's in New London to receive their pay;

Notice by agent Jonathan Otis to crew of the *Experiment,* Nathan Sage, that he will distribute prize money at Middletown.

strayed or stolen
Notice by Jesse Craw that strayed from Mr. Staugher's yard in New London, two large cows;

from Robert Roundey of Windham, a cow.

lost
by William Harris in New London, a pocketbook that contained a note to pay Major William 500 pounds, signed by James Church and Treasurer John Lawrence;

administration of estates
Notice by Jonathan Parker, Administrator of estate of Asher Palmer, deceased and late of Stonington, deceased, to all those indebted to the estate to settle up and creditors to file claims.

libels filed
Notice by Wm. Saltonstall, Register, that libels are filed before, and to be heard by, the Hon. Richard Law, Judge of the Maritime Court for the County of New London:
in favor of Nathan Sage of *Experiment* and Esek Hopkins Jun of schooner *Lively*, their owners and associates against the Brig *Argyle*, late commander William Frigs Jun.; *Charming Sally*, late commander, Robert Clark and the schooner *Dolphin*, late commander John Stanton;
in favor of sloop *Sally,* Seth Warner, its owners and associates against brig *Unio*n, William Haynes, late commander.

please settle accounts
notice by David Belding of East Haddam that those of subscribers of the *Connecticut Gazette* who owe him, he can be found at the houses of Capt. Abner Comstock; Capt. Daniel Lord, Capt. Parsons and Nathaniel Pecks at the dates and times specified.

Notice by Ebenezer Hovey to his customers of the *Gazette* that he proposes to halt delivery for the winter on December 5 and requests that all owing him can pay his neighbor, James Abbot.
****

From *The Gazette,* December 1, 1779

deserted
Notice by William Latham, Captain in the Artillery in Groton that deserted from Fort Griswold, Thomas Carral, in the Artillery; a thick, stout built fellow; 5 feet, 11 inches tall; sandy hair and light hair and eyes; said he was from Dudley in Massachusetts;

Nathan Austin of Preston; a small, slender person; speaks quick.

to be sold
at Edwards Hallam's Wharf in New London, the brig *Jenny*;

at Edwards Hallam's Wharf in New London, the brig *Success;* notice given by Guy Richards, Jun.

wanted
Gentlemen Volunteers to serve on the Brig *Defiance*, Commander Nicoll Fosdick;

a journeyman blacksmith; one who knows ship work would be preferred; apply Pember Calkings in New London.

strayed or stolen
from Michael Powers of New London, a steer;

from Jonathan Murdock of Coventy, a heifer;

from Joseph Chester of New London, North Parish, a young heifer;

from William Moor of New London, a black and white boar shote.

****

From *The Gazette*, December 8, 1779

prizes taken

Yesterday se'nnight, a small British boat came close in with Saybrook Bar and, it being almost calm, sent her boat and took a sloop as it came into the Connecticut River from the eastward, laden with salt. The people on board the sloop attempted to drive her on shore and had got so near that one of them, by running up the bowsprit, jumped on the land and got off;

Sunday last, the privateer Beaver, Capt. Havens, returning from a cruise, brought in with her a brig from Surinam bound for New York laden with a 127 hogsheads of molasses and 240 cases of gin.

to be sold

on Mt. Pleasant, New London by Thomas Allen, Jun. one yoke of fat, four year old oxen, one fat cow, six years old;

at East Haddam Landing, one pair of doubled fortified long 12 pounders, weighing upwards of 3000 weight, suitable for a battery; enquire of Sylvanus Tinker.

come and collect prize money

The Officers and Seamen of Brig *Retaliation*, Capt. Azariah Whittlesey, are advised to go to the agent in Saybrook for their share of the prize money.

wanted

a quantity of salt petre, for which a generous price will be given.

eloped
Notice by Thomas Blackle in New London that his wife Margaret, having behaved in a disrespectful and refractory manner and in numerous situations shamefully treated him and abused him, all of which he has borne with a degree of patience beyond a parallel, to prevent said Margaret from involving him in debt, he does hereby forbid all persons from trusting her on his account or entertaining her because he will pay not debts of her making after today.

strayed or stolen
from Oliver Barber of Hebron, a yoke of steers.

broke into the enclosure
of Elisha Avery of New London, two red yearling heifers.

please pay up
All people, who owe Aaron Bushnell for delivery of the *Gazette*, are asked to pay up.

price of The Gazette to rise
The Printer of this paper had not made an advance of the price of the paper for six months past, his customers sensible that every other item has advanced in price during that same period. but he is now of the necessity of raising it from 5 dollars, the price at the last quarter, to 7 dollars to be paid at entrance. Those not paying at entrance must expect to pay the price the papers are, when they receive the paper. Such as pay in produce at the old accustomed prices (postage always excepted).

****

From *The Gazette* of December 15, 1779

married
Charles Bulkley, Lieutenant in the Continental Navy, to Betsy Hallam.

broke into the enclosure
of Amariah Stanton of Stonington, a horse;

of Thomas Beckwith in East Haddam, a heifer.

taken up
at Fort Trumbull, a horse; notice by Sgt. Ebenezer Chapel.

for sale
by William Stewart of New London, a schooner

notices to collect pay and prize money
to the Officers and Seamen of the *Experiment*, Capt. Nathan Sage, come and collect prize money at the house of Jonathan Otis, agent in Middletown;

to the Officers and Seamen of the *Hancock*, Capt. Lodowick Champlin, come and collect prize money at the house of their agent in Groton;

to the Officers and Soldiers of the Company of Capt. Thomas Stanton of Col. Samuel Chapman's Regiment in the Expedition against Rhode Island, come to the house of Isaac Stanton, Inn Holder in Stonington.

lost
by Theophilus Avery, Jun. of Groton, a small gold watch.

runaway
from Jonah Peirce of Plainfield, a Negro man named Cesar; 25 years of age; somewhat of low stature; about middling size; talks good English and read considerably well.

****

From *The Gazette*, December 22, 1779

accidental shooting
Last Thursday, a soldier in Col. Welles' Regiment stationed here, being employed in cleaning a musket, he imprudently pointed across the main street and snapped it, when it discharged a bullet which went through the body of a Negro man in the street. The Negro is still alive, but his recovery is doubtful.

fire
Monday night last, the dwelling house of Capt. Samuel Johnson, near the Court House in Norwich, was consumed by fire with almost the whole of the furniture, which was very valuable.

died
in Norwich, Joseph Coit, Jun. of that Town.

thefts
Notice by Timothy Green that a coat and other clothes were stolen out of the Printing Office.

stolen from Elias Peck's clothier shop in Colchester, sundry items of clothing.

administration of estates
Notice by Abigail Elliot, Administratrix of the estate of Zebulon Elliot, deceased and late of New London, to all those indebted to the estate to settle up and creditors to file claims.

Notice by William Morgan, Administrator of the estate of Capt. William Morgan, deceased and late of New London, to all those indebted to the estate to settle up and creditors to file claims. A hearing will be held at Clement Leech's in New London.

strayed or stolen
from John Richards of New London, a horse.

for sale
Eighty acres of land in the Goshen Society of Lebanon; two good dwelling houses; a good barn and two orchards; apply to Joseph and Aaron Peabody on the premises.

****

From *The Gazette*, December 29, 1779

ship lost
A schooner owned by the Continental Navy and captained by David Latham of Groton was bound from Philadelphia to Boston

with a load of flour in the late severe snow storm, ran onto Horse Shoe Shoal near Nantucket, when a boat with some of the people were sent on shore, but, as the vessel was not seen afterwards, it is apprehended that it was lost.

inflation
The Society of Marlborough at their late meeting voted the Pastor David Huntington, 3000 thousand pounds for his services the past year, the equivalency of 100 pounds in 1774

married
Giles Mumford of Groton on to Miss Woodbridge, daughter of Doct. Charles Dudley Woodbridge in Stonington.

died
in Colchester, Mrs. Alice Ransom 94 years of Age, widow of Robert Ransom, with whom she lived in the state of marriage for 67 years. She has had 21 children, 112 grandchildren, 220 great grandchildren and seven to the fourth generation for 48 years. Previous to her death, she was a very skilled midwife. Being conscious of her approaching difficulties, she used every opportunity in exhorting her descendants to make sure of an interest in the great Redeemer in whom she had put her trust and from whom, as she often said, had done so much for her.

stolen
Notice by Israel Reeve of New London that stolen from the house of Eliakin Perry of New London were money and clothes; supposed to be taken by a Frenchman, Peter Frow; who is short and well set and pretends to speak very little English; he is also supposed to have taken a horse from Peter Bulkley of Colchester.

sailors needed
the Brig *Spencer*, Captain Michael Mellaly, will sail on a cruise next week.

broke into the enclosure
of Jedidiah Chapel of Chesterfield Society in New London, two sheep.

lost
on the road in New London by Alexander White of Hebron, a sum of money wrapped in an old piece of parchment.

****

ENDNOTES

1. This brief item refers to a week of extraordinary courage and effort on behalf of the Colonial troops. After the fall of New York City in the late summer of 1776, the British pursued a retreating Washington and his army across New Jersey. But not for long. At Trenton, on the Delaware River, Washington issued an order taking up all the boats along that stretch of the River and transported his troops across the river into Pennsylvania. Unable to follow him because they had no craft with which to cross the river, the British halted the chase until spring and, as was the custom among European armies, settled down for the winter and left a detachment of troops in Trenton.

General Washington, however, had not retired for the winter. Aware of America's need for a change in her fortunes and having been reinforced from a number of quarters, he was willing to be bold. He decided to cross the ice filled Delaware River, and surprise one of the British winter camps. On the eve of battle, Thomas Paine's *Crisis* was read to the troops, leaving no doubt as to the importance of the mission or what was expected of them. The next day -- Christmas, 1776 -- Washington with 2,400 men, crossed the Delaware, attacking the 1,400 man Hessian garrison at Trenton. The plan worked better than could have been hoped. A hundred Hessians were killed, 900 were captured and 400 escaped to tell of the American victory. The Americans had four men wounded.

2. "Strayed or stolen" notices were frequent. Horses, cows, bulls, sheep, even swine, wandered off frequently, joining other domesticated herds out of animal instinct. Notices of such animals "breaking into the enclosure of subscriber"are the other side of the coin, the reports of farmers who found those strays among their own herds and flocks. Items of similar ilk for boats, "lost and found" pocketbooks, clothing and items speak also were frequent.

3 New London, North Parish is known as Montville today. It was separated from New London in 1786.

4. A week. Once it was common to record the passage of time by the number of nights rather than days. "Se'nnight" is an abbreviation of the fuller phrase "seven nights", hence a week. Fourteen nights were a

"fortnight". The latter has survived in Britain, while se'nnight lost out to "a week", both here and there.

5. In September of 1774, Committees of Inspection and Observation were established in the towns of the Colonies by the Order of the First Continental Congress. Their task was to enforce the boycott of British good ordered by the Congress and to expose and root out residents with views considered "inimical" to the interests Town, the State and the Nation. These Committees were descended, if you will, from the earlier Committees of Correspondence, a network of towns that relayed information to all the citizens. They would evolve into Councils of Safety at different levels, which became more like governing authorities regarding the War.

6. i.e., a distillery. The Destilhouse in New London was opened a decade earlier as note in *The New London Gazette,* August 5, 1768. It was "to distill choice rums which may be sold low as the hogshead can be imported from New York and Boston at two shillings for single gallon for cash only." Not only was New London a handy place where to begin such a business – sugars and molasses were readily available-- but there was a local "booster" as well "as very considerate amount of ready money are sent out of the colony annually to purchase this useful commodity, it is hoped that the revival of a manufactory so beneficial for the colony will eventually preserve the same."

7. Many prisoners of war, officers among them, were imprisoned and mistreated. Notorious were the British prison ships, mast less hulks lying in New York Harbor, into the lower decks of which were crammed thousands of captured Americans. Each morning at the most notorious, the *Jersey,* the day began by the British guard shouting "Rebels throw out your dead!" They were never disappointed with the number of corpses. Over eleven thousand Americans died in this and the other prison hulks anchored in New York Harbor.

8 A soldier's close fitting coat worn over his uniform derived from the French "to cover all."

9. In Admiralty Law, libel does not mean a slander or defamation as in the Civil Law but a "claim" or, in the Civil law, a complaint for relief.

10. A flag of truce, usually white in color, was flown from the mast of a ship to indicate a desire to confer. Here, it carried American prisoners

captured by the enemy who were to be exchanged for a like number of enemy soldiers captured by Americans.

11. Small pox was not only a killer, but it scarred the survivors for life. In a study over 15% of the notices seeking the return of runaway servants, deserters, escaped prisoners and thieves from New Jersey contain descriptions like "pock mark'd" or "pox fretten", reflecting how many of the survivors of this disease were permanently scarred by it. An outbreak of small pox was to be feared and efforts, even primitive inoculations, were taken to avoid its spread through the population.

By 1770, however, progress had been made in both determining the cause of small pox and preventing it. Yet as can be seen in the pages of *The Gazette*, there were still many cases.

12 Great Neck became part of Waterford in 1801. Parts of it were also called Goshen.

13. Christopher Leffingwell established Connecticut's first paper mill and also manufactured woolen cloth, stockings and chocolates.

14 Many Native Americans remained neutral. Some, including Massachusetts Indians, helped the Americans, but most fought with the British or took advantage of the situation and acted against the colonists on their own. The Cherokee attacked the outlying white settlements in the Carolinas. There also were horrible massacres on the New Jersey frontier, in Pennsylvania and New York. There were the fierce Iroquois from the north, warriors of the Confederate Nations, and their allies, the Mohawks, Onondaga, Senecas, Oneidas, Cayugas, Tuscaroras, Nanticokes and Conoys.

Sir William Johnson, ho was married to an Indian and who was a summer visitor to New London for his health, was the Crown's representative to these Indians for the lucrative fur trading. Britain used the relationship created by Johnson to their benefit, recruiting the Iroquois to cause havoc along the frontier.

15 Captain James Wallace is displayed in the *Gazette* as an arrogant, cruel man, the antithesis of a gentleman like Captain Jacobs. Apparently, the King either did not know that about Wallace or rewarded him for those vices. While Captain Jacobs' future is lost to history, Wallace was knighted upon his return to England in 1777, later

made an Admiral and appointed Commander-in-Chief and Governor of Newfoundland.

16. Lotteries are neither new, nor American born. King James I in 1612, granted the Virginia Colony the right to raise money to help establish settlers in the first permanent English colony at Jamestown. For more than the next century and a half, lotteries – more then two hundred, it is said - played a key part in the financing of roads, libraries, churches, colleges, canals, bridges, both private and public ventures. Princeton, Columbia and the University of Pennsylvania had their beginnings financed by lotteries. Lottery tickets, issued by Continental Congress, even helped to finance the Revolutionary War.

17. New London and Stonington had the first post offices in the State, opening in 1746.

18 The advertisement was also printed in French!

19. This belies the claim that the insurance business began in Connecticut in Hartford in 1794.

20. Any person of mixed ancestry.

21 At the time of the Revolution in America, newspapers had existed for less than a century. During that time, there had been no war between nations that shared a common language and, hence, that could communicate with the other's general populace on a large scale. Therefore, it would seem safe to assume that the war of words -- alternatively, the truth, exaggerations, scoldings, recriminations, lies -- in which Mr. Gaine and his American counterparts of the colonial press were about to engage was the beginning of mass propaganda, today a standard of all warfare. An aim of propaganda and misinformation is to intimidate and undermine the confidence and resolve of enemy troops and civilians alike. At the same time, the press serves up optimistic and encouraging news accounts for its own citizens

There were no neutral newspapers in America during the Revolutionary War. A paper's political affiliations could be quickly gleaned from the subtleties of its expressions, such as its use of the term "rebels", rather than "patriots". Hugh Gaine, owner, publisher, editor and distributor of the *New York Mercury* was a case in point. He was pro British, although after the war he had no desire to go back to England and lived the rest of his life in America. The most notorious

Loyalist journal was *Rivington's New York Gazetteer,* later called *Rivington's New York Loyal Gazette,* and finally *The Royal Gazette,* all published at Hanover Square in New York City by the same man, James Rivington. He might have been the most hated man in America. These first two years of *The New York Gazette coincided* with the birthing of the Revolution.

In the beginning, Rivington had reported on events with moderation and impartiality. Soon, however, he became increasingly Tory, loyal to the Crown and disdainful of the mob. His remarks in the press towards the rebels became more derogatory, his comments more cutting and taunting and his conduct toward the American cause more offensive.

But, Rivington's tale had a surprising ending. When the British evacuated New York City and the Americans literally feet behind, General Washington met publicly with several individuals, shaking their hands and embracing them so that all who watched would know that these were Friends, not enemies, of American Liberty. Needless to say, the citizens were incredulous, upon seeing General Washington greet in that same familiar way, James Rivington, the detested editor of *The Royal Gazette,* whose news was always anti rebel and pro British. Washington had calculated correctly. Rivington's slurs on the American Cause, both fired up the Rebels, and added greatly to the trust that the British high command gave him. Rivington, together with Robert Townshend, his partner in the British Coffee House, where many a secret was discovered, had been a member of Tallmadge's Culper Spy Network.

22. Jesuit Bark, or Powder, was first introduced to the European population by Jesuit missionaries. They had encountered its use by the Peruvian Indians in South America. It was a remedy for malaria and is the source of today's quinine.

23 Duncan Stewart was the well respected Collector of His Majesty's Customs for the Port of New London, as well on the Board of Commissioners of His Majesty's Customs in America.

24. Hell Gate is a narrow, rocky tidal strait in New York City. It connected Long Island Sound, Harlem River, the East River and Upper Bay of New York Harbor. A British ship could pass relatively easily and safely (once it got through Hell Gate) from New York City to New London, Newport and Boston without having to go into the Ocean and around Long Island .

The name "Hell Gate" is a corruption of the Dutch phrase *Hellegat*, which reportedly could mean either "hell's gate" or "bright gate/passage". The former would be apt because converging tide-driven currents from waterways above made the navigation hazardous.

25. Runaway notices also described another skin condition of the period, also now a memory only: "He is much scarified under one of his cheek bones caused by the King's Evil." The disease, with the ominous name, is better known in medical circles as *cervical lymphadenitis* or *scrofula*. Tubercular in nature, it is characterized chiefly by swelling and degeneration of the lymphatic glands, especially around the neck area. It is rare in the United States today because of the elimination of tubercle from the milk and the prevention of mass infections in childhood. Heliotherapy --getting outside in the sun -- was a traditional method of treatment.

26. The Susquehanna Purchase involves a portion of Connecticut's history seemingly forgotten today. The Susquehanna and Delaware Companies were among a number of land companies formed in Eastern Connecticut, especially by the citizens of Colchester and Windham in the early 1750s for the purpose of developing the Wyoming Valley and Susquehanna territories in Pennsylvania. It was well received and Towns sprung up — at least on paper.

Connecticut based its claim to these lands to its charter in 1662 from King Charles II to the territory between the 41st and 42nd degree of north latitude running from Narragansett Bay to the Pacific Ocean. A tract of that land was purchased in 1754 by John Henry Lydius, a Dutch trader, from the Iroquois who owned it by right of conquest from the Susquehannas. Preparations were made for development, when a massacre of settlers by Indians in Pennsylvania in 1763 resulted in a proclamation by Connecticut Governor Fitch prohibiting further settlement, until the Indians were pacified. In the meanwhile, Eliphalet Dyer of Windham was sent to England in an unsuccessful attempt to secure confirmation of the land grant.

It was 1769 before any definite settlement was made. But, almost immediately, the settlers became embroiled in bloody clashes with rival settlers from Pennsylvania, who saws it differently. They claimed the lands by virtue of a grant from Charles II which gave William Penn the territory between 39 degrees 43 minutes and 43 degrees North Latitude, overlapping Connecticut's claim. They argued that the 1754 purchase from the Indians by Connecticut land speculators was a brazen swindle with the help of the Iroquois who sold land they did not own.

After the Revolution, Article 9 of the enacted Articles of Confederation appointed Commissioners to hold hearing and resolve the conflict. On November 18, 1782, it handed down a decision, known as the Trenton Decree, in favor of Pennsylvania on December 30, 1782. Many thought it a predetermined political decision, not a judicial determination.

27. Getting paper itself was sometimes difficult. It was only until 1765 when the *Gazette* could purchase Connecticut made paper, made from old rags in a long, laborious process. Buying paper could be hard. It was scarce and expensive. It was not until 1765 that Connecticut even had a paper mill. Even then, making paper was not easy. The wood pulp, with which we are familiar, did not appear until nearly a century later. Cotton and linen rags were the "pulp". It took a lot of time and work First, rags had to be collected from several sources: including "rag pickers" who went from house to house, asking for rags, which they then sold to paper mills and ads in the newspapers themselves to buy them. Then the rags were cut up and placed in a vat full of a special solution, where they soaked until the solution had broken down the cloth fibers to only tiny pieces. A framed screen was lowered into the vat and gathered the matted fibers and then left it to dry. This made a single sheet of paper!

28. Esek Hopkins was Commander in Chief of the Fleet throughout the American Revolutionary War. Born in what is Rhode Island, he had been a sea captain, commanded a privateer in the French and Indian War, and served as a deputy to the Rhode Island General Assembly. With the War, he went back to sea, being appointed Commander in Chief of the Fleet authorized by the Continental Congress to protect American commerce, taking command of eight small merchant ships that had been hastily altered as men of war. After a very successful assault on Nassau and New Providence and the capture of a number of prizes, his fleet was mostly blockaded in Narragansett Bay by the superior British sea power.

Hopkins had a contrary side which critics attacked. He had disregarded Congress' direction to rid the Chesapeake of British cruisers, instead raiding New Providence. There were other allegations of inaction, especially in an encounter with the HMS *Glasgow*. Because of the continuing debacle, on January 2, 1778, Hopkins was relieved of his command permanently.

29. To help finance the war and in an attempt to quell their subversive activities, the Continental Congress in 1776 declared that the property of Loyalists was subject to seizure. Within five years, every state passed similar "confiscation acts". Only South Carolina later reimbursed the Loyalists for the property taken. Ultimately, the British Parliament indemnified the others.

30. Part of the famous Lee family of Virginia, Henry Lee would come to be known Light Horse Harry Lee and is considered by many to have been the best cavalry officer in American history. A true hero, he fought with valor throughout the war. Upon independence, he returned to Virginia, where he served several years as Governor of the State. His son, Robert E. Lee, who many consider the greatest American general, commanded the Confederate troops during the Civil War.

31. This probably refers to Paul and Barnabas, missionaries to the Gentiles in Galatians 2:1-10). The two had been given "the right hand of fellowship" by highly esteemed leaders of the Christian community on Jerusalem "when they recognized the grace given to them." The Right Hand of Christian Fellowship is a practice performed by many sects of Christian as an extension of Brotherhood into the Church.

32. Benedict Arnold was born in 1741 in Norwich and distinguished himself early in the capture of Fort Ticonderoga (1775), the Battles of Valcour Island on Lake Champlain in 1776, the battles of Danbury and Ridgefield in Connecticut and the Battle of Saratoga in 1777, where he was severely wounded.

33. Niantic was part of New London at the time.

34. This refers to spinning wool, which begins with shearing the sheep. Skirting the fleece is next which involves removing the un-spinnable stuff, wool that is too short or too greasy. Scouring the wool follows where the wool goes into a vat, is covered with water several times, the dirty water draining out a hole in the bottom of the vat. After a warm water wash to remove excess lanolin, the wool is spread it out and dried. A wool carder, using wire bristled cards, gets all of the burrs out of the wool and the two cards and brushes them to make the wool soft and fluffy. The more a carder could do, the more a spinner, who got it next, could convert the fibers into a continuously twisting yarn.

35. Bleeding was the treatment of choice in Colonial America. Fevers, inflammations of the stomach, throat, and eyes, asthma, sciatic pains, coughs, epilepsy and rheumatism, bruises and even those drowned or suffocated were all treated by bleeding. The thought was that lessening the amount of blood in the body was beneficial. Bleeding was usually accomplished with a lancet, usually on the arm. Blood was normally drawn until the patient became faint or even unconscious.

36 England had General William Howe and his brother Admiral Richard Howe, as well as Sir Henry Clinton. The American forces had General George Clinton (also Governor of New York) and, his brother General James Clinton and General Robert Howe of North Carolina.

37. This practice of filing a "grievance" at perceived unfair treatment by the Government, still exists in the form of "Grievance Day" when property owners can protest the real estate taxes assessed against them.

38. Portage bill is not legislation but a shipping document, a statement by the ship master at the end of a voyage, showing the total earnings of each member of the crew.

39. Elisha Hinman was a sailor through and through. Born in Stonington, he first went to sea at fourteen years of age and, by nineteen was a captain in the Europe and the West Indies trade. He sailed under Capt. Esek Hopkins (see endnote 28, *supra*) and was severely wounded in engagement with the *HMS Glasgow.* Appointed one of the first captains in the United States navy, he commanded several ships including the *Alfred,* which in March, 1778, was captured. Hinman was taken to England and imprisoned. He escaped to France, returned to America, and was honorably acquitted for the loss of his ship.

40. After the British withdrew from Philadelphia in June 1778 Washington had appointed Arnold the military commander of the city. Resentful toward Congress for passing him over for promotion and reimbursing him his wartime expenses, widower Arnold, who had become enamored of 18 year Peggy Shippen, a Loyalist's daughter, hosted grand parties and fell deeply into debt. That led to shady financial schemes. Congress began investigating his accounts and Arnold sought and received the command of West Point. He attempted to deliver West Point to the British but was thwarted.

41. Moses Cleavland or Cleveland was born in Canterbury. A lawyer, politician, soldier, and surveyor, he founded the city of Cleveland, while surveying the Western Reserve in 1796.

42. The custom of appointing a special day known as a fast day has been in vogue in New England since the Puritans and was fairly must limited to the region. They had brought with them from England the custom of appointing special days for fasting and prayer. Originally, it was set by the clergyman from the pulpit for his congregation. Then the Governor selected a date for all in the colony to observe and proclaimed in the newspapers.

43. In making linen out of flax, the farmer's wife combed handfuls of dried fiber through combs to grade the fibers. The short, coarse fibers, called tow, were used for coarse linen, while the longer fibers made finer linen. The tow was bundled together and carded before spinning.

44. Tuberculosis or TB was popularly known as "consumption" for a long time. It is certainly less known today than cancers, heart diseases, diabetes and other killers. However, before the discovery of antibiotics, it was the worse killer. In 1882, for example, one of every seven deaths in Europe was caused by it. By the turn of the century, it was estimated that more than 80% of the U. S. population were infected before age 20, and tuberculosis was the single most common cause of death. Even as late as 1938 there were more than 700 TB hospitals in the United States.

45. Occupying Philadelphia meant that the Delaware River had to be brought under control or, otherwise, the troops holding the city could not be supplied. Two American forts, Fort Mercer at Red Bank, below Glouster on the Jersey side of the Delaware, and Fort Mifflin, on Mud Island, near the opposite shore, threatened the British supply line. Hence, the British had to remove them, which it did through intense cannonading. The Americans fought back with galleys, commanded by Commodore John Barry, which set afire some of the British war ships.

46. Because the Continental Congress was unable to levy taxes to pay for the war, it relied on the printing press to issue nearly $250 million in Continental dollars. It was backed only by the good faith of the Congress; Soon, there was too much money competing for too few goods. The result was inflation.

Inflation is not really rising prices, although it seems that way, but that's not quite right. Inflation is not caused by rising prices. Rather, rising prices are a symptom of inflation. Too much cash for too little goods. For example, the price of *The Gazette* went way up – if you paid cash. But if you paid in country foods or other barter, it stayed the same.

PROPER NAMES

A
ABBEON, Daniel– 11/14/77
ABBOT, James - 11/24/79
ABBOT, John - 2/21/77
ABBOTT, Col. Joseph - 5/20/79
ABNER, Capt. - 1/30/78
ABORN, Col. Samuel - 4/8/79
ACGEL, William - 4/4/77
ACKLY, Nathan - 11/27/78
ADAM, Mr. - 7/24/78
ADAMS, Alexander P. - 1/16/78; 2/5/79
ADAMS, Elias - 8/14/78
ADAMS, Eliashid - 9/18/78; 8/25/79
ADAMS, James - 12/25/78
ADAMS, Miss Lydia - 9/22/79
ADAMS, Nathaniel - 9/5/77
ADAMS Jun., Nathaniel - 7/4/77
ADAMS, Wm. - 2/21/77
ADGAIN, Matthew - 10/24/77
ADSHED, James - 12/25/78
ALDEN, Joab - 10/2/78
ALDEN, John - 8/14/78
ALDEN, Mrs. - 7/24/78
ALICE, Thomas - 4/3/78
ALLEN, Amasa - 6/12/78
ALLEN, Cady - 2/21/77
ALLEN, Christopher - 8/8/77; 5/20/79
ALLEN, Capt. D. - 4/29/79
ALLEN, Ebenezer - 7/17/78; 1/8/79; 4/29/79
ALLEN, Elisha - 9/29/79
ALLEN, James - 9/22/79
ALLEN, Jason - 1/17/77; 1/30/78; 5/15/78; 8/15/77; 2/5/79; 7/28/79
ALLEN, Jun, Jason - 1/8/79

ALLEN, John - 10/27/79
ALLEN, Mary - 1/8/79
ALLEN, Oliver - 1/24/77
ALLEN, Phineas - 2/21/77
ALLEN, Thomas - 4/25/77; 5/16/77; 8/21/78; 9/25/78; 10/23/78; 6/2/79
ALLEN, Jun., Thomas - 6/27/77; 7/11/77; 12/8/79
ALLEN, William - 12/25/78
ALLEN, Captain - 6/13/77
ALLON, Thomas - 3/20/78; 5/1/78
ALLYN, Christopher - 8/15/77
ALLYN, Ephraim - 10/2/78
ALLYN, James - 10/2/78
ALLYN, Sr. James - 10/2/78
ALSWORTH, James - 2/14/77
ALVORD, Samuel - 6/16/79
AMES, John - 6/12/78
AMES, Nathaniel - 3/7/77
AMIEGS, Colonel - 9/18/78
ANDERSON, John - 8/14/78
ANDRUS, Samuel - 9/22/79
ANDRUS, Jun., Zebadiah - 6/5/78; 5/20/79
ANEW, John – 11/14/77
ANGEL, Jonathan - 10/13/79
ANGEL, Col. - 9/22/79
ANGEL, Mr. - 8/25/79
APTHORP, Charles Ward - 5/27/79; 8/11/79
ARCHER, Benjamin - 8/14/78
ARMSTRONG, Rev. Mr. – 3/6/78
ARNOLD, Benedict - 3/27/78; 2/26/79
ARNOLD, Gideon - 8/14/78; 10/31/77
ARNOLD, Simon - 4/25/77

ARNOLD, Capt. Thomas - 8/22/77
ARTHUR, John - 10/10/77
ASHER, Meyers - 12/12/77
ASHLEY, Abner - 10/31/77
ASHNER, Philip - 5/20/79
ATGOR, Aaron - 8/14/78
ATKINS, Joel - 1/31/77
ATWOOD, Isaac - 8/14/78
AUSTIN, Nathan - 12/1/79
AVERY, Amos – 11/28/77
AVERY, Col. Ebenezer - 9/5/77; 1/15/79
AVERY 3d, Ebenezer - 5/23/77
AVERY, Capt. Elijah – 11/28/77
AVERY, Elisha - 12/8/79
AVERY, G. - 4/11/77
AVERY, Griswold - 3/7/77; 4/29/79; 11/24/79
AVERY, James - 10/9/78
AVERY, Latham - 7/3/78
AVERY, Nathan - 8/22/77
AVERY, Park - 12/18/78
AVERY, Robert - 5/16/77
AVERY, Samuel - 7/24/78
AVERY Jun., Simon - 1/24/77
AVERY, Stephen - 4/17/78
AVERY, Jun., Theophilus - 12/15/79
AVERY, Thomas – 1/24/77; 3/13/78
AVERY, William - 6/13/77; 9/12/77; 11/14/77; 11/17/79
AYELELS,; John - 9/15/79; 10/20/79

B
BABCOCK, Adam - 5/23/77
BABCOCK, Amos - 9/5/77
BABCOCK, Elisha - 3/14/77
BABCOCK Joshua - 5/16/77; 12/12/77; 1/30/78; 2/6/78; 10/2/78; 12/11/78; 4/29/79
BABCOCK Mercy - 5/16/77
BABCOCK Oliver - 2/14/77; 5/16/77
BACKUS, Ebenezer - 1/10/77; 7/3/78
BACKUS, Mr. - 7/24/78
BACON, Beriah - 4/11/77
BACON, Broadhurst - 6/12/78
BACON, Pierpont - 1/10/77; 5/20/79
BAILEY, Abraham - 9/1/79
BAILEY, Ezekiel - 4/11/77
BAKER, Abel - 5/29/78
BAKER, Palsey - 9/29/79
BALCAM, Joseph - 8/5/78
BALDAN, Mr. - 11/17/79
BALDIN, Jun.,Theohpilus. – 11/28/77
BALDWIN, Ebenezer - 4/11/77
BALDWIN, William - 7/28/79
BALEY, Elijah - 2/6/78
BALEY, James- 2/6/78
BALEY, Jun., Nathan - 7/8/79
BALL, Samuel - 4/4/77
BANKS, Hannah - 1/30/78
BANKS, Jonathan - 12/25/78
BANKS, William - 1/30/78
BARBER, Lt. David - 1/16/78
BARBER, John - 9/5/77; 2/6/78
BARBER, Oliver - 12/8/79
BARBER, Dr. Thomas - 2/28/77
BARBER, Mr. - 7/24/78
BARKER, Samuel - 3/19/79
BARRICK, William - 8/8/77
BARROW, Edmund - 8/29/77.
BARRY, Elizabeth - 10/2/78; 4/29/79
BARSTOW, John - 2/21/77
BARTLET, Dr. Moses - 4/4/77; 10/31/77

BASKER, David - 11/17/79
BASSET, Isaac - 12/11/78
BATES, Eleazer - 1/10/77; 1/31/77
BATES Bates, John - 7/28/79
BAXTER, Nathan - 9/19/77
BEACH, Miles - 9/4/78
BECKWITH, Elisha - 4/8/79
BECKWITH, Miss Elizabeth - 1/29/79
BECKWITH, Rev. George - 8/14/78; 9/5/77
BECKWITH, Jedidiah- 8/29/77; 10/13/79
BECKWITH, Jesse - 9/12/77; 8/28/78; 4/15/79
BECKWITH, Nathan - 8/14/78
BECKWITH, Phineas - 12/11/78
BECKWITH, Samuel - 9/5/77
BECKWITH, Thomas - 12/15/79
BECKWITH, Timothy - 9/5/77
BEDFORD, Mr. - 9/5/77
BEEBE, Desiree - 12/18/78; 8/25/79
BEEBE, Elenathan - 7/31/78
BEEBE, Ezekiel - 12/4/78
BEEBE, Jabez - 4/17/78
BEEBE, Jonathan - 7/24/78; 10/2/78
BEEBE, Noah – 12/26/77
BEEBE, Samuel - 3/21/77; 12/18/78; 3/12/79 ;8/25/79
BELCHER, Nathan - 7/11/77
BELCHER, William - 1/24/77
BELDEN Belden [see Belding], David - 12/4/78; 12/25/78
BELDEN, Ez. P.- 1/24/77
BELDEN Belden, Samuel - 5/13/79; 7/14/79
BELDING, David [see Belden] – 12/5/77; -1/30/78; 11/24/79
BELLOWS, – - 9/5/77

BELTON, Jonas - 1/3/77; 1/10/77; 1/24/77; 8/29/77; 11/28/77
BENNET, Job - 2/14/77
BENNET, Robert . – 11/21/77
BENNET, Spencer - 6/12/78
BENSON, William - 4/8/79
BENTLEY, Nathaniel - 7/3/78; 9/18/78
BENTLEY, Capt - 6/19/78
BERRY, William - 4/8/79
BETTS, Mr. - 7/24/78
BICKNELL, Moses - 10/20/79
BICKNELL, Samuel - 3/12/79
BICKNELL, Stephen - 10/20/79
BIDDLE, Capt. - 10/10/77; 4/17/78
BIDWELL, Allen - 5/27/79
BIGELOW, Captain - 7/18/77
BIGELOW, Mrs. - 1/31/77
BIGLAND, William - 11/27/78
BILL, Abigail - 11/17/79
BILL, Benajah - 1/10/77
BILL, Benjamin – 3/13/78
BILL, Beriah - 2/21/77
BILL, Christopher – 3/13/78
BILL, David B. - 1/16/78
BILL, Eliphalet - 1/10/77
BILL, James - 4/24/78
BILL, Mrs. Samuel - 3/19/79
BILL, Mrs. Temperance - 1/16/78
BILLINGS, Daniel - 11/17/79
BILLINGS, Capt. Henry - 7/18/77; 11/13/78
BILLINGS, Jesse - 10/2/78
BILLINGS, Joseph - 2/5/79
BILLINGS, Stephen - 9/22/79
BILLINGS, Capt. Roger - 12/12/77; 2/6/78; 10/9/78
BINGHAM, Lt Samuel - 1/10/77
BINGHAM, Simeon - 6/20/77
BINGHAM, William - 6/20/77

BINGHAM, Mr. - 5/29/78
BISBEE, Capt. - 11/13/78
BISHOP, Asa - 11/27/78
BISHOP, Daniel - 4/11/77
BISHOP, Lt. Ebenezer - 7/11/77
BISHOP, Elijah - 4/18/77
BISHOP, Henry - 2/28/77
BISHOP, Israel - 8/14/78
BISHOP, Lt. Nathaniel - 4/25/77
BISHOP, Capt. Nicholas - 7/28/79
BISHOP, Reuben - 2/21/77
BISSEL, Galas - 11/17/79
BISSEL, Hezekiah - 1/16/78; 5/20/79; 7/28/79; 8/18/79
BLACKLE, Margaret - 12/8/79
BLACKLE, Thomas - 12/8/79
BLACKSEE, Enos - 5/9/77
BLACKWELL, Joseph - 4/29/79
BLACKWOOD, Thomas - 1/16/78
BLANCH, John - 4/29/79
BLEBS, Capt. Jabez - 9/26/77
BLISS, Capt. Elisha - 7/17/78
BLISS, Ellis - 10/20/79
BLISS, John - 3/12/79
BLISS, Landlord - 10/24/77
BLOGGET, Benjamin - 1/1/79
BLOGGETT; Dr. - 1/1/79
BLOMER, John - 9/25/78
BLOSS, Elizabeth – 2/20/78
BLOSS, James – 2/20/78
BOELL, John - 2/21/77
BOIX, Emanuel – 12/5/77
BOLLES, Isaiah - 1/31/77
BOLLES, Jeremiah - 8/14/78
BOLLES, John - 3/7/77; 7/11/77; 9/26/77; 6/12/78; 2/26/79
BOLLES, Sen., John - 9/26/77
BOLLES, 2d, John - 4/8/79
BOLLES, Joseph, - 1/29/79
BOLLES, Richard - 8/14/78
BOLLES, Samuel - 6/27/77; 7/4/77

BOLLES, Miss Zeporrah - 1/29/79
BOLLES, Mrs. - 3/7/77
BOND, John - 5/9/77
BOOKER, Samuel - 5/1/78
BORDON, Peleg - 6/20/77
BOSTON - 3/14/77
BOTTOM, Lt. Elisha - 8/15/77
BOWDISH, Asa - 5/9/77
BOWERS, John - 8/14/78
BOYNTON, Aephia - 9/15/79; 10/27/79
BOYNTON, Samuel - 9/15/79; 10/27/79
BRADDICK, John – 2/13/78; 4/3/78; 12/25/78
BRADFORD, Abigail - 6/26/78; 7/24/78
BRADFORD, James - 4/29/79; 11/17/79
BRADFORD, Samuel - 1/3/77
BRADFORD, William - 6/26/78; 7/24/78
BRADLEY, Abraham - 9/4/78
BRADLEY, Joshua - 11/17/79
BRADLEY, Col. Philip B. - 5/9/77
BRAHAM, James - 5/23/77
BRAINERD, Daniel - 1/17/77; 10/24/77
BRAINERD, Elijah - 4/25/77
BRAINERD, Ezra, - 4/25/77
BRAINERD, Jabez - 4/25/77
BRAINERD, Nehimiah - 4/25/77
BRAINERD, Prudence - 10/24/77
BRAINERD, Stephen - 12/12/77; 3/12/79
BRAMAN, James - 5/9/77
BRANCH Branch, Aholiab - 9/19/77
BRANCH, Capt. Moses – 3/6/78
BRAND JR., Samuel - 7/3/78
BRANSON, Benjamin - 8/1/77

BREED, Gershom - 1/10/77; 4/18/77
BREED, John M. - 4/18/77; 7/3/78; 6/23/79; 6/9/79; 8/11/79
BREWSTER, Abel - 4/29/79
BREWSTER, Asa – 11/14/77
BREWSTER, Elisha - 1/24/77; 4/25/77
BREWSTER, Jonathan - 7/28/79; 8/11/79
BREWSTER, Capt. John - 1/10/77
BREWSTER, Jonas - 2/21/77; 5/9/77; 5/23/77
BREWSTER, Samuel - 3/19/79
BRIAN, Mr. - 7/24/78
BRIGGS, William - 9/19/77
BROCKWAY, William - 5/1/78; 4/8/79
BROKWAY, Gideon - 6/20/77
BROOKS, Jonathan - 11/13/78
BROOKS, Samuel - 8/11/79
BROOKS, William - 7/10/78; 4/29/79
BROOKS, Capt. - 10/20/79
BROOME, John - 5/2/77
BROOME, Samuel - 5/2/77;
BROWN, Abiel - 9/5/77
BROWN, Andrew - 9/19/77
BROWN, Jun., Beriah - 3/27/78
BROWN Jun., Daniel - 5/16/77
BROWN, Jedidiah - 4/18/77
BROWN, Jesse - 8/18/79
BROWN, John - 3/14/77; 4/4/77; 8/1/77; 10/10/77; 2/6/78; 10/2/78
BROWN, Jonathan - 9/29/79
BROWN, Mary - 2/6/78
BROWN, Samuel - 6/27/77
BROWN, Stephen - 2/21/77
BROWN, Thomas - 4/22/79
BROWN, Timothy - 12/25/78
BROWN, William John - 5/27/79

BROWN, Capt. - 10/24/77
BROWN, Mr. - 3/14/77; 7/21/79
BROWNE, James - 10/13/79
BROWNE, Joseph - 2/12/79
BROWNING, Wm. - 4/11/77
BRUMMICUM; William - 5/9/77
BRUNCE, Capt. - 4/17/78
BRUNSON, Asa - 5/9/77
BUCHANAN, James - 7/10/78
BUCHANAN, Mr. - 10/24/77
BUCK, Justus - 7/28/79
BUCK, Thomas - 11/17/79
BUCKINGHAM, John - 4/10/78; 7/28/79
BUCKLEY, Charles - 2/19/79
BUCKLIN, Jun., Joseph – 11/7/77
BUDD, Joseph . – 11/21/77
BUDDINGTON, Capt. Eliphalet - 2/12/79
BUEL, Samuel - 9/19/77
BUELL, Lt John - 4/4/77
BUELL Capt. - 7/24/78
BUFFET, Josiah - 5/22/78
BULKLEY, Capt. Charles - 6/27/77; 12/15/79
BULKLEY, Chauncey - 4/25/77
BULKLEY, Eliphalet - 5/13/79
BULKLEY, John - 8/28/78; 9/1/79
BULKLEY, Joshua - 8/14/78
BULKLEY, Peter - 12/29/79
BULKLEY, Roger - 1/10/77; 6/12/78; 6/9/79
BULKLEY, William - 5/9/77
BULKLEY, Dr. - 5/16/77
BULKLEY, Capt. - 3/21/77; 7/3/78
BULL, Asher - 4/29/79
BULL, David – 2/27/78
BURGOYNE, Gen. – 2/13/78
BURKE, Simeon - 7/4/77
BURKE, Capt. - 12/4/78

BURNAP, Abraham - 3/21/77
BURNHAM, Benjamin - 2/21/77
BURNHAM, Jonathan - 7/24/78
BURNHAM, Joseph - 11/27/78
BURROWS, Anna - 7/21/79
BURROWS, Jun. Capt. Hubbard - 1/10/77
BURROWS, Nathan - 7/21/79
BURROWS, Paul - 8/29/77
BUSH, Captain - 10/31/77
BUSHNELL, Aaron - 2/26/79; 12/8/79
BUSHNELL, Aston - 2/26/79
BUSHNELL, Jun., Benajah - 12/4/78
BUSHNELL, Handly - 4/10/78
BUSHNELL, Nathan- 7/1/79
BUSHNELL Jun. Nathan - 12/5/77; 5/30/77; 5/29/78; 2/26/79
BUSHNESS, Eushbius - 10/31/77
BUTLER, Benjamin - 4/4/77
BUTLER, David - 5/27/79
BUTLER, Capt. Elijah - 2/6/78
BUTLER, Simon - 9/5/77
BYARD, William - 8/11/79

C
CABOT, Marston - 11/17/79
CABRIER - 5/29/78
CADY, John - 7/21/79
CADY, Peneul - 8/14/78
CALKINS, Mrs. Abigail - 6/6/77
CALKINS, Frederick - 4/29/79
CALKINS, Pember - 6/6/77; 6/27/77; 12/1/79
CALKINGS, Capt. Jonathan - 2/7//77; 5/9/77 4/24/78; 10/16/78
CAMBY, James - 9/25/78
CAMERON, Charles - 5/22/78
CAMP, A. - 9/25/78

CAMPBEL, Allen - 9/18/78
CAREW, Daniel - 7/1/79
CAREW, Palmer - 4/24/78
CAREY, Rev. - 1/15/79
CARN, Joseph - 5/9/77
CARPENTER, Elijah - 12/25/78
CARPENTER, Eph. - 6/13/77; 6/20/77
CARPENTER, Henry - 8/14/78
CARPENTER, Joshua - 6/13/77; 6/20/77
CARRAL, Thomas - 12/1/79
CARRIER; Isaac - 5/23/77
CARY, Ens. Ephraim - 1/16/78
CARY, Mr. - 7/24/78
CASE, Abraham - 7/4/77
CASE, William – 11/14/77
CASEY, Capt. -4/17/78; 5/8/78
CASWELL, Joseph - 2/26/79
CELSTON, John - 11/3/79
CESAR - 3/7/77; 12/15/79
CHAMPION, Israel - 4/25/77
CHAMPION, Captain - 5/23/77; 4/24/78
CHAMPLAIN, Colonel Joseph - 9/25/78
CHAMPLIN, Capt. Bowdwich - 7/28/79
CHAMPLIN, Edward - 9/12/77; 5/1/78; 8/28/78; 4/15/79
CHAMPLIN, Elihu - 11/27/78
CHAMPLIN, Elijah - 11/6/78; 4/8/79
CHAMPLIN, George - 4/17/78; 7/3/78
CHAMPLIN, Jeffrey - 5/6/79
CHAMPLIN, John - 10/24/77; 7/3/78; 4/1/79
CHAMPLIN, Joseph - 9/1/79

CHAMPLIN, Capt. Lodowick - 9/15/79; 10/20/79; 12/15/79
CHAMPLIN, Samuel - 7/18/77; 1/30/78; 2/13/78; 1/8/79; 5/13/79; 8/18/79; 10/20/79
CHAMPLIN, Mrs. Samuel - 1/22/79
CHAMPLIN, Silas - 8/11/79
CHAMPLIN, Mrs. - 1/17/77
CHAMPLIN, Capt - 1/31/77; 2/7//77; 4/25/77; 8/8/77; 5/8/78; 6/5/78; 2/26/79; 7/28/79; 9/1/79; 9/29/79
CHAMPLIN, Lt. - 7/1/79
CHANDLER, Charles C. - 4/4/77; 5/2/77; 5/20/79; 7/21/79
CHANDLER, Hezekiah - 9/25/78
CHANDLER, Seal - 9/25/78
CHANDLER, William - 9/25/78
CHAPEL, Sgt. Ebenezer - 12/15/79
CHAPEL, Isaac – 11/14/77
CHAPEL, Jedidiah - 12/29/79
CHAPMAN, Abisha - 4/11/77
CHAPMAN, Caleb - 4/25/77
CHAPMAN, David - 1/17/77
CHAPMAN, Edward - 1/17/77; 1/31/77
CHAPMAN, Ezra - 2/12/79
CHAPMAN, Col. Jabez - 8/21/78
CHAPMAN, Major James - 2/28/77 ;8/22/77; 1/16/78
CHAPMAN, Jedidiah - 4/11/77
CHAPMAN, Jeremiah - 1/29/79; 2/19/79
CHAPMAN, John - 11/14/77; 4/29/79; 8/4/79
CHAPMAN Jun., John - 8/25/79
CHAPMAN, Libbeus - 4/11/77
CHAPMAN, Lt. Nathaniel - 10/3/77
CHAPMAN, Perins - 5/30/77
CHAPMAN, Peter – 12/5/77
CHAPMAN, Richard - 2/28/77; 7/18/77; 5/1/78; 10/27/79; 11/17/79
CHAPMAN, Ritner - 10/10/77
CHAPMAN, Col. Samuel - 12/15/79
CHAPPEL, Comfort - 12/11/78
CHAPPEL, Thomas - 12/25/78
CHASE, Zacheus - 4/11/77
CHASSE, Jun., James - 8/14/78
CHAUCERY, Nathan - 1/16/78
CHEETS, Miriam - 9/5/77
CHESEBROUGH, Amos - 3/26/79; 5/13/79
CHESEBROUGH, Mrs. Bridget - 5/9/77
CHESEBROUGH, Cuss - 5/27/79
CHESEBROUGH, Elihu - 5/2/77; 5/15/78
CHESEBROUGH, Peleg - 4/17/78
CHESTER, Caleb - 2/14/77
CHESTER, James - 2/14/77
CHESTER, Jason - 5/22/78
CHESTER, Jonathan - 12/11/78
CHESTER, Joseph - 12/1/79
CHESTER, Mrs. Thankful - 2/14/77
CHESTER, Thomas - 6/20/77; 10/17/77
CHESTER Jun, Thomas - 9/25/78
CHESTER, Capt. - 5/15/78
CHEW, Samuel - 7/25/77; 9/26/77
CHEW, Capt. – 12/26/77; 4/17/78
CHILD, Captain Josiah - 5/9/77
CHILD, Nathan - 11/27/78
CHILD, Shubael - 8/11/79
CHILDS, Capt. Elisha - 5/20/79; 10/20/79
CHILLSON, Benjamin - 7/24/78
CHRET, Madam - 7/4/77
CHRISTIN, Edward - 9/25/78

CHRISTOPHERS, Christopher - 1/17/77
CHRISTOPHERS, John - 5/15/78
CHRISTOPHERS, Peter - 5/15/78
CHRISTOPHERS, Richard - 5/15/78
CHURCH, James - 11/24/79
CHURCH, Silas - 1/31/77
CILLES, John - 9/25/78
CLARK, Abel - 1/30/78
CLARK, Anne - 1/16/78
CLARK, Charles - 8/8/77
CLARK, Danford - 4/10/78
CLARK, Capt. Daniel - 1/16/78
CLARK, Francis - 1/31/77
CLARK, John - 7/11/77; 11/14/77; 4/24/78; 3/5/79
CLARK, Deacon Joseph - 1/31/77
CLARK, Nathaniel - 1/30/78; 4/29/79
CLARK, Robert - 10/20/79; 11/24/79
CLARK, Stephen - 6/26/78
CLARK; Maj. - 11/27/78
CLARKE, Ethan - 2/14/77; 11/14/77
CLARKE, Phineas - 2/14/77
CLAUGH, O. - 5/20/79
CLEFT, L. - 2/21/77
CLEFT, Capt. - 5/16/77
CLEMENT, Jeremiah - 1/10/77; 7/11/77; 10/9/78
CLEVELAND, Aaron - 4/24/78; 5/20/79
CLEVELAND, Moses - 4/8/79
CLEVELAND, Samuel - 8/25/79
CLEVELAND, Tim - 2/21/77
CLIFT, Lt. Lemeul - 5/30/77
CLIFT, Waterman - 10/31/77
CLIFT, Capt. Wills - 5/23/77
CLINTON, George - 11/27/78

CLINTON, General Henry - 3/26/79
CLOVER, Col. - 7/31/78
CLY, Stephen - 2/21/77
COBB, Moses - 4/29/79
COBB, Simeon - 5/9/77
COBBS, James - 10/24/77
COFFIN, Henry - 12/25/78
COFFIN,, Isaac - 9/25/78
COIT, Benjamin - 8/14/78
COIT; Daniel - 1/29/79
COIT, Capt. Joseph – 2/13/78
COIT, Jun., Joseph - 12/22/79
COIT, Samuel - 6/20/77; 8/8/77; 9/19/77; 10/10/77; 11/14/77; 11/21/77
COIT, William - 1/17/77; 2/7//77; 8/14/78
COIT, Widow - 1/29/79
COLBERT, William - 4/29/79
COLE, Marcus - 1/24/77
COLEGROVE, Christopher - 8/14/78
COLEMAN, Edward S. - 2/21/77
COLFAX, Wm. - 1/24/77
COLLIER, Richard - 1/10/77; 12/19/77
COLLINS, Daniel - 1/24/77; 10/24/77
COLLINS, Silas - 12/25/78
COLT, Harris - 5/27/79
COMSTOCK, Abner - 9/12/77; 10/31/77; 5/1/78; 8/28/78; 4/15/79; 11/24/79
COMSTOCK, Amos - 1/30/78
COMSTOCK, Benjamin - 3/5/79
COMSTOCK, James – 12/19/77
COMSTOCK, Mary - 3/5/79
COMSTOCK, Capt. Samuel - 4/8/79
COMSTOCK, Mr. - 7/24/78
CONE, Ebenezer - 4/25/77

CONE, William - 4/25/77; 11/7/77
CONE, Capt. - 10/3/77; 9/22/79
CONGDEN, Joseph - 9/22/79
CONKLIN, Edward - 2/5/79; 2/12/79; 4/8/79; 5/20/79
CONKLING, Jacob - 4/11/77
CONKLING, Joseph - 10/10/77; 11/14/77; 11/21/77; 11/28/77; 5/8/78; 6/5/78 6/26/78; 7/3/78; 7/10/78; 7/24/78; 12/4/78
CONKLING, Capt. - 5/30/77; 8/1/77; 8/8/77; 9/19/77; 6/2/79
CONSTANT, William - 6/13/77
CONVERS, Benjamin - 8/14/78
CONVERSE, Paine - 1/8/79
COOK, Elijah - 8/14/78
COOK, Nathaniel - 7/24/78
COOK, Jun. Nicholas - 4/10/78
COOPER, Nathan - 4/29/79; 11/17/79
COOPER, Lt. Samuel - 4/4/77
COOPER, Mr. - 11/24/79
COPP, Samuel - 4/29/79; 11/17/79
CORNWALL, Elizabeth - 11/17/79
CORNWELL, Elisha - 4/25/77
COSSWALL, Rev. Mr. – 3/6/78
COTTERIL, John - 5/22/78
COTTON, Thomas - 10/24/77; 11/14/77
COX, Ephraim - 2/5/79
CRANDAL, Asa - 8/22/77; 3/13/78
CRANDLE, Christopher - 4/29/79
CRANE, Col. John - 3/20/78
CRANE, Josiah - 11/17/79
CRANE, Capt. Samuel - 5/20/79
CRARY, John - 10/9/78; 5/22/78
CRARY, Oliver - 1/10/77

CRARY, Robert - 2/21/77; 5/29/78; 10/9/78
CRARY, Capt.- 6/19/78
CRAS, Capt. Samuel - 5/20/79
CRAW, Jesse - 11/24/79
CRESEA, Joseph - 11/6/78
CROCKER, Freeman - 4/1/79
CROCKER, John - 4/24/78; 11/20/78
CROSBY, Jonathan - 7/17/78
CROSBY, Levi - 1/10/77
CROSSING, William - 2/26/79
CROWEL, Edward - 4/11/77
CULVER, Daniel - 5/22/78
CULVER, Hannah - 5/22/78
CULVER, James - 4/29/79
CULVER,, John - 4/24/78
CULVER, Samuel - 9/26/77
CULVER, Stephen - 11/13/78
CULVER, Capt. - 3/19/79
CUNNINGHAM, CORNELIUS - 3/21/77
CURDY, John M. - 7/14/79
CURTIS, Henry - 10/31/77
CYRUS - 11/27/78

D

D'ESTAING, Count - 10/16/78; 11/20/78
DANIELS, Asa - 7/18/77
DANIELS, Thomas - 9/18/78
DANIELSON Jun., Samuel - 5/20/79
DANIELSON, Landlord - 10/24/77
DANSLY, Asa - 2/12/79
DARBY, John - 12/25/78
DARBY, Nathaniel - 1/17/77
DARBY, Rufus – 12/26/77; 1/2/78
DARBY, Thomas - 5/30/77
DARRAL, Thomas - 1/16/78

DARREL, Miss Polly - 2/28/77
DARREL, Samuel - 9/15/79; 10/20/79
DARROW, Capt. Christopher - 1/17/77; 4/11/77
DARROW Jun., Christopher - 1/24/77
DARROW Edmond - 1/10/77; 7/17/78; 9/29/79
DARROW, Jonathan - 8/14/78
DARRY, Jeremiah - 12/25/78
DART, Solomon - 1/10/77; 12/11/78
DAVENPORT, James - 3/27/78; 10/2/78; 4/29/79
DAVIS, Elizabeth - 9/5/77
DAVIS Davis, James - 10/10/77; 12/12/77
DAVIS, Henry - 10/10/77
DAVIS, Joseph - 4/17/78
DAVIS Jun., Joseph - 9/8/79
DAVIS, Levi - 4/18/77
DAVIS, Samuel - 1/1/79
DAVISDSON, Capt. – 3/6/78
DAY, Lt. David - 3/12/79
DAYTON, Capt. Ebenezer - 5/1/78; 5/15/78; 5/22/78; 6/12/78; 7/3/78
DEANE, Barnabas - 5/2/77
DEANE, Mrs. Elizabeth - 6/27/77
DEANE, Silas - 6/27/77
DEARBORN, Col. - 2/19/79; 4/8/79 1
DEBOW, Capt. - 1/29/79
DEE, William - 4/11/77
DEGGET, Nathan - 8/14/78
DELIVAN, Samuel - 9/22/79
DELOP, James - 7/28/79
DEMING, Jonathan - 5/16/77; 5/6/79
DEMING, John - 5/15/78

DEMING, Lt. Pownall - 2/21/77; 7/18/77
DENISON, Capt. Daniel – 8/1/77; 2/13/78
DENISON, Daniel Jun – 2/13/78
DENISON 3d, Daniel - 8/1/77
DENISON, Elisha - 2/12/79
DENISON, Ester – 2/13/78
DENISON, Miss Grace - 12/18/78
DENISON, Capt. James - 1/29/79
DENISON, John - 8/8/77; 9/12/77; 11/14/77; 12/19/77; 2/12/79; 4/1/79; 5/6/79; 9/1/79; 9/22/79
DENISON 2d, John. – 11/28/77; 12/19/77
DENISON 3rd, John - 2/6/78
DENISON 4th, John - 11/28/77; 3/27/78; 3/12/79
DENISON 2d, Joseph - 2/6/78
DENISON, Samuel - 8/5/78
DENNIS, Jun., George - 7/17/78
DENNIS Dennis, John - 1/10/77; 1/24/77; 4/4/77; 7/11/77
DENNIS, William - 4/8/79
DERING, Thomas - 1/10/77; 2/6/78; 12/25/78
DERRY, Ned - 12/25/78
DERRY - 8/11/79
DESHON, Capt. Daniel - 1/16/78
DESHON, John - 1/17/77; 8/22/77; 1/30/78; 7/1/79; 9/15/79
DESHON, Richard - 8/22/77; 10/24/77; 11/14/77; 11/21/77 1/16/78
DESHON, Capt. - 12/25/78
DESOLPH, Amamsa - 7/17/78
DESOLPH, Mark Anthony - 7/17/78
DEVOTION, John - 4/18/77; 3/20/78

DEWEY, Josiah - 2/21/77; 3/21/77; 8/14/78; 9/18/78
DEWITT, Jacob - 8/14/78; 8/11/79
DEWY, Daniel - 6/6/77
DEXTER, John – 3/13/78
DICK - 1/31/77; 11/14/77
DICKINSON, Capt. - 3/14/77
DICKSON, James - 6/6/77
DIKE, Nathaniel - 7/21/79
DIMOCK, Lot - 9/1/79
DIXON, Jun., James - 8/14/78
DOANE, Elisha - 12/25/78
DOBOLL, Nathan - 3/21/77
DODGE, John - 2/21/77
DODGE, Joseph - 5/22/78
DODGE,, Peregrine - 1/10/77
DODGE, Capt. - 7/3/78
DOE, John - 5/20/79
DOLBEARE, John - 5/29/78
DOOLITTLE, Capt. Thomas - 8/14/78
DOOLITTLE, Isaac - 7/31/78
DORCEN, Joseph - 7/28/79
DORR, Edward - 6/12/78
DORR, Lydia - 6/20/77
DORR, Mrs. Mary - 4/18/77
DORR, Matthew - 11/14/77; 6/12/78
DORRANCE, David - 1/24/77; 2/5/79
DORRANCE 3d, James - 6/20/77
DORRANCE, John - 5/27/79
DORRANCE, Samuel - 6/20/77
DOUGLAS, James - 2/28/77
DOUGLAS, Jonathan – 12/5/77
DOUGLAS, Miss Lucy - 4/18/77
DOUGLAS, Nathan - 4/18/77; 6/6/77; 8/15/77; 11/14/77; 11/21/77;1/30/78; 5/15/78; 6/19/78; 9/25/78; 1/8/79; 2/12/79; 6/16/79; 9/8/79; 9/22/79

DOUGLAS, N. - 2/7//77
DOUGLAS, Richard - 1/24/77; 4/11/77
DOUGLAS, Robert - 2/28/77
DOUGLAS, William - 8/25/79
DOUGLASS, Douglass, Spera - 4/18/77
DOUGLASS, Douglass, Thomas - 6/23/79; 7/8/79
DOUGLASS, Douglass, William - 4/17/78
DOUGLASS, Capt. - 3/19/79
DOWNER, Elisha - 5/15/78
DOWNER, Dr. Joshua - 5/22/78; 6/12/78; 7/24/78; 10/9/78; 8/11/79; 8/25/79; 9/22/79
DOWNY, James - 9/25/78
DRAKE, Lt. Simeon - 9/22/79
DU GRACES, Mons. Restais - 4/29/79
DUBOLT, Jun., Nathan - 7/4/77
DUDLEY, Moses - 1/22/79
DUDLEY, Dudley, William - 4/10/78; 1/22/79
DUDLEY, Mr. - 7/24/78
DUNBAR, Moses - 3/21/77
DUNHAM, Daniel - 5/20/79
DUNHAM, Solomon - 5/27/79
DUNLAP, Robert - 5/23/77; 7/4/77
DUNLAP, Capt. - 11/6/78
DUNLOP, Betsy - 10/10/77
DUNN, Paul - 5/27/79
DUNN, Samuel - 11/6/78
DUNN, Captain - 5/27/79
DUNPHY, William - 10/10/77
DURKEE, Jun., Jno. - 2/21/77;
DURKEE, Col. - 2/21/77; 2/28/77; 4/4/77; 4/18/77; 4/25/77; 5/2/77; 5/9/77; 5/23/77; 5/30/77; 7/11/77; 7/18/77; 10/3/77; 4/24/78 12/11/78
DUTTON, Ebenezer - 3/27/78

DUTTON Dutton, Timothy - 3/5/79
DYAR, Elijah - 10/24/77; 6/23/79
DYAR, John - 10/24/77; 6/23/79
DYER, Caleb - 4/29/79
DYER, Eliphalet - 7/10/78; 10/2/78; 7/28/79; 8/11/79
DYER, Jabez - 8/11/79
DYER, Nathaniel - 9/12/77; 10/16/78
DYER, Oliver - 7/10/78
DYER, Thomas - 10/2/78
DYER, William - 5/2/77; 5/16/77

E

EARLE, John - 9/5/77
EATON, Calvin - 8/14/78
EATON, Ebenezer - 2/21/77; 4/17/78
EATON, Gavin - 4/17/78
EATON, Joseph - 1/15/79
EATON, Nathaniel - 2/21/77; 4/17/78
EATON, Capt. - 5/29/78; 7/24/78
EATON, Mr. - 6/20/77
EDGERTON, Asa - 10/2/78; 5/6/79
EDRIDGE, Charles - 9/5/77
EDRIDGE, Mrs. - 9/5/77
EDWARDS, Pierpont - 9/19/77
EELS, Rev Nathaniel - 9/5/77
ELDERKIN, Jedidiah - 3/27/78
ELDERKIN, John - 1/10/77; 1/24/77; 8/29/77; 4/29/79
ELDERKIN, Joshua - 5/9/77; 10/2/78; 7/8/79
ELDERKIN, Capt. Vine - 6/6/77
ELDRIDGE, Charles - 10/2/78
ELDRIDGE, Jun. Charles - 5/23/77

ELDRIDGE, Christopher - 9/5/77
ELDRIDGE, Daniel - 9/5/77; 9/11/78; 1/8/79
ELDRIDGE, James - 1/24/77; 4/25/77; 10/2/78
ELIOT, Jacob - 5/20/79
ELIOT, Zebulon - 7/11/77; 9/12/77; 12/22/79
ELLERY, W. - 5/2/77
ELLES, Martin - 1/30/78
ELLIOT, Abigail - 12/22/79
ELWOOD, James - 8/14/78
ELY; Christopher - 1/24/77; 5/16/77
ELY, Major Daniel - 5/16/77
ELY, Elihu - 5/22/78
ELY, Col. John - 1/10/77; 2/7//77; 2/14/77; 4/11/77; 7/11/77; 7/18/77; 8/15/77; 9/19/77; 11/21/77; 9/18/78
ELY, Samuel - 10/31/77; 11/13/78; 5/20/79
EMERSON Foster, Rev. Mr. – 3/6/78
EMMERSON, Joseph - 10/3/77
EMMONS, John - 4/25/77
EMMONS, Joseph – 9/5/77; 12/26/77; 12/4/78
EMMONS, Mr. - 7/24/78
ENGLISH, Freedom - 6/6/77
ENGLISH, Richard - 6/6/77
ENGS, William - 11/17/79
ENOS, David – 3/6/78
ENOS, Colonel – 2/20/78
EROST, David - 8/25/79
ESLING, Rudolf - 4/11/77
ETON, William - 9/25/78
EVENS, Jacob - 3/20/78
EVERIT, Jesse - 8/18/79
EVETT, Ebenezer - 10/23/78
EVETT, Jonathan - 10/23/78
EYLLYS, Col. - 5/16/77
EYMAN, William - 11/17/79

F

FAIRBANKS, John - 12/25/78
FAIRBANKS, Phineas - 4/24/78
FANNING, Charles - 2/21/77
FANNING, Gilbert - 2/12/79; 11/17/79
FANNING, Mary - 10/20/79
FANNING, Roger - 9/22/79
FAREBANKS, Benjamin - 8/14/78
FARGO, Joshua - 1/16/78
FARMER, Charles - 12/25/78
FARR, Benjamin, - 10/13/79
FAULKNOr, Samuel - 8/14/78; 9/18/78
FEIMO, Mr. – 2/27/78
FELCH, John - 6/20/77
FELLOWS, Isaac – 2/13/78
FELSHAW, Capt,- 6/19/78
FENNO, Ephraim - 1/10/77
FENT, Daniel - 2/6/78
FIELDING, William - 5/2/77; 6/27/77
FIELDS, Isaac - 1/24/77; 2/21/77
FINCH, Captain Andrew - 7/18/77
FISH , Aaron - 7/17/78
FISH, John - 7/17/78
FISH, Rev. - 3/21/77
FISK, Bezaleel - 3/7/77
FITCH, Andrew - 2/21/77
FITCH, Benjamin - 4/10/78
FITCH, Elisha - 4/11/77
FITCH, Jun., Jabez - 8/25/79
FITCH, Nathaniel - 8/14/78
FITCH, Capt. Theophilus – 3/13/78
FITZGERALD, Thomas - 5/2/77
FLINT, Abner - 10/2/78
FLINT, Nathaniel - 7/24/78
FLINT, Royal – 11/7/77

FLINT, Mr. - 7/24/78
FLYNN, Edward - 10/13/79
FOOT, Aaron - 3/12/79
FOOT, Adonijah - 3/12/79
FOOT, Asa - 8/8/77
FORD, James, - 6/12/78
FORD, Widow - 6/12/78
FORDHAM, Capt. - 5/8/78
FORSYTHE, Timothy - 11/17/79
FORSYTHE, Mr. - 4/8/79
FORTUNE, Thomas - 9/25/78
FORTUNE, Mr. - 2/26/79
FOSDICK, Nicoll - 12/1/79
FOSDICK, Th. U.- 1/24/77
FOSDICK, Capt. - 9/29/79
FOSTER, Daniel - 3/21/77
FOSTER, Rev. Mr. Isaac – 3/6/78
FOSTER, John - 1/10/77; 7/3/78; 9/22/79
FOSTER, Michael - 6/27/77
FOSTER, William - 4/24/78; 11/17/79
FOTOR, Peter - 7/24/78
FOWLER, Joseph - 4/25/77
FOWLER, Morris - 1/10/77; 10/10/77; 10/24/77; 11/14/77
FOX, Daniel - 8/14/78
FOX, Jun., Daniel - 1/16/78
FOX, Elisha - 4/10/78; 2/19/79; 3/5/79
FOX, George - 2/5/79
FOX, Jun. Samuel - 7/1/79
FRANKLIN, Abel - 8/14/78
FRANKLIN, Benjamin – 3/13/78
FRASER, Robert - 7/17/78
FREDERICK, John - 10/13/79
FREEBURN, Isaac - 7/28/79
FREEMAN, Daniel - 5/16/77
FREEMAN, Elizabeth – 1/23/78
FREEMAN, Enoch - 9/18/78
FREEMAN, James – 1/23/78
FRIGS Jun., William - 11/24/79
FRINK, Mrs. Grace - 2/21/77

FRINK, Nathan - 10/27/79
FROW, Peter - 12/29/79
FUCKER, Thomas - 5/27/79
FULLER, Abidiah - 1/24/77
FULLER, Asa - 8/14/78
FULLER, Joseph – 11/21/77
FULLER, Nodiah - 10/3/77
FULLER, Roger - 7/8/79
FULLER, Rev. - 10/10/77

G

GAINE, Hugh - 5/16/77
GALAND, Labe - 5/29/78
GALLUP, Elisha - 5/22/78; 4/1/79
GALLUP, Joseph – 2/27/78; 4/3/78
GALLUP, Col. Nathan - 1/3/77; 4/15/79; 5/20/79; 9/22/79
GALLUP, Jun, Nathan - 1/10/77
GARDNER, Benjamin - 6/13/77
GARDNER, David - 6/13/77
GARDNER, Phoebe - 10/2/78
GARDNER, Samuel - 4/25/77
GARRICK, William - 1/24/77; 4/4/77; 7/11/77
GARY, Benjamin - 10/24/77
GATES, Daniel – 11/7/77
GATES, John - 5/30/77
GATES, Levi – 4/25/77; 11/7/77
GATES, Nehemiah - 3/12/79
GATES, Timothy - 4/25/77; 9/5/77; 12/26/77
GEER, Abner - 7/17/78
GEER, Amos - 1/3/77
GEER, Lemuel - 10/9/78
GELSTON, David - 7/24/78
GELSTON, John - 4/4/77; 7/21/79
GIBSON, George - 5/20/79
GIBSON, Robert - 8/25/79

GIBSON, Roger - 1/17/77; 10/9/78; 5/20/79
GILBERT, Bradford - 3/5/79
GILBERT, Nehemiah - 8/14/78
GILBERT, Jun. Thomas - 3/5/79
GILBERT, Col. - 3/5/79
GILBERT, Capt. - 4/8/79
GILBERT, Mr. - 3/26/79
GILL; Capt William - 11/6/78
GILLIT, Ebenezer - 4/10/78
GILLIT, Edward - 4/10/78
GILLS, John - 4/18/77
GLOVE, Samuel - 2/7//77
GLOVER, Grover - 4/24/78
GODDARD, Ebenezer - 11/10/79
GODDARD, Miss Polly - 11/10/79
GOLD, James – 11/21/77
GOODBODY, John - 7/11/77
GOODELL, Lt. Silas - 5/16/77
GOODMEN, Jeremiah - 10/31/77
GOODRICH, Capt. Oliver - 11/13/78
GOODWELL, Reuben - 1/8/79
GOODWIN, Daniel - 6/5/78
GOODWIN, Capt. - 9/25/78
GOOLD, John - 10/17/77
GORDON, Benjamin - 8/25/79
GORDON, Deacon - 5/29/78
GORE, Amos - 8/14/78
GORTON, Benjamin - 8/15/77
GORTON, Collins - 5/2/77; 8/29/77; 9/19/77; 10/10/77
GORTON, William - 8/29/77
GOSNER, Christian - 10/2/78; 4/29/79; 11/17/79
GRAHAM, John - 12/4/78
GRANGER, Peter - 5/27/79
GRANT, Joshua - 9/12/77; 8/11/79
GRANT, William - 9/25/78
GRANVILLE, Mr. - 9/5/77
GRAVES, Benjamin - 4/25/77

GRAVES, Mary - 4/25/77
GRAVES, Samuel - 9/5/77; 11/17/79
GRAVES, Mr. - 7/24/78
GRAY, Major Ebenezer - 9/18/78
GRAY, James - 4/29/79
GRAY, Samuel - 4/4/77; 3/13/78; 7/28/79
GRAY, Simeon - 4/4/77
GRAY, Thomas - 9/25/78
GREEN, Mrs. Abigail - 3/5/79
GREEN, Amos - 4/25/77
GREEN, Francis - 11/17/79
GREEN, Griffin - 11/17/79
GREEN, Capt. James - 10/24/77
GREEN, Jedidiah - 5/23/77
GREEN, John - 9/25/78; 10/23/78
GREEN, Jonas - 9/26/77
GREEN, Samuel - 9/26/77
GREEN, Timothy - 1/10/77; 10/17/77; 1/16/78; 2/13/78; 3/13/78; 11/6/78; 2/19/79; 3/5/79; 4/29/79; 10/13/79; 10/20/79; 12/22/79
GREENE, Benjamin - 10/13/79
GREENE, Christopher - 8/5/78; 9/22/79
GREENE, General - 7/31/78
GRIFFETH, James. – 11/28/77
GRIFFEY, James - 10/13/79
GRIFFIN, Abner - 8/28/78
GRIFFIN Jun, Jaspar - 10/2/78
GRIFFIN, Inn Holder – 11/21/77
GRIFFING, Abner - 9/12/77; 1/30/78; 5/1/78; 4/15/79; 5/27/79
GRIFFING, George - 4/18/77
GRIFFING, John – 12/5/77; 5/27/79
GRIFFING, Capt. Peter - 4/24/78; 6/16/79

GRIFFING, Mr. - 7/24/78
GRIMES, Mr. – 2/27/78
GRISWOLD, Andrew - 1/10/77; 2/21/77
GRISWOLD, Samuel - 4/11/77
GRISWOLD, William - 12/4/78
GROSVENOR, Caleb – 12/19/77
GROSVENOR, Ebenezer - 5/6/79
GROSVENOR, Elijah - 10/27/79
GROSVENOR, Major - 2/28/77
GROSVENOR, Mr. - 3/12/79
GRUNMAN, Thomas - 12/25/78
GUINEA - 8/14/78
GUION, Thomas - 12/25/78
GURLEY, Jacob B - 5/27/79.
GUSTIN, Deacon Thomas - 7/18/77

H
HACKER, Henry - 12/25/78
HACKER, Capt. - 4/3/78
HALE, Isaac - 8/5/78
HALE, Joseph - 9/1/79
HALL, Daniel - 1/10/77
HALL Lt. James - 3/20/78
HALL, John - 2/21/77
HALL, Thomas - 9/12/77; 10/3/77
HALL, William - 6/13/77; 10/13/79
HALLAM, Betsy - 12/15/79
HALLAM, Edward - 1/31/77; 2/21/77; 4/11/77; 9/5/77; 1/16/78; 12/11/78; 4/8/79; 6/2/79; 12/1/79
HALLAM, John – 1/2/78; 4/17/78
HALLAM, Captain Robert - 9/22/79
HALLOCK, George - 5/22/78

HALSEY, Jeremiah - 2/7//77; 2/14/77; 12/5/77; 12/12/77; 8/14/78
HAMILTON, Alexander - 6/23/79
HAMILTON, Guidon - 11/17/79
HAMILTON, John - 7/24/78
HAMILTON, Robert - 2/21/77
HANDEE, Capt. - 5/16/77
HANDY, Josiah - 4/4/77
HANKS, Benjamin - 5/16/77; 4/10/78; 4/1/79
HARBERSON, Dominick - 9/25/78
HARDING, Seth - 4/18/77; 9/19/77; 3/19/79
HARDING, Thomas - 7/28/79
HARDING, Capt - 10/17/77
HARKNESS, John - 5/22/78; 5/29/78; 10/9/78; 1/15/79; 9/1/79
HARKNESS, Mr. - 7/24/78;
HARMAN, John - 2/21/77
HARRINGTON, Abraham - 8/14/78
HARRINGTON, Farrington - 7/1/79
HARRIS, Daniel - 9/19/77
HARRIS, James - 4/1/79
HARRIS, Jeremiah - 5/29/78
HARRIS, John - 1/17/77; 2/7//77; 8/22/77; 3/26/79
HARRIS, Joseph - 1/16/78; 9/1/79
HARRIS, Capt. Peter – 1/2/78
HARRIS, Miss Polly – 1/2/78
HARRIS, Sarah - 5/15/78
HARRIS, Thomas - 8/15/77; 2/27/78; 5/15/78
HARRIS, Walter - 1/10/77
HARRIS, William - 11/24/79; 11/10/79
HARRIS, Capt. - 4/18/77
HARRISON, William - 4/18/77

HART, John - 12/25/78
HART, Samuel - 6/26/78
HART, Rev. Mr. - 7/21/79
HART, Major - 9/22/79
HARTINGTON, Abraham - 10/13/79
HARTSHORN, David - 10/31/77
HARTSHORN, Ebenezer - 10/31/77
HARTSHORN, Jonathan - 6/5/78
HARVEY, Asa - 4/25/77
HARVEY, John - 1/31/77
HARVEY, Joseph - 1/3/77; 1/31/77
HARVEY, Rhoda - 1/31/77
HASCALL, David - 8/14/78
HASKIN, Aaron - 5/22/78
HASSARD, Stephen - 5/2/77
HATCH, Elijah - 10/23/78
HATCH, Mr. - 12/25/78
HAUGHTON, Ebenezer - 8/14/78
HAUGHTON, James - 1/30/78; 5/15/78; 1/8/79; 7/28/79
HAUGHTON, Mr. - 4/24/78
HAVENS, Capt. William - 7/4/77; 9/5/77; 6/19/78; 7/17/78; 1/29/79; 2/5/79; 2/12/79; 4/22/79; 5/20/79; 7/8/79; 9/8/79; 12/8/79
HAWKINS, Edward - 8/14/78
HAWKINS, Capt. - 2/7//77
HAWLEY, Capt. - 6/6/77
HAYDEN, Ebenezer - 12/4/78
HAYES, Ezckiel - 9/5/77
HAYNES, William - 10/20/79; 11/24/79
HAYS, Dr. Peter - 10/20/79
HAZEN, Jacob - 2/7//77
HAZZARA, George - 1/29/79
HAZZARD, Lt. - 8/11/79
HEBARD, Nathaniel - 4/18/77
HEFFORD, Samuel - 1/3/77
HELLEN, Alexander - 9/25/78

HELMS, OLIVER - 6/27/77
HEMPSTED, John - 4/11/77; 4/18/77; 10/9/78; 6/9/79
HEMPSTED, Joshua - 3/14/77; 5/15/78; 1/8/79; 7/28/79
HEMPSTED Jun., Joshua - 7/24/78; 6/23/79
HEMPSTED, Nathaniel - 4/29/79
HEMPSTED, Robert - 3/12/79
HEMPSTED, Lt. Samuel - 9/22/79
HENDEE, Asa - 6/6/77
HENRY, John - 1/10/77; 7/18/77; 12/19/77; 6/9/79
HENRY, Mr. - 5/22/78
HENSHAW, Benjamin – 4/18/77; 11/14/77; 12/26/77; 4/10/78; 9/25/78
HERBERT, Eliphalet - 2/6/78
HERRICK, Richard - 12/25/78
HERTELL, John - 6/6/77 8/5/78
HEWARD, Nathan - 3/7/77
HEWIE, Israel - 4/29/79
HEWITT, Richard - 8/21/78
HICKOK, Benjamin - 10/20/79
HIGGINS, Jedidiah – 12/26/77
HIGGINS, Mr. - 10/20/79
HIGS, Abel – 11/7/77
HILL, Henry - 1/24/77
HILLARD, John - 5/13/79; 11/17/79
HILLHOUSE, John C. - 5/20/79
HILLHOUSE, Mrs. Sarah - 3/21/77
HILLHOUSE, William - 3/21/77; 9/12/77; 4/17/78; 4/15/79; 5/20/79; 7/1/79; 9/15/79
HILLIMAM, Lt. Henry ???? - 4/4/77
HINE, Abel - 7/8/79
HINGSTON, William - 5/20/79
HINMAN, Elisha - 5/30/77; 10/10/77; 7/17/78; 2/26/79; 5/20/79; 6/2/79; 6/16/79; 8/18/79; 10/20/79
HINMAN, Noble - 1/10/77; 1/17/77; 2/28/77; 4/25/77; 5/2/77; 6/27/77; 11/14/77; 11/20/78; 12/4/78; 12/25/78
HISCOCK, Thomas - 12/12/77; 2/6/78
HISCOX, Simeon - 9/12/77
HITES, Capt John - 10/3/77
HOARD, James - 7/17/78
HOBART, Eliphalet - 7/4/77; 4/29/79
HODGES, Nathan - 7/24/78
HOIT, James - 5/22/78
HOLBROOK, Deacon, John - 9/4/78
HOLMES; Eliphalet - 1/24/77
HOLMES, James - 10/3/77
HOLMES, John - 10/10/77; 12/12/77
HOLMES, Powell - 10/3/77
HOLMES, Samuel - 5/30/77; 9/4/78
HOLMES, Dr. Seth - 8/15/77; 1/30/78; 5/15/78
HOLMES, Capt. Thomas - 5/30/77
HOLMES, Jun., Thomas - 1/10/77; 5/30/77
HOLMES, Mr. - 3/12/79
HOLSTON, Zedrick - 12/25/78
HOLT, Benj. - 2/21/77
HOLT, Ebenezer - 4/24/78
HOLT, James - 2/21/77; 3/27/78
HOLT, Jun., Joshua - 11/13/78
HOLT, Joseph - 4/29/79
HOLT, Nathaniel - 4/24/78
HOLT, Stephen - 2/26/79
HOPKINS, Esek - 1/30/78
HOPKINS, Jun, Esek - 10/6/79; 10/20/79; 11/3/79; 11/24/79
HORNER, George - 10/2/78

HORSFORD, Aaron - 4/25/77
HORTON, Mr. - 11/21/77; 5/6/79
HOUGH, David - 4/11/77
HOUGH, John - 8/15/77
HOUSE, Lt. Simeon - 9/19/77
HOUSTON, Purnel - 10/2/78
HOVEY, Ebenezer - 12/5/77; 11/6/78; 11/27/78; 11/24/79
HOVEY, Samuel - 12/25/78
HOWARD, Daniel - 1/16/78
HOWARD, James - 5/1/78; 5/6/79
HOWARD, John - 8/11/79
HOWARD, Nathan - 1/16/78
HOWARD, Sarah - 1/16/78
HOWARD, William - 3/13/78; 9/11/78
HOWE, General - 1/10/77; 2/7/77; 5/16/77; 5/23/77
HOWE, Doctor - 11/27/78
HOWEL, Mr. - 9/25/78
HOWELL, Stephen - 3/20/78
HOXSIE, Jun., Benjamin - 7/11/77
HUBBARD, Elijah – 11/7/77
HUBBARD, James – 12/19/77
HUBBARD, Jeremiah - 4/25/77
HUBBARD Jun., John – 11/7/77
HUBBARD, Mrs. Lydia - 11/27/78
HUBBARD, William - 11/27/78
HUDMEL, Ezekiel - 12/25/78
HUDSON, John – 8/8/77; 11/14/77; 11/21/77; 4/17/78
HUDSON - 3/7/77
Hughes, James - 8/15/77
HULBERT, John- 2/6/78
HULL, Abid - 9/25/78
HUMFREE, Elijah - 1/22/79
HUNGERFORD, Green - 4/25/77
HUNGERFORD, Lemuel – 2/13/78

HUNGERFORD, Robert - 4/25/77; 10/3/77
HUNT, Eliplez. – 11/28/77
HUNTINGTON, Andrew - 2/28/77; 4/4/77; 3/13/78; 4/24/78; 7/8/79
HUNTINGTON, Benj. – 2/13/78
HUNTINGTON, Jun., Benjamin - 4/25/77
HUNTINGTON, Caleb - 7/17/78
HUNTINGTON, David - 12/29/79
HUNTINGTON, Rev. Eliphalet - 2/21/77; 2/28/77
HUNTINGTON, Elisha – 2/13/78
HUNTINGTON, Jabez - 1/10/77; 4/18/77
HUNTINGTON, Col. Jed - 1/17/77; 1/24/77; 2/28/77; 4/4/77; 4/11/77; 4/18/77; 4/25/77
HUNTINGTON, Joshua - 8/1/77
HUNTINGTON, Levi - 7/14/79
HUNTINGTON, Lydia - 6/6/77
HUNTINGTON, Nehimiah - 4/11/77
HUNTINGTON, Roger - 11/17/79
HUNTINGTON, Samuel - 10/13/79
HUNTINGTON, Simon - 7/1/79
HUNTINGTON, General - 7/24/78; 9/11/78; 10/20/79
HUNTLEY, William – 12/5/77
HURD, Capt. - 10/20/79
HURLBUT, George - 2/12/79
HURLBUT, Joseph - 3/6/78; 4/10/78; 3/12/79; 3/26/79; 5/13/79
HUTCHINSON, Asa - 8/14/78
HYDE, Benjamin - 1/10/77; 6/2/79
HYDE, Daniel - 1/10/77; 5/30/77; 6/2/79
HYDE, Jr, Elijah - 4/4/77

HYDE, James - 4/11/77
HYDE, Capt Jedidiah - 2/21/77; 5/23/77
HYDE, Joseph - 4/11/77
HYDE, Martha - 4/18/77; 2/27/78
HYDE, Peleg - 8/29/77
HYDE, Samuel -1/10/77
HYDE, Jun. Samuel - 1/10/77
HYDE, Silas - 4/18/77; 2/27/78
HYDE Jun., Thomas - 4/11/77
HYDE, Walter - 1/10/77
HYDE, Col. - 10/24/77
HYMAN, Nicholas - 11/17/79

I

INGALS, Ephraim - 2/21/77; 11/27/78
INGEL, Landlord – 11/21/77
INGRAHM, Samuel - 11/17/79
INGRAM, Simon - 4/29/79
IRONS, Frnic - 8/8/77
ISHAM, Joseph - 2/6/78
IVERY, Samuel - 10/2/78

J

JACKSON, Thomas - 7/4/77; 9/15/79; 10/20/79
JACOBS; Capt. - 3/14/77; 3/21/77
JAMES, Isaac - 8/15/77
JAY, John - 10/13/79
JEFFERY, Jun., Charles - 10/31/77
JEFFERY, Edward - 5/23/77, 9/12/77; 4/17/78
JEFFERY, John - 5/1/78
JEFFERY, Samuel - 1/10/77
JENKS, Charles - 5/20/79
JENKS, Capt. - 6/9/79
JENNINGS, J - 8/29/77.

JEWETT, David - 1/10/77
JEWETT, Capt. Joseph - 3/20/78
JEWETT, Lucretia - 3/20/78
JINKS, Silvanus - 12/25/78
JOHN - 11/27/78
JOHNES, Obidiah - 2/6/78
JOHNSON, James - 2/7//77; 9/25/78; 11/17/79
JOHNSON Jun., James - 4/24/78
JOHNSON, John - 10/17/77
JOHNSON, Joshua - 5/23/77
JOHNSON, Capt. Samuel - 12/22/79
JOHNSON, Stephen - 4/11/77; 10/3/77; 4/24/78; 4/1/79
JOHNSON, Thomas - 5/23/77
JOHNSON, Jun., Thomas - 5/23/77; 3/19/79
JOHNSON, Col. – 3/6/78; 4/29/79
JONES, Amos – 12/19/77
JONES, Miss Patty - 4/29/79
JONES, Samuel – 2/20/78
JONES, Thomas - 6/27/77;7/17/78; 11/13/78
JONSON, Jerusha - 4/18/77
JORDAN, Stephen - 6/20/77
JOREM, Benjamin - 2/28/77; 3/6/78
JOSLIN, Jesse - 8/14/78
JOYCE, John - 12/25/78
JUTESON, S. - 9/5/77

K

KEE, John - 8/14/78
KENDRICKS, Captain – 12/26/77
KENEY, John - 8/22/77
KENNEDY, James - 12/25/78
KENNEDY, Capt. Thomas - 4/11/77; 10/2/78
KENNY, Herman - 9/15/79

KERR, Capt. John - 4/17/78; 5/8/78; 5/15/78; 5/22/78; 6/26/78
KETY, Capt. Calvin - 1/30/78
KEY, Zurishhaddai - 8/29/77
KEYES, Keyes, Maj. John - 5/20/79
KEYES, Stephen - 1/24/77
KEYS, Keys, Captain - 9/19/77
KILBY, Samuel - 8/8/77
KILLEY, Samuel - 9/25/78
KIMBALL, John - 7/8/79
KING,, Jabez - 5/27/79
KING, James - 6/20/77
KING, Jeremiah - 12/4/78
KING, Mary - 4/18/77
KING, Capt. - 10/6/79; 10/13/79
KINGSBERRY, Capt. Ebenezer - 5/20/79
KINGSBURY, Ephraim - 4/18/77
KINGSBURY, Nathaniel - 4/11/77
KINGSBURY, Dr. Obidiah - 4/18/77
KINGSBURY, Sarah - 4/18/77
KINGSBURY, Sandford - 7/28/79
Kinne, Lt. Ezra - 9/1/79
KINNEY, Benomi - 8/14/78
KINSMAN, Jeremiah - 4/11/77
KINSMAN, John – 12/26/77
KINYON, David - 5/15/78
KINYON, Thomas - 5/15/78
KNEELAND, Dr. Hez - 1/30/78; 10/23/78
KNEELAND, Jun. Hez. - 10/23/78
KNIGHT, Caleb - 5/29/78; 1/15/79
KNIGHT, Joseph - 6/20/77; 2/27/78
KNOWLTON, Jun, Stephen - 5/1/78
KNOX, Michael - 9/25/78

KNOX, Mr. - 6/20/77

L
LADLE, Adam - 11/3/79
LAMB, John – 11/14/77
LAMB Lamb, Samuel - 1/29/79
LANDON, Jason - 10/10/77
LANE, Hez. - 5/20/79
LANGDON, Sarah - 2/6/78
LARK, Covel - 9/22/79
LATHAM, Daniel - 1/15/79
LATHAM, David - 12/29/79
LATHAM, James - 1/24/77; 3/7/77
LATHAM, Lucy - 1/24/77
LATHAM, William - 12/1/79
LATHAM, Captain - 7/18/77
LATHROP, Azariah – 2/21/77; 11/28/77; 9/22/79
LATHROP, Daniel - 3/27/78; 9/29/79
LATHROP, Elijah - 4/11/77
LATHROP, Elisha - 1/10/77; 2/21/77
LATHROP 3d, Elisha - 5/16/77; 8/29/77
LATHROP, Joshua - 3/27/78
LATHROP, Thomas - 4/18/77
LATHROP, Zapaniah - 1/3/77
LATHROP, Capt.- 6/19/78
LATHROP, Mr. - 7/24/78
LATIMER, David - 1/10/77; 9/1/79
LATIMER, Col. Jonathan - 4/11/77; 5/2/77; 7/25/77; 11/21/77; 6/12/78
LATIMER, Picket - 7/3/78
LATIMER, Samuel - 8/22/77; 1/16/78; 7/1/79; 10/13/79
LAW, Andrew - 7/17/78
LAW Law, Richard - 1/24/77; 2/21/77; 4/17/78; 5/8/78;

5/22/78; 7/3/78; 7/17/78;
9/25/78; 11/6/78; 2/12/79;
4/8/79; 4/22/79; 5/20/79;
7/28/79; 8/11/79; 9/15/79;
10/20/79; 11/3/79; 11/24/79
LAWIS, Phineas - 8/14/78
LAWRENCE, John - 11/24/79
LAX, William - 8/15/77
LAY, Amos - 4/25/77
LAY Lay, Elisha - 6/12/78
LAY Lay, Capt. Lee - 12/4/78
LAY Lay, Capt. - 4/25/77
LAYALL, Jonathan - 3/20/78
LEACH, Corporal Benjamin - 3/20/78
LEACH, Ebenezer - 3/21/77
LEAKE, John - 5/20/79
LEAVENS, James - 10/9/78; 11/27/78
LEDYARD, Ebenezer - 2/26/79
LEDYARD, Major - 1/1/79
LEDYARD, Mrs. - 2/26/79
LEDYARD, Messrs - 2/7//77; 9/18/78
LEE, Rev. Andrew - 2/21/77
LEE Lee, Benjamin - 3/14/77; 4/18/77; 11/14/77
LEE, Elisha - 2/21/77; 10/3/77
LEE, Ezra - 1/24/77; 7/4/77
LEE, H. - 4/29/79
LEE, General Henry – 2/20/78
LEE, Martin - 4/8/79
LEE, Mary - 9/12/77; 11/14/77;5/1/78; 8/28/78; 10/3/77
LEE, Widow Mary - 4/15/79; 7/28/79
LEE, William – 11/14/77
LEE, Capt. - 4/18/77
LEECH, Clement - 5/15/78; 1/8/79; 7/28/79; 11/24/79; 12/22/79
Leeds, Anna - 4/17/78

LEEDS, Jedidiah - 10/31/77; 1/29/79
LEEDS Leeds, Jonathan - 5/30/77; 4/17/78
LEEDS Leeds, William - 12/11/78; 1/1/79; 4/8/79; 6/16/79; 7/21/79; 8/18/79
LEEDS Leeds, Lt. - 4/17/78
LEETS, Mr. - 6/20/77
LEFFINGWELL, . Christopher - 3/14/77; 6/13/77; 7/11/77; 7/25/77; 8/14/78; 9/18/78; 11/13/78; 6/23/79
LEFFINGWELL, Daniel - 9/18/78
LEFFINGWELL, Elisha - 7/1/79
LEFFINGWELL, Matthew - 1/10/77
LEFFINGWELL, Phineas - 11/20/78
LEIGH, Jonathan - 2/21/77
LEIGHTON, Capt. Samuel - 7/24/78
LEONARD, Samuel - 2/21/77
LESTER, Amos - 12/25/78
LESTER, Andrew - 6/20/77
LESTER, David - 1/3/77; 6/13/77; 9/12/77
LESTER, Eliphalet - 9/22/79
LESTER, Mrs. Lucy - 9/22/79
LESTER, Mary - 9/19/77
LESTER, Phineas - 2/21/77; 5/1/78
LESTER, Simeon - 7/11/77; 9/19/77
LESTER, Thomas - 1/10/77; 6/13/77; 9/5/77; 9/12/77
LESTER, Timothy - 5/20/79
LETELIER, Charles - 4/15/79
LEVINE, Dominico - 12/25/78
LEWIS Jun., Elijah - 10/23/78
LEWIS, Elisha - 9/5/77
LEWIS, Jr., Elisha - 9/25/78
LEWIS, Emanuel - 4/11/77

LEWIS, Capt. Israel - 3/20/78
LEWIS, Jabez - 3/21/77
LEWIS, John - 8/14/78
LEWIS, Joseph - 3/14/77; 5/9/77; 1/29/79; 2/19/79
LEWIS, Capt. Robert - 5/9/77
LEWIS, Capt. - 4/25/77; 5/9/77
LITTLE; Deodat - 5/16/77
LITTLE, James - 5/30/77
LIVINGSTON, William A. - 11/17/79
LOCK, Timothy - 11/6/78
LOMIS, Abraham - 7/4/77
LOMIS, Caleb - 7/11/77; 3/5/79
LOMIS, 2d, Caleb - 9/5/77
LONDON - 9/5/77; 1/23/78; 7/3/78
LONGWORTHY, John - 10/2/78
LOOMIS, Israel - 11/27/78
LOOMIS, P. - 12/25/78
LOPER, Abraham - 12/12/77; 2/6/78
LOPEZ, Abra. - 4/11/77
LOPEZ, Mr. - 6/12/78
LORD, Daniel - 9/12/77; 5/1/78; 8/28/78; 11/24/79
LORD, Enoch - 4/4/77
LORD, Jabez - 9/25/78
LORD, James - 1/24/77
LORD, John - 6/27/77
LORD, Richard - 4/4/77
LORD, Samuel P. - 11/10/79
LORD, Solomon - 8/1/77; 10/31/77; 8/5/78
LORD, Rev. Doctor - 3/27/78
LORD, Mr. - 7/24/78
LORE, Capt. Jabez - 8/18/79
LORING, William - 1/16/78
LOUDON, Samuel - 1/17/77
LOVEJAYS, Nehemiah - 8/14/78
LOVER, Joseph - 5/16/77
LOWREY, Alexander - 5/27/79
LUCAS, Mrs. Mary - 2/21/77

LYMAN, Eliphalet - 7/17/78
LYNES, Abel - 12/25/78
LYON, Asa - 6/27/77; 9/19/77
LYON, Jonathan - 6/27/77
LYON, Peter - 9/25/78
LYONS, Ephraim - 7/4/77
LYONS, Mr. - 4/4/77

M

M'CLELLAN, Samuel - 1/10/77
M'CLELLAN, Col. - 7/17/78; 11/6/78; 12/4/78
M'CURDY, John - 4/18/77
M'CURDY, Lyade - 7/24/78
M'DANIELSON, Robert - 12/25/78
M'DOUGLALL, Alexander - 12/25/78
M'FALL, William - 6/13/77
M'LARTY, Robert - 5/20/79
M'NINCH, David - 11/17/79
MACKALL, Hobart - 7/28/79
MAIN, Amos – 12/5/77; 12/12/77; 4/1/79
MAIN, Jeremiah - 9/1/79
MALL, Nathaniel - 9/25/78
MALONY, James - 5/2/77
MAN, Zadock - 8/14/78
MANNING, Hezekiah - 10/2/78
MANAWARING, Asa - 1/29/79; 2/19/79; 2/26/79; 3/26/79; 5/20/79
MANAWARING, Lydia - 5/16/77
MANAWARING, Oliver - 7/31/78
MANAWARING, Thomas - 5/16/77; 10/10/77; 12/12/77
MANAWARING, William - 1/15/79; 4/11/77; 11/10/79; 9/22/79
MANAWARING, Mrs. - 1/15/79
MARSH Jun., Nathaniel - 4/4/77
MARSON, William - 5/20/79

MARSON, Mr. - 1/10/77
MARTIN, Abigail - 7/24/78
MARTIN, Anderson - 1/10/77
MARTIN 3d, George - 10/27/79
MARTIN, John - 12/25/78
MARTIN, Nathan - 1/16/78
MARTIN - 10/17/77
MARTIN, Rev. - 5/23/77
MARSTON, John, – 11/14/77
MARVIN, Capt. Dan - 6/20/77; 4/17/78
MARVIN, Elihu - 2/21/77
MARVIN, Matthew - 11/27/78
MARVIN, R. - 9/4/78
MASON, Elias - 5/1/78
MASON, Elnathan - 7/24/78
MASON, James - 5/16/77
MASON, Col. - 11/17/79
MASTERS, Richard - 7/4/77
MATHER Jun., Samuel – 3/21/77; 12/26/77; 1/2/78
MATSON, Nathaniel - 10/31/77; 5/1/78; 8/28/78; 4/15/79; 7/1/79
MATSON, William – 9/12/77; 11/7/77
MATTESON, Allen - 7/28/79
MATTHEWS, John - 2/21/77
MATTOCKS, Sam'l - 6/5/78
MAY, Eleazer – 1/23/78
MAY, George - 9/15/79
MAY, Robert - 11/17/79
MAYTON, Capt. Reuben - 3/5/79
MCCARY, Capt. Richard - 4/8/79
MCCLOUD, Alexander - 9/25/78
MCCOLLUM; Daniel - 4/29/79
MCCULLOUGH, Col. - 1/8/79
MCGHILL, Elelazer - 7/24/78
MCGREGORY, Jn. - 2/21/77
MCKEEVE, William r - 9/25/78
MCNEIL, Neil - 8/11/79
MCNEIL McNeil, Capt, - 2/19/79

MEAD, Dr. Amos - 10/9/78
MEGRINGER, Captain John - 5/30/77; 7/11/77
MELALLY, Michael - 3/27/78; 7/3/78; 2/26/79; 12/29/79
MERREL, Alexander - 6/9/79; 10/27/79
MERRIL, Hezekiah - 10/10/77
MERROW, Elisha - 2/7//77
MICHAEL, Captain – 3/13/78
MICHEL, J.- 5/29/78
MIGHELLS, John - 9/5/77
MIGHELLS, Mary - 9/5/77
MILES, Mr. - 3/26/79
MILLARD, Nathaniel - 7/24/78
MILLARD, Oliver - 7/24/78
MILLARD, Sarah - 7/24/78
MILLER, Burnet - 10/10/77
MILLER, Captain David - 7/8/79
MILLER, Elisha - 1/3/77; 3/12/79
MILLER, Gabriel - 12/25/78
MILLER, Jeremiah – 12/19/77
MILLER, John - 5/9/77; 12/11/78
MILLER, Nicholas - 10/10/77
MILLER, Nicodemus - 4/8/79
MINARD, Philip - 12/4/78
MINARD, Samuel - 3/5/79
MINER, Jun., Charles - 10/10/77
MINER, Ephraim – 2/7//77; 2/21/77; 8/1/77; 3/6/78; 3/13/78; 3/27/78; 6/12/78; 12/25/78; 3/19/79; 9/22/79
MINER, Ester - 1/8/79
MINER, Hugh - 5/23/77
MINER, John - 7/24/78 12/25/78
MINER, Capt. Simeon - 11/24/79
MINER, Stephen - 1/16/78
MINER, Mr. - 11/13/78
MING, Thomas - 5/22/78
MINOR, Nathaniel- 2/6/78
MITCHEL, Isaac - 12/25/78

295

Mitchell, Hez. - 6/6/77
MOAGS, Jacob - 10/2/78
MOFFAt, Dr. Thomas - 4/10/78
MONRO, James – 12/26/77; /1/79
MOOR, John - 6/9/79
MOOR, William - 1/22/79; 12/1/79; 12/18/78
MOORE, Nathan- 2/21/77; 9/25/78
MORE, Caley - 5/23/77
MORE, Mr. - 2/26/79
MORGAN, Benjamin - 5/9/77
MORGAN, Jun., Benjamin - 5/16/77
MORGAN, Christopher - 1/16/78
MORGAN, Elihu - 7/4/77
MORGAN, Henry - 9/29/79; 10/13/79
MORGAN, John - 4/11/77; 9/22/79; 10/20/79
MORGAN, Joseph - 9/11/78
MORGAN; Phebe - 3/27/78
MORGAN, Solomon - 12/25/78
MORGAN, Temperance - 1/16/78
MORGAN, Capt. William - 7/4/77; 1/16/78; 9/11/78; 1/1/79; 12/22/79
MORGAN, Jun. William - 12/22/79
MORGAN, Elder - 6/27/77
MORSE, Joseph - 11/6/78
MORTIMORE, Mr. - 4/15/79
MORTON, James - 9/19/77
MOSELY, Ebenezer - 7/28/79
MOSELY, Samuel - 3/7/77
MOSS, John - 9/25/78
MOSS, Robert - 9/25/78
MOTT, Jeremiah - 7/28/77
MOTT, John - 9/5/77
MOTT, Col. Samuel - 5/20/79
MOUSE, Simeon - 1/24/77

MULLENDINE, Mary - 4/18/77
MUMFORD, Miss Catherine - 4/29/79
MUMFORD, David - 12/12/77; 8/28/78
MUMFORD, Giles - 12/29/79
MUMFORDd, Peter - 10/24/77; 11/14/77
MUMFORD, Robinson - 4/25/77; 5/2/77; 5/23/77; 9/12/77; 2/26/79; 3/26/79; 4/1/79
MUMFORD, Thomas - 8/29/77; 12/12/77; 3/20/78; 4/17/78; 7/17/78; 4/15/79; 4/29/79; 5/20/79; 6/16/79; 9/29/79; 10/20/79
MUMFORD, Capt. - 6/9/79
MUMFORD, Ensign – 2/20/78
MUMFORD, Mr. - 9/1/79
MUNRO, Joshua - 4/29/79; 11/17/79
MUNSON, Levi - 4/29/79
MURDOCK, Amos - 10/3/77
MURDOCK, Jonathan - 12/1/79
MURDOCK, John - 3/20/78
MURPHY, Mr. - 6/2/79
MYERS, Arthur - 10/10/77

N
NED - 10/24/77
NETON, Samuel - 9/5/77
NEVINS, Capt. David - 1/17/77; 1/24/77
NEWELL, Norman - 5/9/77
NEWMAN, John Holly - 11/24/79
NEWMAN, Dr. John Newman - 11/24/79
NEWPORT - 2/19/79
NEWTON, Jun. Christopher - 8/15/77
NEWTON Israel – 12/19/77

NICHOLS,- David - 12/11/78
NICHOLS, William - 9/25/78
NICHOLS, Capt. - 5/2/77
NILES, Frederick - 9/18/78
NILES, James – ½3/78
NILES, Nathan - 5/20/79
NILES, Robert - 1/3/77; 7/25/77; 8/1/77; 8/8/77; 9/19/77; 4/15/79
NILES, Thomas N. - 1/3/77
NILES, Capt. - 7/25/77
NINAH - 4/10/78
NOBLE, William - 9/25/78
NOBLES, Nathan - 2/21/77
NOEL, Mons. - 11/17/79
NORMAN, John - 7/17/78
NORTON, Bariah - 4/29/79; 11/17/79
NORTON, John - 8/14/78
NOYCE, Joseph - 4/29/79
NOYES, James - 11/17/79
NOYES, William - 5/20/79
NULBERT, John - 7/24/78
NUTTING, John - 12/25/78
NYE, Capt. Thomas - 4/17/78; 5/8/78

O

OCCUM, Martha - 8/29/77
OLCOTT, Mr. - 7/24/78
OLIVER, John - 4/15/79
OLMSTED, Capt. Icabod - 4/25/77; 10/3/77; 11/7/77
OLMSTED, Joseph - 9/25/78
OLMSTED, Oliver - 9/1/79
OLMSTEAd, Capt. Stephen - 5/15/78; 6/12/78; 8/14/78
OLMSTED, Jun, Stephen - 8/14/78
OLMSTEAD, Mr. - 7/24/78
OLNEY, Lt. Commander Jeremiah - 9/22/79
ORFORD - 8/1/77

OTBERLTBROW, Samuel - 9/25/78
OTIS, James - 1/30/78
OTIS Otis, Jonathan - 11/24/79; 12/15/79
OWENS, John - 1/30/78; 1/1/79
OWENS, Joseph - 4/11/77

P

PACKARD, Nathaniel – 12/19/77
PACKARD, Benejab – 1/2/78
PACKARD, Benjamin – 12/19/77
PACKARD, Capt. Daniel - 2/6/78; 4/8/79
PACKWOOD, Miss Fanny - 11/10/79
PACKWOOD, Capt. Joseph - 2/7//77; 7/25/77
PACKWOOD, Capt. William - 11/10/79
PAGE, Thomas - 2/6/78; 10/20/79
PAINE, Amos - 7/21/79
PALMER, Asa - 6/27/77
PALMER, Asher - 11/24/79
PALMER, Elijah - 5/9/77
PALMER, George - 12/18/78
PALMER, Jun., Jonathan - 5/20/79; 11/17/79
PALMER, Joseph - 6/2/79
PALMER, Joseph Pearse, - 6/2/79
PALMER, Mary - 10/20/79
PALMER, Nathan - 7/18/77; 7/31/78
PALMER, Peris - 2/6/78
PALMER, Richard – 1/23/78
PALMER, Thomas - 4/29/79; 11/17/79

PALMER, Capt. - 2/21/77; 7/18/77
PALMER, Mr. - 8/22/77
PALMES, Capt. Edward - 10/17/77; 1/16/78
PANEVART, John - 5/29/78
PANNIMAN, James - 12/12/77
PARISH, Nehemiah - 8/25/79
PARK, Rev. Joseph - 3/21/77
PARK, Moses - 1/8/79
PARK, Zebulon - 1/8/79
PARK, Mr. - 7/24/78
PARKE, John - 9/18/78
PARKER, Jonathan - 11/24/79
PARKER, Joseph - 5/9/77
PARKER, M. - 11/17/79
PARKER, Capt. Samuel - 5/9/77
PARKER, Thomas - 9/25/78
PARKER, Timothy - 10/9/78; 4/1/79; 5/27/79
PARKER, William - 10/20/79
PARKER, Capt. - 8/25/79; 10/6/79
PARKHURT, Abraham - 5/16/77
PARKS, John - 8/14/78
PARKS Jun , John - 2/21/77; 3/21/77
PARKS, Thomas - 5/13/79
PARMALEE, Bryan - 8/14/78
PARMELS, John - 7/1/79
PARSONS, Elijah – 12/5/77; 5/27/79
PARSONS, Joseph - 10/20/79
PARSONS, Col. Marshfield - 9/12/77; 10/17/77; 1/30/78; 4/17/78; 5/1/78; 7/24/78; 8/28/78
PARSONS, Capt. Moses - 8/8/77
PARSONS, Samuel - 2/28/77; 1/16/78
PARSONS, Gen. Samuel H. - 2/28/77; 5/9/77; 7/11/77; 8/22/77; 2/19/79; 4/29/79

PARSONS, Capt. - 10/3/77; 5/23/77; 11/24/79 -
PARSONS, Lt. - 11/24/79
PATRICK, Jacob - 8/14/78
PATTEN, John - 1/31/77
PATTEN, William - 1/31/77
PATTERSON, Robert - 4/25/77
PAYNE, Benjamin - 8/11/79
PEABODY, Aaron - 12/22/79
PEABODY, Joseph - 12/22/79
PEARCE, John - 2/7//77
PEARSE, Nathaniel - 5/6/79
PEATMAN, John - 12/25/78
PECH, Lee - 9/26/77
PECK, Darius - 8/22/77
PECK, Elias - 12/22/79
PECK, Elizabeth - 2/21/77
PECK, Joseph - 2/21/77
PECK, Jun. Joseph - 2/21/77
PECK, Nathaniel - 11/24/79
PECK, Adj. Gen., William - 2/26/79
PEIRCE, Jonah - 12/15/79
PELTON, Jun., Ebenezer - 10/20/79
PELTON Pelton, Thomas - 1/10/77
PEMBERTON, Miss Issana - 7/21/79
PEMBERTON, Patrick G. - 6/20/77.
PEMBERTON, Thomas - 12/25/78
PENFIELD, Mr. 7/24/78
PENNIMAN, James - 9/1/79; 11/17/79
PENNY, Jonathan - 2/6/78
PENNY, Thomas- 2/6/78
PERCIVAL, Francis - 12/12/77; 1/16/78

PERCIVAL, Capt. Timothy - 7/28/79
PERGINE, John - 5/20/79
PERKINS, Andrew - 8/22/77; 4/10/78; 11/6/78
PERKINS, David - 10/13/79
PERKINS; Eben - 1/24/77
PERKINS, Elisha - 8/5/78; 5/20/79
PERKINS, Capt. Hez. - 8/18/79
PERKINS, Isaac - 3/27/78
PERKINS,' Capt. Jabez - 4/10/78; 10/9/78; 11/13/78; 9/1/79
PERKINS, Widow Joanna - 1/10/77
PERKINS, John - 4/11/77; 10/2/78
PERKINS, Mrs. Kezia - 6/20/77; 1/16/78
PERKINS, Levi - 8/14/78; 7/17/78
PERKINS, Luke - 1/10/77; 1/17/77; 6/20/77; 1/16/78
PERKINS, Phebe - 3/27/78
PERKINS, Rufus - 11/17/79
PERKINS, Lt. Simon - 9/18/78
PERKINS, Solomon - 5/20/79
PERKINS, Captain - 3/20/78
PERKINS, Mr. 1/10/77; 1/24/77
PEROW - 4/8/79
PERRY, Eliakin - 12/29/79
PERSONS, Joseph - 7/1/79
PETERS, Nathan - 2/21/77
PHELP, Seth - 2/21/77
PHELPES, Alexander - 12/11/78
PHELPES, Mary - 12/11/78
PHELPS, Charles - 5/2/77; 9/5/77; 10/31/77
PHELPS, Joel - 6/27/77
PHELPS, John - 11/10/79
PHELPS, Moses – 2/13/78
PHELPS, Samuel - 10/31/77

PHILIPS, Jonathan - 12/12/77
PHILIPS, Joshua - 12/12/77
PHILLIPPS, John - 12/12/77; 2/6/78
PHILLIPS, Barnard – 11/28/77; 12/25/78
PHIMMER, Ebenezer - 8/14/78
PHIPPS, David - 11/17/79
PICK, Nathaniel - 4/15/79
PICOT, P. - 4/29/79
PIERCE, Abel - 10/10/77
PIERCE, Benomi - 11/17/79
PIERCE, Moses - 5/30/77
PINKHAM, Daniel - 12/25/78
PINKHAM, Sylvanus - 9/18/78
PINYARD, Matthias - 12/25/78
PIRKINS, Abraham - 10/31/77
PLATT Platt, Jeremiah - 5/2/77
PLATT, Noah - 4/10/78
PLUMB, Samuel - 10/2/78
PLUMBLEY; Oliver - 5/30/77
POMP - 4/15/79
POMPE, Darkis - 11/17/79
POMROY, Noah - 8/8/77
POND, William - 7/3/78
PORTER, John - 12/11/78; 9/29/79; 10/20/79
PORTER, Moses – 2/27/78
POST, Joseph - 4/25/77
POST, Nathaniel - 12/4/78; 7/28/79; 8/11/79; 9/15/79; 10/20/79
POTTER, Ebenezer - 4/11/77
POTTER, Peter - 12/25/78
POTTER, Stephen - 8/29/77
POTTER, Mrs. - 4/29/79
POWERS, Jun, Icabod - 3/27/78; 9/18/78
POWERS, Joshua - 11/3/79
POWERS, Michael - 12/1/79
POWERS, Samuel - 4/11/77
PRATT, Allen - 12/11/78
PRATT, Jedidiah - 4/29/79

PRENTICE, Amos - 10/20/79
PRENTICE Prentice, Mercy - 4/29/79
PRENTICE Prentice, Col. Samuel - 4/17/78; 1/8/79
PRENTICE Prentice, Capt. Stephen -[see also Prentis] 5/15/78
PRENTICE Prentice, Col. - 2/28/77; 9/19/77; 8/22/77
PRENTIS, Joseph - 8/15/77; 5/15/78; 1/8/79
PRENTIS, Capt. Stephen [see also Prentic] - 8/15/77; 7/28/79
PRENTIS, Mr. - 8/25/79
PRESCOTT, General - 7/18/77
PRESTON, Lydia - 7/1/79
PRESTON, Capt. Stephen- 1/30/78
PRICE, Samuel - 4/8/79
PRICE, William - 9/25/78
PRICOTT, Capt. - 11/17/79
PRIMUS - 7/4/77
PRINCE, William - 4/11/77; 4/17/78; 8/11/79
PRINCE - 4/25/77; 5/6/79
PRIOR, Elisha - 12/11/78
PUNDERTON, Ebenezer - 8/11/79
PUTNAM, Charles – 11/28/77

Q
QUAM - 7/8/79

R
RAINEY, Thomas – 2/13/78
RANDAL, Amos - 5/16/77
RANDAL, Benjamin - 9/8/79
RANDAL, Ichabod - 10/13/79
RANDAL, Jonathan - 1/10/77
RANDAL, Thomas - 2/12/79

RANDALL, Rufus - 11/27/78
RANSOM, Mrs. Alice - 12/29/79
RANSOM, Joshua – 12/19/77
RANSOM, Robert - 12/29/79
RANSOM, Mr. - 7/28/79
RATHBONE, Wait - 10/10/77
RATHBORN, Benjamin – 12/19/77
RATHBUN, Capt. John - 10/2/78
RATHBUN, Jr., John - 5/2/77; 11/14/77; 3/20/78
RAWSON, Rev. Mr. Grindal - 4/11/77
RAYMEND, John - 4/29/79
RAYMOND Raymond, John - 7/28/79
RAYMOND, Jun., John - 1/8/79
RAYMOND, Joshua - 4/11/77; 6/13/77; 6/20/77; 7/4/77
RAYMOND, William - 1/24/77
RAYNSFORD, Captain - 7/28/79
READ, Abijah - 3/21/77
REED; Enoch - 1/24/77; 8/22/77
REED, William - 8/4/79
REEVE, Israel - 12/29/79
REID, William - 8/11/79
REMSEN, Capt. Abraham - 9/22/79
REYNOLDS; Elisha - 1/1/79
RHODES, James - 3/12/79
RICE, Daniel - 6/6/77
RICE, Elisha - 5/9/77
RICHARDS, D. - 2/26/79
RICHARDS, David - 9/12/77
RICHARDS Jun., David - 9/11/78
RICHARDS, Elisha - 4/1/79
RICHARDS, Guy - 4/11/77; 1/16/78; 11/24/79
RICHARDS, Jun. Guy - 9/8/79; 12/1/79
RICHARDS, John - 8/22/77; 1/16/78; 4/17/78; 11/13/78; 12/22/79

RICHARDS, Peter - 2/19/79; 4/29/79; 8/18/79
RICHARDS, Samuel - 5/23/77; 7/4/77; 12/19/77
RICHARDS, William - 9/19/77; 1/24/77; 4/4/77
RICHARDS, Capt. - 10/13/79
RICHER, Benjamin - 12/25/78
RIGHTBEE; John - 9/19/77
RILEY, John - 8/14/78
RIPLEY, John - 10/13/79
RIPLEY, Capt.- 6/19/78
ROBBINS, Moses - 1/15/79
ROBBINS, Robert - 1/10/77
ROBBINS, William - 12/25/78
ROBERTS, Eliphalet - 6/20/77
ROBERTS, Griffith - 9/25/78
ROBERTSON, William - 9/15/79
ROBINS, William - 5/22/78
ROBINSON, Capt. Abner - 11/6/78
ROBINSON, Benjamin - 9/1/79
ROBINSON, John - 10/13/79; 10/27/79
ROBINSON, Capt. Samuel - 11/13/78
ROBINSON, Thomas – 11/28/77
ROBINSON, William - 11/17/79
ROCKWELL, John - 12/18/78
RODMAN, Daniel - 8/11/79
ROE, Alex - 9/19/77
ROGERS, Jun., Ebenezer- 2/6/78
ROGERS, Edmund - 7/1/79
ROGERS, Captain Ezehiel - 7/4/77
ROGERS, Harris - 11/10/79
ROGERS, James - 4/11/77; 8/29/77; 10/27/79
ROGERS, Jehiel - 12/18/78
ROGERS, John - 5/23/77; 2/6/78; 1/15/79; 1/29/79
ROGERS, Jonathan- 2/6/78
ROGERS, Joseph - 4/29/79; 9/15/79
ROGERS, Martha - 9/15/79
ROGERS, Obidiah - 6/20/77
ROGERS, Peter - 8/22/77
ROGERS, Rustford - 1/10/77
ROGERS, Captain Samuel - 10/16/78; 3/5/79; 10/6/79
ROGERS, Thomas – 3/7/77; 3/6/78
ROGERS, Uriah - 8/21/78
ROGERS, William - 1/29/79
ROGERS, Col. Zabdiel - 7/17/78; 8/11/79
ROGERS, Capt. - 4/15/79
ROLAND, Capt - 4/25/77; 6/12/78
ROOR, Col. Jesse - 5/20/79
ROOR, Ephraim - 10/27/79
ROSE, John - 10/24/77
ROSE, Nathaniel - 5/23/77; 10/3/77
ROSECARRY, James - 9/25/78
ROSS, Ezra - 7/10/78
ROSSETER, Dr. Appleton Wolcos - 7/28/79
ROSSETER, Rev. Mr. Asher - 1/16/78
ROSSETER, Elnathan - 2/12/79; 3/12/79
ROUILLARD, Mr. - 7/24/78
ROUNDEY, Robert - 11/24/79
ROUSE, Elias - 6/9/79
ROUSE, John - 8/18/79
RUDD, Jonathan - 7/25/77; 10/2/78
RUDD, Samuel - 7/25/77
RUDE, Zephaniah - 5/8/78
RUSS, Stephen - 4/25/77
RUSSEL, Rev. David - 10/20/79
RUSSEL, Elisha - 10/10/77
RUSSEL, Giles – 11/28/77; 10/20/79

RUSSEL, Prudence - 12/12/77
RUSSEL, William - 3/12/79
RUSSELL, Joseph - 9/25/78
RUSSELL, Lieutenant Colonel - 2/28/77
RUSSELL, Rev. Mr. – 3/6/78
RUTGARD, John - 5/22/78

S

SABIN, Jonathan - 3/7/77
SABIN, Zeb- 9/5/77
SAFFORD, Solomon - 1/10/77; 4/11/77
SAGE, Giles - 2/26/79
SAGE, Michael - 3/27/78
SAGE, Capt. Nathan - 11/27/78; - 1/1/79; 2/5/79; 2/12/79; 8/18/79; 10/6/79; 10/20/79; 11/24/79; 12/15/79
SAGE, Col. - 3/27/78; 6/5/78
SALISBURY, Jonathan - 11/6/78
SALMON, Jonathan - 8/14/78; 11/6/78
SALTER, John - 5/27/79
SALTONSTALL, Capt. Dudley - 3/7/77; 4/17/78; 5/8/78; 6/2/79
SALTONSTALL, Gilbert - 3/7/77
SALTONSTALL, Gen. Gurdon – 6/27/77; 12/19/77; 9/11/78; 7/1/79; 9/15/79; 10/20/79
SALTONSTALL, Nathaniel - 5/20/79; 7/1/79
SALTONSTALL, Roswell - 1/10/77; 8/22/77
SALTONSTALL, Winthrop - 1/17/77; 1/24/77; 2/21/77; 6/13/77; 6/20/77; 8/8/77; 9/5/77; 9/12/77; 9/19/77; 10/10/77; 11/14/77; 11/21/77;-4/17/78; 5/8/78; 5/22/78; 7/17/78; 9/25/78; 11/6/78; 2/12/79; 4/8/79; 4/22/79; 5/20/79; 7/1/79;

7/28/79; 8/11/79; 9/15/79; 10/20/79; 11/3/79; 11/24/79
SAM - 7/3/78
SANDLER, James - 9/25/78
SARLS, Thomas - 9/22/79
SAUNDERS, Jun., David – 3/13/78
SAVAGE, Capt. Abijah - 1/16/78
SAXTON, Judah - 5/23/77
SCOTT, Henry - 1/16/78
SCOVEL, Lemuel - 12/12/77
SCOVELL, Nathan - 1/10/77
SCRANTON, Thomas – 11/14/77
SCULL, John - 12/25/78
SCULL, Nicholas - 12/25/78
SEARE, Mr. - 4/25/77
SEARS, Edward - 12/25/78
SEBORD, Jacob - 7/18/77
SEIDMORE, Isaac - 5/22/78
SELDEN, Elijah - 1/24/77
SELDEN, Elisabeth - 6/13/77
SELDEN, Ezra - 1/24/77; 5/16/77; 6/20/77; 4/17/78; 5/27/79
SELDEN, Samuel - 6/13/77
SELDEN, Jun, Samuel - 6/13/77
SELDEN Selden, Col. - 2/21/77
SERGEANT, Capt. - 3/20/78
SETHSBEL, Mrs. Eunice - 1/22/79
SEYMOUR, Moses - 9/4/78
SELDEN, Capt. Thomas - 5/22/78
SELDEN, Col. - 5/2/77
Shadder, David - 5/22/78
SHAPELY, Adam - 4/10/78; 2/26/79; 11/17/79
SHAPELY, Daniel - 3/26/79
SHARPER - 7/4/77; 9/19/77
SHAUNEY, Mr. – 2/27/78
SHAW, Daniel - 10/17/77
SHAW, John - 12/25/78

SHAW, Nathaniel - 7/25/77; 5/1/78; 9/11/78; 12/18/78; 4/15/79; 5/20/79; 5/27/79; 9/15/79
SHAW, Jun., Nathaniel - 1/3/77; 3/7/77; 4/11/77; 10/10/77; 4/17/78; Shaw, Thomas - 4/17/78; 2/19/79; 4/29/79
SHAW, Mr. - 8/21/78; 7/8/79
SHEFFIELD, George - 2/28/77; 3/13/78
SHEFFIELD, James - 8/22/77; 3/13/78
SHELDEN, Katherine - 7/24/78
SHELDON, Col. Elisha - 5/22/78
SHEPARD, Joseph - 5/20/79
SHEPARD, Col. William - 3/5/79
SHEPARD, John - 8/15/77
SHEPPARD, John - 1/10/77
SHERBURNE, Col. Henry - 1/16/78; 2/19/79; 3/5/79
SHERMAN, Christopher - 4/4/77
SHERRIL, Henry - 4/11/77
SHERRY, Roger - 2/21/77
SHERWOOD, Mr. – 3/6/78
SHIPMAN, Capt. B. - 7/8/79
SHIPMAN, Edward - 5/20/79
SHIPMAN, John - 9/15/79
SHIPMAN Jun., John - 1/22/79; 2/12/79
SHIPMAN, Samuel - 1/22/79
SHOLES, Levi – 11/7/77
SHORT, John - 1/17/77
SI - 5/27/79
SILBER, Nathaniel - 12/25/78
SILL, Richard - 1/17/77; 3/7/77
SIMINDS, Jacob - 2/21/77
SIMONDS, Benjamin - 12/25/78
SIMONS, Remembrance - 9/19/77
SKINNER, Jonathan - 7/21/79
SKINNER, William - 4/11/77; 9/12/77

SLUMAN, Joseph - 9/5/77; 12/26/77
SMEDLEY, Samuel - 4/29/79
SMEDLEY, Capt. - 4/18/77; 4/25/77; 8/14/78
SMITH, Abilzer - 7/4/77
SMITH, Amos. - 4/8/79
SMITH, Anna - 7/24/78
SMITH, Basheba - 4/1/79
SMITH, Charles - 4/25/77; 8/28/78
SMITH, Christopher - 4/11/77
SMITH, Daniel - 12/25/78
SMITH, David - 1/15/79
SMITH, Edward - 6/19/78
SMITH, Ephraim – 12/5/77
SMITH, Ezeckiel - 2/21/77
SMITH, Hez. – 12/26/77
SMITH, Jabez - 2/7//77
SMITH Jun., Jabez - 2/21/79
SMITH, Captain James - 8/15/77; 5/22/78; 2/12/79
SMITH 2d, James - 2/26/79
SMITH, John - 1/17/77; 7/18/77; 9/25/78; 12/25/78; 11/17/79
SMITH, Josiah - 4/29/79; 11/17/79
SMITH, Joseph - 11/13/78; 4/22/79
SMITH, Moses - 8/22/77
SMITH, Nathan – 3/13/78
SMITH, Jun., Nathan – 11/7/77
SMITH, Lt. Nehemiah - 8/25/79
SMITH, Oliver - 4/11/77; 6/27/77; 10/2/78; 11/13/78; 5/20/79; 6/23/79
SMITH, Remembrance - 11/17/79
SMITH, Dr. Reuben - 7/8/79
SMITH, Seth – 12/5/77
SMITH, Capt. Simeon - 5/20/79
SMITH, Capt. - 3/14/77
SMITH, Mrs. - 1/15/79

SMITH, Mr. - 7/24/78
SOLLY, Nathan - 8/8/77
SOPER, John - 5/16/77
SOULE, Jonathan - 5/1/78
SOULE, Mary - 5/1/78
SOUTHWORTH, Constant - 5/27/79
SOUTHWORTH, Martin - 1/31/77
SPALDING, Ebenezer - 12/4/78
SPENCE, William - 7/28/79
SPENCER, Amaziah - 2/14/77
SPENCER, David - 1/24/77
SPENCER, Ebenezer - 9/5/77; 12/26/77
SPENCER, Isaac - 1/24/77
SPENCER, Simeon - 8/14/78
SPICER, Nathan - 10/10/77
SPINK, Richard - 5/1/78
Spooner, Basheba - 7/10/78
Spooner, Joshua - 6/12/78; 7/10/78
SQUIRE, Isaac - 4/11/77
SQUIRES, Francis - 9/15/79; 10/20/79
STANIS, William - 12/25/78
STANLEY, Jun., Caleb - 10/27/79
STANNARD, Peter - 4/10/78
STANTON, Amariah - 12/15/79
STANTON, Amos - 6/20/77
STANTON, Andrew - 9/25/78; 5/13/79
STANTON, Anne - 7/31/78
STANTON, Isaac - 7/31/78; 12/15/79
STANTON, John - 10/20/79; 11/24/79
STANTON, Joseph - 3/27/78
STANTON, Capt. Nathaniel - 6/27/77; 7/24/78
STANTON, Lt. Robert - 5/13/79
STANTON, 2d Samuel - 6/20/77
STANTON, Sarah - 9/25/78

STANTON, Capt. Theophilus - 6/19/78; 7/31/78
STANTON, Thomas. – 11/21/77; 12/12/77; 12/15/79
STANTON, 2d, Thomas - 5/9/77
STANTON, 4th, Thomas - 1/17/77
STANTON, Col. - 2/7//77
STANTON, Mr. - 7/24/78
STANUAR, Mr. - 7/24/78
STAPLES, Capt. - 9/19/77
STARK, William - 4/11/77
STARKWEATHER, Joseph - 9/29/79
STARR, Elijah – 12/5/77
STARR, Capt. Jabez - 8/18/79
STARR, Jun., James - 3/27/78
STARR, Jonathan - 8/22/77; 7/1/79
STARR, Joshua - 1/17/77; 3/6/78; 7/17/78
STARR, Richard - 4/10/78
STARR, Thomas - 3/27/78
STARR, Col. - 2/5/79; 10/20/79
STAUGHER, Mr. - 11/24/79
STEDMAN, James - 7/4/77; 9/19/77
STEDMAN, Nathan - 1/10/77; 5/30/77; 8/4/79
STEDMIN, Benj. - 10/10/77
STEELWOOD, Richard - 12/25/78
STERRY, Roger - 2/21/77; 8/14/78
STEVENS, Elnathan - 1/3/77; 2/7/77
STEWART, Duncan - 7/4/77
STEWART, Stephen - 12/25/78
STEWART, William - 1/10/77; 4/18/77; 10/17/77; 7/17/78; 12/11/78; 5/6/79; 6/23/79; 12/15/79
STICKLAND, Samuel - 11/24/79

STILMAN, Capt. - 4/25/77; 7/18/77
STOCKHOLM, Capt. Amos - 7/4/77
STOCKHOLM, Andrew - 4/29/79
STOCKIN, Elisha - 1/16/78
STOCKIN, Zebelulon - 1/16/78
STODDARD, Ichabod - 1/10/77
STODDARD, Israel - 5/20/79
STODDARD, James – 11/14/77
STODDARD, John - 9/11/78; 10/9/78
STODDARD, Lucretia - 9/22/79
STODDARD, Nathan - 2/19/79; 3/5/79
STODDARD, Ralph - 1/3/77; 11/14/77
STODDARD, Richard, Capt. - 6/9/79
STODDARD, Mr. - 6/26/78
STONE, Henry - 8/14/78
STONE, William - 4/29/79; 11/17/79
STORRS, Dan - 11/27/78
STORRS, Capt. Exp. - 5/20/79
STORY, William - 2/26/79
STRAIGHT, William - 8/14/78
STRICKLAND, Peter- 8/15/77; 1/30/78
STRICKLAND, Thomas - 1/3/77
STRONG, Beriah - 4/18/77
STRONG, Hephzibah - 2/6/78
STRONG, Jedediah - 10/24/77; 2/6/78
STRONG, Joseph - 3/27/78; 2/26/79
SULLIVAN, F. - 5/20/79
SULLIVAN, Maj. Gen. - 2/26/79
SUMMER, Samuel - 4/10/78
SUMMER, Lt. George - 11/6/78
SUNDAY, Nathaniel - 8/14/78
SWAN, Jesse - 8/25/78
SWAN Swan, John - 4/4/77;

SWAN Swain, Paul - 1/1/79
SWAN Swan, Robert - 5/2/77
SWAN Swan, Thomas - 6/27/77; 7/4/77;
SWAN Swan, Timothy - 12/11/78
SWIFT, John -8/21/78
SWIFT, Thomas - 10/2/78
SWIFT, Col. - 4/29/79

T

TABER, Job - 8/21/78
TABER, Samuel - 1/17/77; 4/18/77; 4/24/78; 6/9/79
TABOR, Pardon - 2/21/77; 2/28/77; 4/4/77
TAINTER, John - 1/3/77; 1/10/77; 1/23/78; 2/6/78
TAINTER, Mr. - 7/24/78
TALBOT, Capt. Silas - 11/6/78; 8/11/79; 9/15/79; 10/20/79
TALLCOTT, Matthew - 10/10/77
TALLMAN, Benjamin - ½9/79; 2/5/79
TALLY, Samuel - 1/22/79
TALMAN, Samuel - 6/20/77
TAYLOR, Jared - 6/19/78
TAYLOR, John - 6/2/79
TAYLOR, Samuel - 10/31/77
TAYLORr, William - 9/25/78
TEEFRY, William - 12/25/78
TERRET, William - 1/9/78
TESTER, Mr. - 4/29/79
TEW, Capt. Henry - 1/10/77; 11/17/79
TEW, Paul - 3/7/77; 7/21/79
THAYER, George - 4/29/79
THOMAS, Absalom - 10/13/79
THOMAS, Ebenezer - 4/11/77
THOMAS, Henry - 9/25/78
THOMPSON, Charles - 4/29/79

THOMPSON, Nathan - 9/5/77; 7/24/78; 1/8/79
THOMPSON, Thomas - 2/26/79
THOMSON, Charles- 1/30/78; 2/6/78
THOMSON, James - 4/3/78
THOMSON, John - 11/10/79
THOMSON, Robert - 8/14/78
THOMSON, Mr. - 7/24/78
THORP, Andrew - 8/14/78
THROOP, Jun., Benjamin - 1/24/77
THROOP, Dan - 2/19/79
THROOP, Col. - 7/25/77
THURBER, Benjamin - 10/20/79
THURSTON, George– 11/14/77; 3/27/78
TIER, James - 9/25/78
TIFFANY, Timothy- 4/18/77; 5/8/78
TILDALE, Elijah - 4/4/77
TILDEN, Daniel - 1/16/78
TILLER, James - 2/6/78
TILLEY, John - 5/6/79
TILLEY, Joseph - 6/2/79
TILLY, James - 12/12/77
TILTON, John - 5/20/79
TINKER, 3rd, John - 1/3/77
TINKER, Edward - 4/11/77; - 10/2/78
TINKER, Capt. Jehiel - 8/22/77
TINKER, Stephen - 9/5/77
TINKER, Sylvanus - 6/5/78; 7/31/78; 12/8/79
TINKER, William - 10/10/77
TISDEL, Elkanah - 5/20/79
TITUS, Timothy - 8/14/78
TOBET, Samuel - 5/22/78
TOM - 6/12/78
TOMPSON, James - 6/2/79
TOMPSON, Capt. - 10/10/77
TONE, Mr. - 7/24/78
TORTOCOLOM, Barn. - 8/14/78

TOTTON, James - 4/29/79
TOUSE, Sgt. John - 3/20/78
TOUSSONT, Louis - 10/27/79
TOZER, Jun., Samuel – 1/3/77; 1/23/78
TRACY, Dr. Elisha - 6/20/77
TRACY, Frederick - 7/14/79
TRACY, Jabez - 5/15/78
TRACY, Dr. Jedidiah - 6/16/79
TRACY, John - 1/24/77
TRACY, Samuel - 2/21/77
Trayer, Nicholas - 12/25/78
Treman, Henry - 2/5/79
Trffin, Joshua - 1/16/78
Tripp, James - 2/6/78
Truman, Jonathan - 7/24/78
TRUMBULL, David – 4/4/77; 3/13/78; 4/24/78; 12/11/78
TRUMBULL, Governor - 2/28/77; 4/18/77; 4/25/77; 5/16/77; 4/3/78; 7/31/78; 8/11/79; 10/20/79
TRUMBULL, Col. Joseph - 5/1/78; 7/31/78
TRYON, Major - 4/24/78
TUCKER, Job - 1/3/77
TUCKER, Samuel - 1/3/77
TULLY, Mr. - 8/11/79
TURNER, Isaac - 6/9/79
TURNER, James - 10/23/78
TURNER, John - 5/9/77; 12/25/78
TURNER, Matthew - 10/23/78
TURNER, Thomas - 4/25/77
TURNER, Wm. - 9/5/77
TYLER, Abraham - 4/25/77
TYLER, Elisha - 10/10/77
TYLER, Joseph – 11/28/77; 5/13/79
TYLER, Capt. Moses - 10/9/78
TYLER, Brig. Maj. Gen - 7/1/79; 7/21/79
TYLER, Col. - 5/16/77

U
UNDERWOOD, James - 1/15/79
UNDERWOOD, William - 1/9/78

V
VAIL, Capt. John - 9/5/77
VANCE, William - 11/17/79
VANFANT, Christopher - 4/4/77
VAUGN, John - 3/7/77
VEIL, Capt. Joseph - 5/8/78
VENDIERO, Thomas - 12/25/78
VENTRUS, John - 4/25/77
VERUM, General - 7/24/78
VIVEE, Peter - 10/20/79

W
WADE, Capt. - 5/8/78
WAIT, Daniel - 2/21/77; 4/18/77; 10/3/7
WAIT, Marvin - 1/17/77; 3/7/77; 4/11/77; 10/17/77; 1/16/78; 8/14/78; 2/19/79; 4/29/79; 5/13/79; 11/17/79
WAIT, Jun., Richard - 12/11/78; 11/17/79
WAIT, Thomas - 2/28/77; 3/14/77
WAITEMOUR 3d, William - 8/14/78
WALCH, Thomas - 2/7//77
WALES, Ebenezer - 2/21/77; 5/9/77
WALES, Elisha – 12/19/77
WALES, Capt. Nathaniel - 5/20/79
WALES Jr., Nathaniel - 7/28/79
WALKER, Jonathan - 5/23/77
WALKER, Joseph - 5/27/79

WALLACE, Sir James - 3/21/77; 7/3/78
WALLS, Col. Jonathan - 9/22/79; 9/29/79
WALTON, Jun., William - 8/14/78
WARD, Billious - 9/25/78
WARD, Ebenenzer - 12/25/78
WARD, John - 9/5/77
WARD, Samuel - 2/14/77
WARD, William - 9/25/78
WARNER, Oliver - 4/29/79
WARNER, Seth - 10/20/79; 11/24/79
WARNER, Capt. - 10/6/79
WARREN, Joseph - 4/8/79
WARREN, Moses - 3/19/79
WARRIN, Ephraim - 8/14/78
WASHINGTON, George - 1/3/77; 2/28/77; 11/27/78
WASSEEN, John - 8/14/78
WATERMAN; Mrs. Bashseba - 1/22/79
WATERMAN, Elazer - 4/11/77
WATERMAN, Joseph - 3/27/78; 1/22/79; 5/13/79
WATERMAN, Jno. - 2/21/77
WATERMAN, Richard - 7/28/79
WATERMAN, Mr. – 2/13/78
WATERS, William - 5/2/77
WATERS, Mr. - 7/24/78
WATROUS, Gurdun - 10/13/79
WATTLES, Andrew - 6/6/77
WATTLES, William - 9/15/79
WATTLES, Capt. - 4/25/77
WAY, Jun., Ebenezer - 1/16/78
WEAVER, William - 4/29/79; 11/17/79
WEBB, James - 1/16/78
WEBB, Joseph - 5/2/77
WEBB, Josiah - 12/25/78
WEBB, Nathaniel -2/21/77; 5/2/77; 5/9/77

WEBB, Thomas - 12/25/78
WEBB, Col. - 5/9/77; 5/23/77; 10/3/77; 12/26/77
WEBB, Mr. - 7/24/78
WEBSTER, George - 5/22/78
WEBSTER, Israel - 5/16/77
WEBSTER, P. - 5/16/77
WEGLOW, Pater - 5/22/78
WELCH, John - 2/19/79
WELCH, William - 4/24/78
WELD, Rev. Aeljah - 3/21/77
WELD, John - 3/21/77
WELDEN, Capt. - 9/29/79
WELLES, Col. - 12/22/79
WELLS, Amos - 1/3/77
WELLS, Anthony - 11/17/79
WELLS John Howell - 1/10/77
WESCOT, Eleazer - 6/6/77
WESCOTE, Capt. John - 2/6/78
WESCOTT, Capt. Jabez - 12/12/77
WEST, David - 5/16/77
WEST, Judah - 2/5/79
WESTON, Elijah - 10/2/78
WETMORE, Prosper - 7/11/77; 9/5/77; 10/10/77; 11/7/77; 12/11/78
WHALEY, Alex. - 4/29/79
WHEAT, Samuel - 8/11/79
WHEATLEY, Andrew - 2/7/77; 2/21/77; 5/16/77
WHEATLEY Wheatley, Jane - 2/7//77; 5/16/77
WHEATLEY Wheatley, John - 2/7//77 ; 5/16/77
WHEATON, Comfort – 12/19/77
WHEELER, Hosea - 12/12/77
WHEELER, Charles - 4/22/79; 9/22/79
WHEELER, Cyrus - 6/13/77
WHEELER, Hosea - 2/6/78
WHEELER, John - 10/10/77
WHEELER, Paul - 7/3/78

WHEELER, Obidiah - 4/15/79
WHEELER, Paul - 6/13/77
WHEELER, Thomas - 6/27/77
WHEELER, William - 11/13/78
WHEELER, Mr. - 7/24/78
WHEELOCK, Rev. Eleazar – 3/13/78
WHIPPLE, Abraham - 2/26/79
WHIPPLE, Christopher – 12/26/77; 2/27/78
WHIPPLE, David – 11/28/77
WHIPPLE, Isaaih – 1/2/78; 12/19/77
WHIPPLE, Thomas - 5/2/77; 3/27/78; 11/17/79
WHITE, Aaron - 1/30/78
WHITE, Alexander - 12/29/79
WHITE, Amos - 4/25/77; 7/17/78; 2/26/79
WHITE, Enoch - 4/4/77
WHITE, Jacob - 3/7/77; 1/8/79
WHITEMORE, Daniel - 8/22/77
WHITING, William - 4/18/77; 11/14/77; 4/10/78
WHITMAN, Col. - 2/26/79
WHITNEY, Matthias - 8/14/78
WHITNEY, Nehemiah - 8/14/78
WHITNEY, Capt. William - 8/25/79; 9/22/79
WHITNEY, Capt. - 7/17/78
WHITTLESEY, Azihiah - 9/15/79; 12/8/79
WHITTLESEY, Chauncey - 7/8/79; 8/11/79
WHITTLESEY, Newton - 7/8/79
WHITTLESEY, Capt. - 10/6/79
WICK, Sylvanus - 7/24/78
WICKHAM, Thomas - 1/10/77
WIEMPAY, Charles - 5/23/77
WIFT, Col. - 6/6/77
WIGGER, Ely - 12/11/78
WIGHTMAN, Allen – 11/14/77
WILEY, John - 4/25/77

WILLIAM, Joseph – 11/14/77
WILLIAMS, Capt. Amariah - 5/27/79
WILLIAMS, Amos - 4/18/77
WILLIAMS, Elisha - 1/10/77; 4/11/77
WILLIAMS, Elizabeth. -- 11/21/77; 11/21/77
WILLIAMS, George - 6/27/77; 7/4/77
WILLIAMS, Capt. Henry - 3/5/79
WILLIAMS, Jonathan - 8/22/77
WILLIAMS, John -5/23/77; 2/6/78; 4/17/78; 11/13/78; 11/27/78; 6/23/79
WILLIAMS 3d, John - 12/19/77; 2/26/79; 9/22/79
WILLIAMS, Joseph - 8/14/78; 7/14/79
WILLIAMS, Mary - 11/13/78
WILLIAMS, Nathaniel - 1/3/77
WILLIAMS Jun., Nathaniel - 6/20/77
WILLIAMS, Robert - 2/21/77
WILLIAMS, Thomas - 7/4/77; 10/31/77
WILLIAMS, William - 7/8/79; 11/3/79
WILLIAMS, Lt. Zedock - 9/19/77
WILLIAMS, Rev. Mr. – 3/6/78
WILLIAMS, Col. - 5/2/77; - 5/15/78
WILLIAMS, Jun, Ensign - 1/10/77
WILLIS, Nathaniel - 4/18/77
WILLOUGHBY, Elijah - 5/22/78
WILLSON, John - 8/14/78
WILSON, David - 10/3/77
WILSON, Jonathan - 3/27/78
WILSON, Joshua - 7/18/77
WILSON, Marham - 9/25/78
WILSON, Thomas - 12/4/78; 2/26/79; 4/29/79

WINSLOW, Isaac - 5/27/79
WINTER, Timothy - 11/6/78
WINTHROP, Joseph - 12/11/78
WINTWORTH, William - 4/18/77
WISTER, Nathan – 1/2/78
WITTER, Jacob - 10/20/79
WITTER Witter, Lt. Nathan – 12/26/77
WOMPEY, John - 2/14/77
WOOD, Ebenezer - 11/17/79
WOOD, John - 9/29/79
WOOD, Thomas - 8/14/78
WOODBRIDGE, Miss Charlotte - 12/29/79
WOODBRIDGE, Dudley - 1/9/78; 1/16/78; 6/2/79; 8/4/79; 12/29/79
WOODBRIDGE, Joseph - 7/17/78; 7/24/78; 12/4/78
WOODBRIDGE, Paul - 12/18/78; 10/20/79
WOODBRIDGE, Jun. Paul - 12/18/78
WOODBRIDGE, Samuel - 1/9/78; 6/2/79; 8/4/79
WOODBRIDGE, Sarah - 10/20/79
WOODBRIDGE, William - 1/10/77
WOODBURY, James - 12/25/78
WOODER - 11/3/79
WOODWARD, Sarah - 8/4/79
WOODWORTH, - 2/7//77
WOOLMAN, Mills - 4/29/79
WOOLSEY, Phineas - 12/25/78
WOOSTER, Maj. Gen. - 5/9/77
WORTHINGTON, Elias - 1/3/77; 7/18/77
WORTHINGTON, Jun., Elias – ½3/78; 2/6/78
WORTHINGTON, Col. William - 5/20/79
WRIGHT, Miss Demise - 7/25/77

WRIGHT, Lt. Dudley - 6/13/77; 7/25/77; 8/8/77; 12/5/77
WRIGHT, Ebenezer - 7/10/78
WRIGHT, Joel - 3/14/77
WRIGHT, John - 5/9/77; 6/27/77; 8/8/77
WRIGHT, Jun., John - 10/31/77
WRIGHT, Joseph - 5/16/77
WRIGHT, Lydia - 3/14/77
WRIGHT Wright, Capt. Seth - 3/14/77
WRIGHT, Capt. – 2/27/78

WYLIE, Ensign John - 12/12/77; 2/6/78
WYLLYS, Col - 4/24/78; 5/1/78
WYLLYS, Mr. - 5/2/77; 5/23/77; 6/13/77

Y

YEAMONS, David – 12/5/77
YELDALL, Dr. - 5/16/77
YOUNG, Elijah - 8/14/78

PLACE NAMES

Albany - 10/10/77; 3/27/78
Antigua - 6/12/78
Antirim, Ireland - 6/2/79
Ashford - 3/14/77; 4/4/77; 4/25/77; 12/19/77; 12/26/77; 3/27/78; /24/78; 8/14/78; 11/27/78; - 3/12/79; 4/1/79; 5/20/79

Baltimore - 12/25/78
Barbados - 1/31/77; 4/17/78
Bay State - 10/13/79
Beakman Patent – 11/7/77
Bedford - 1/31/77; 4/18/77; 5/30/77; 12/12/77; 6/5/78; 6/12/78; 3/5/79
Bermuda - 6/19/78; 7/8/79; 9/15/79; 10/6/79; 10/20/79
Beverly - 12/25/78
Black Rock - 6/6/77
Block Island - 4/25/77; 8/22/77; 6/12/78; 6/19/78; 4/15/79
Blue Point; - 10/6/79; 10/13/79
Bolton - 6/6/77; 5/22/78; 6/16/79
Boston - 4/18/77; 5/30/77; 8/22/77; 9/19/77; 12/26/77; 2/13/78; 2/27/78; 5/8/78; 6/26/78; 8/28/78; 9/25/78; 10/16/78; 11/20/78; 12/4/78; 12/25/78; 5/27/79; 6/2/79; 7/1/79; 7/28/79; 8/18/79; 8/25/79; 9/15/79; 10/20/79; 10/27/79; 12/29/79
Branford - 7/24/78; 7/1/79
Canaan - 9/1/79
Canada Society of Windham - 9/19/77; 9/11/78
Canterbury - 2/21/77; 3/21/77; 6/20/77; 7/4/77; 8/15/77; 9/5/77; 10/24/77; 12/26/77; 5/1/78; 5/29/78; 6/26/78; 7/24/78; 8/14/78; 9/18/78; 12/4/78; 12/11/78; 12/25/78; 7/28/79; 8/25/79; 10/13/79
Cape Ann - 8/8/77; 12/25/78
Cape Francois - 5/27/79
Cape Hatteras - 2/21/77
Cape May - 8/8/77
Cedar Hill - 2/26/79
Chapel's Hill, in New London - 4/3/78
Charleston, South Carolina – 1/23/78; 12/25/78
Charlestown, Rhode Island - 3/21/77; 7/11/77
Chatham - 1/10/77; 4/4/77; 4/11/77; 5/23/77; 9/5/77; 10/31/77; 11/7/77;12/12/77 4/24/78; 5/1/78; 5/15/78; 6/12/78; 8/14/78
Chelsea in Norwich - 1/10/77; 7/17/78
Cheshire - 7/17/78
Chester, Saybrook - 7/28/79

Chesterfield Society in Lyme - 1/3/77; 5/9/77; 8/29/77; 10/31/77; 11/21/77
Chesterfield, New London - 5/9/77; 6/13/77
City Island, NY - 4/10/78
Coaxet in Dartmouth - 4/17/78
Cohas - 4/10/78
Cohasset, Massachusetts - 8/8/77
Colchester - 1/3/77; 1/10/77; 3/7/77; 4/4/77; 5/9/77; 5/16/77; 6/6/77; 6/27/77; 7/11/77; 7/18/77; 7/25/77; 8/8/77; 11/21/77; 12/5/77; 12/19/77; 1/23//78; 1/30/78; 2/6/78; 5/15/78; 5/22/78; 7/24/78; 8/14/78; 8/28/78; 10/2/78; 11/27/78; 2/5/79; 3/5/79; 3/12/79; 5/6/79; 5/13/79; 5/20/79; 6/9/79; 7/8/79; 7/28/79; 9/8/79; 12/22/79; 12/29/79
Colchester, Westchester Parish - 3/5/79; 3/12/79
Connecticut River - 2/21/77; 2/28/77; 3/7/77; 7/18/77; 2/6/78; 2/20/78; 6/12/78; 9/11/78; 12/4/78; 8/11/79; 9/1/79; 10/13/79; 12/8/79
Cork - 7/1/79; 9/15/79
Coventry - 3/21/77; 5/9/77; 5/23/77; 8/22/77; 10/3/77; 10/31/77; 11/28/77; 2/6/78; 5/20/79; 7/28/79; 9/1/79; 9/15/79; 10/13/79; 10/27/79; 11/17/79; 12/1/79
Coventry, North Parish - 4/25/77

Crane's Island, Long Island - 10/24/77

Danbury - 5/9/77; 10/20/79
Darby - 6/6/77
Dartmouth - 4/17/78
Delaware - 1/9/78
Delaware River - 1/3/77; 6/19/78
Dominica - 5/30/77; 9/19/77
Dudley, Massachusetts - 12/1/79

East Guilford - 10/23/78
East Haddam - 1/3/77; 1/10/77; 1/17/77; 1/31/77; 2/14/77; 4/4/77; 4/11/77; 4/18/77; 4/25/77; 5/16/77; 7/18/77; 8/8/77; 8/22/77; 9/5/77; 9/12/77; 10/3/77; 10/17/77; 10/24/77; 10/31/77; 11/7/77; 11/14/77; 12/19/77; 12/26/77; 1/16/78; 1/30/78; 2/6/78; 2/13/78; 3/20/78; 3/27/78; 5/1/78; 5/15/78; 6/5/78; 6/12/78; 7/24/78; 7/31/78; 8/21/78; 9/18/78; 10/2/78; 12/4/78; 7/28/79; 8/4/79; 8/25/79; 9/1/79; 9/22/79; 11/3/79; 11/10/79; 11/24/79; 12/15/79
East Haddam Landing - 2/26/79; 12/8/79
East Haddam, Millington Parish - 1/10/77; 4/25/77; 6/6/77; 10/17/77; 7/24/78; 11/27/78
East Hartford - 11/3/79

East Haven - 7/24/78
East Indies - 4/25/77
Egg Harbor - 12/25/78; 9/29/79
Eight Mile River - 4/11/77
Enfield - 6/20/77; 11/14/77; 2/13/78
Eustatia - 12/25/78
Exeter, Rhode Island - 5/22/78; 5/6/79

Fairfield - Ct. 1/10/77; 6/6/77; 7/24/78
Fairfield, Virginia - 12/25/78
Farmington - 4/25/77; 5/23/77; 9/5/77; 3/20/78
Fire Island Inlet - 5/15/78; 6/12/78
Fisher's Island - 2/7//77; 3/14/77; 3/21/77; 7/25/77; 8/1/77; 8/29/77; 9/19/77; 7/21/79
Fisher's Island Point - 7/1/79
Fisher's Island Sound - 3/7/77
Fishkill - 3/20/78; 7/8/79
Four Mile River - 10/20/79
France - 2/21/77; 6/27/77; 12/26/77; 3/13/78; 5/29/78; 12/25/78; 2/19/79

Gales Ferry - 8/15/77; 8/22/77; 1/16/78; 2/6/78
Gardiner's Bay - 3/26/79
Gardiner's Island - 1/10/77; 2/21/77; 12/18/78; 3/26/79; 4/8/79
Georgia - 1/9/78

Germantown - 6/2/79
Glasgow - 7/1/79
Goshen - 10/10/77; 12/26/77; 2/19/79
Goshen in Lebanon - 2/5/79;
Goshen, New London, Great Neck – 3/6/78
Goshen Point - 2/26/79
Goshen Reef - 7/25/77; 5/1/78
Governors Island - 4/10/78
Greenwich New Town, Rhode Island - 1/1/79
Groton - 1/3/77; 1/10/77; 1/17/77; 11/24/77; 1/31/77; 2/14/77; 3/14/77; 3/21/77; 4/4/77; 4/11/77; 5/9/77; 5/16/77; 5/23/77; 5/30/77; 6/13/77; 6/20/77; 7/4/77; 8/15/77; - 8/22/77; 8/29/77; 9/5/77; 9/12/77; 9/26/77; 10/10/77; 10/31/77; 11/7/77; 11/14/77; 11/28/77; 12/5/77; 12/12/77; 12/19/77; 1/2/78; 1/16/78; ½3/78; 2/6/78; 2/27/78; 3/13/78; 3/20/78; 3/27/78; 4/3/78; 4/17/78; 5/1/78; 7/3/78; 7/17/78; 7/24/78; 7/31/78; 8/5/78; 8/14/78; 8/28/78; 9/11/78; 9/18/78; 10/2/78; 12/4/78; 12/11/78; 12/18/78; 12/25/78; 1/1/79; 1/8/79; 1/15/79; 1/22/79; 1/29/79; 2/26/79; 4/15/79; 4/22/79; 4/29/79; 5/13/79; 5/20/79; 6/16/79; 6/23/79; 7/8/79; 7/21/79; 8/4/79; 8/18/79; 8/25/79; 9/1/79; 9/22/79; 9/29/79; 10/13/79; 10/20/79;

11/17/79; 12/1/79; 12/15/79; 12/29/79
Groton, First Society– 3/13/78; 4/10/78
Guadloupe - 5/30/77
Guilford - 6/20/77; 7/24/78; 1/22/79; 4/15/79; 7/1/79; 7/28/79
Guinea - 4/25/77

Haddam - 1/10/77; 1/31/77; 4/25/77; 1/23/78
Hadlyme - 1/10/77
Halifax - 5/30/77; 4/17/78; 9/15/79
Hanover Parish, Norwich - 5/30/77
Hartford – 3/21/77; 5/2/77; 5/9/77; 10/10/77; 2/13/78; 2/27/78; 5/1/78; 6/5/78; 3/5/79; 3/12/79
Hartford County – 2/13/78
Hartford Ferry - 10/27/79
Hartford West Division - 9/29/79
Harvard in Worcester county - 4/24/78
Hebron - 1/17/77 ; 9/19/77; 2/20/78; 4/24/78; 5/8/78; 8/14/78; 7/8/79; 10/20/79; 12/8/79; 12/29/79
Hebron, First Society - 5/8/78 - 5/8/78
Hell Gate - 7/25/77
Hispaniola - 2/21/77
Hoboken, NJ - 1/29/79
Hoebuck - 1/29/79

Hopkinton - 1/10/77; 4/25/77; 1/14/77; 3/20/78; 3/27/78; 9/22/79
Horse Shoe Shoal - 12/29/79
Huntington, Long Island - 7/4/77; 9/18/78

Ireland - 2/7//77; 6/13/77; 4/24/78; 6/2/79

Jamaica - 9/19/77; 12/26/77; 1/16/78 3/6/78; 6/12/78; 9/15/79; 10/20/79
Johnson, Rhode Island– 11/14/77
Jordan Bridge - 2/7//77
Jordan Plain, New London - 4/29/79

Killingly - 5/16/77; 9/5/77; 9/19/77; 12/19/77;1/9/78; 3/6/78; 3/27/78; 5/1/78; 6/19/78; 7/17/78; 7/24/78; 8/14/78; 12/11/78; 1/15/79; 1/22/79; 5/20/79; 7/21/79
Killingsworth - 1/3/77; 2/7//77; 2/21/77; 2/28/77; 6/20/77; 9/12/77; 7/24/78; 11/13/78; 5/20/79
Killingsworth, North Parish - 10/20/79
Kinderhock - 10/10/77,
King County, Rhode Island. – 11/28/77; 3/27/78

Lancaster - 12/25/78
Lebanon - 1/3/77; 1/10/77;
3/14/77; 4/4/77; 4/25/77;
5/16/77; 5/30/77; 6/6/77;
6/13/77; 6/20/77; 10/3/77;
10/24/77; 12/12/77; 1/16/78;
2/6/78; 3/13/78; 4/10/78;
4/24/78; 7/17/78; 7/24/78;
7/31/78; 8/14/78; 10/2/78;
12/11/78; 2/5/79; 2/19/79;
2/26/79; 5/20/79; 6/2/79;
7/28/79; 10/13/79; 10/20/79;
12/22/79
Lebanon, Goshen Society -
12/22/79
Lichfield - 7/8/79
Lincoln Township, New
Hampshire - 10/9/78
Litchfield County - 10/10/77;
12/26/77; 9/4/78
Liverpool - 10/10/77
London - 9/19/77; 5/8/78;
9/15/79; 10/20/79
Long Bridge - 8/22/77
Long Island Sound - 3/21/77;
5/9/77; 5/23/77; 5/30/77
7/25/77; 8/1/77; 10/24/77;
2/6/78; 9/4/78; 9/11/78;
12/4/78; 2/5/79; 3/26/79;
4/8/79
Long Island - 1/10/77;
2/7/77; 3/7/77; 4/11/77;
7/4/77 ; 8/1/77; 9/12/77;
10/24/77; 10/31/77;
12/26/77; 1/30/78; 2/6/78;
2/20/78; 2/27/78; 3/6/78.
3/20/78; 4/10/78; 4/24/78;
5/15/78; 8/14/78; 9/18/78;
12/4/78; 12/25/78; 2/5/79;
2/12/79; 3/12/79; 3/26/79;

6/16/79; 8/11/79; 9/22/79;
10/6/79; 10/13/79
Long Point, Stonington -
3/12/79
Lyme - 1/3/77; 1/10/77;
1/31/77; 2/7/77; 2/28/77;
3/14/77; 4/4/77; 4/11/77;
4/18/77; 5/9/77; 5/16/77;
6/6/77; 6/13/77; 6/20/77;
6/27/77; 7/4/77; 7/11/77;
8/22/77; 8/29/77; 9/5/77;
9/12/77; 1/8/79; 2/19/79;
3/12/79; 3/19/79; /8/79;
4/15/79; 5/20/79; 5/27/79;
7/14/79; 7/28/79; 9/15/79;
10/20/79; 11/3/79
Lyme, East Society - 4/25/77
Lyme, First Society -
6/12/78; 9/4/78; 11/27/78
Lyme, North Quarter –
11/21/77; 12/26/77; 5/8/78;
8/14/78
Lyme, Second Society -
3/14/77

Mammocock - 8/15/77;
10/27/79
Manchester, Eng. - 8/29/77
Manchester, Vermont -
10/13/79
Mansfield - 2/21/77; 6/27/77;
7/4/77; 9/5/77; 7/17/78;
8/5/78; 9/18/78; 10/2/78;
10/9/78; 11/27/78; 5/6/79;
5/20/79; 5/27/79; 9/1/79;
10/20/79
Mansfield, First Society –
5/16/77; 2/13/78

Mansfield, Old Society - 4/4/77
Marble Head, Massachusetts - 6/6/77; 7/18/77; 12/25/78
Marlborough in Colchester- 1/30/78
Marlbrough Society in Hebron - 1/17/77;
Martha's Vineyard – 2/13/78; 3/6/78
Martinico - 3/21/77; 4/17/78; 6/19/78
Maryland - 1/9/78; 12/25/78
Massachusetts - 2/7/77; 2/21/77; 5/9/77; 5/30/77; 6/6/77; 8/8/77; 12/25/78; 12/1/79; 4/22/79; 5/27/79
Massachusetts Bay - 1/9/78
Middletown - 1/10/77; 1/31/77; 3/7/77; 3/14/77; 5/23/77; 8/22/77; 9/19/77; 10/10/77; 11/7/77; 12/26/77; 1/16/78; 1/30/78; 2/6/78; 2/13/78; 2/27/78; 3/27/78; 4/24/78; 6/5/78; 6/19/78; 7/3/78; 8/14/78; 9/25/78; 11/27/78; 12/11/78; 12/25/78; 4/29/79; 7/8/79; 8/11/79; 8/18/79; 11/24/79; 12/15/79
Middletown, North Society of - 1/16/78
Middletown South Farms - 4/11/77
Middletown, Upper House - 6/19/78
Middletown, New Jersey - 2/28/77
Milford - 9/26/77; 7/24/78; 12/25/78

Millstone Point - 8/14/78
Mohegan - 8/15/77
Montauk Point - 6/19/78
Mount Pleasant in New London, Great Neck - 6/27/77; 7/11/77; 12/8/79
Mystic, Massachusetts - 5/9/77
Mystic River - 4/17/78; 7/24/78; 4/8/79; 5/13/79; 5/20/79; 9/1/79; 10/20/79

Nantes, France – 12/26/77
Nantucket - 12/25/78; 1/1/79; 12/29/79
Narragansett Beach - 8/22/77; 11/24/79
Narragansett - 2/7//77; 2/21/77; 5/16/77; 10/10/77; 8/21/78
New Concord - 11/17/79
New England – 3/6/78; 3/20/78; 6/12/78; 8/5/78
New Guilford - 2/6/78
New Hampshire - 1/9/78; 10/9/78
New Hartford - 10/10/77
New Haven - 1/3/77; 3/7/77; - 3/21/77; 5/9/77; 9/19/77; 6/12/78; 7/24/78; 7/31/78; 9/25/78; 12/25/78; 7/8/79; 7/1/79
New Jersey - 1/9/78; 12/25/78
New London - 1/3/77; 1/10/77; 1/17/77; 11/24/77; 1/31/77; 2/7//77; 2/21/77; 2/28/77; 3/7/77; 4/4/77; 4/11/77; 4/18/77; 4/25/77;

5/2/77; 5/9/77; 5/16/77; 5/23/77; 5/30/77; 6/6/77; 6/13/77; 6/20/77; 6/27/77; 7/4/77; 7/11/77; 7/18/77; 7/25/77; - 8/1/77; 8/8/77; 8/15/77; 8/22/77; 8/29/77; 9/5/77; 9/12/77; 9/19/77; 9/26/77 1/2/78; 1/16/78; 1/23/78; 1/30/78; 2/6/78; 2/13/78; 2/27/78; 3/6/78; 3/13/78; 3/27/78; 4/3/78; 4/10/78; 4/17/78; 4/24/78; 5/1/78; 5/8/78; 5/15/78; 5/22/78; 5/29/78; 6/5/78; 6/12/78; 6/19/78; 6/19/78; 6/26/78; 7/3/78; 7/17/78; 7/24/78; 8/5/78; 8/14/78;8/21/78; 8/28/78; 9/11/78; 9/18/78; 9/25/78; 10/2/78; 10/9/78; 10/16/78; 10/23/78; 11/13/78; 12/4/78; 12/11/78; 12/18/78; 12/25/78; 1/1/79; 1/8/79; 1/22/79; 1/29/79; 2/5/79; 2/12/79; 2/19/79; 2/26/79; 3/5/79; 3/12/79; 3/19/79; 3/26/79; 4/1/79; 4/8/79; 4/15/79 4/22/79; 4/29/79; 5/6/79 5/13/79; 5/20/79; 6/2/79; 6/9/79; 6/16/79; 7/1/79; 7/8/79; 7/14/79; 7/21/79; 7/28/79; 8/4/79; 8/11/79; 8/18/79; 8/25/79; 9/1/79; 9/8/79; 9/15/79; 9/22/79; 9/29/79; 10/13/79; 10/20/79; 10/27/79; 11/10/79; 11/17/79; 11/24/79; 12/1/79; 12/8/79; 12/15/79; 12/22/79; 12/29/79

New London, Chesterfield Society - 12/29/79
New London County - 5/9/77; 6/13/77; 9/5/77; 2/13/78; 4/17/78; 10/9/78; 11/6/78; 12/25/78; 2/12/79; 4/8/79; 4/22/79; 4/22/79; 5/20/79; 7/28/79; 8/11/79; 9/15/79; 10/20/79; 11/3/79
New London, Great Neck - 2/21/77; 2/28/77; 3/14/77; 4/11/77; 5/2/77; 6/27/77; 7/11/77; 8/29/77; 9/19/77; 10/10/77; 10/24/77; 11/14/77; 10/3/77; 10/10/77; 10/17/77; 10/24/77 11/7/77; 11/14/77; 11/21/77; 11/28/77; 12/5/77; 12/12/77; 12/19/77; 12/26/77; 3/6/78; 4/3/78; 4/10/78; 4/24/78; 3/5/79
New London North Parish - 1/3/77; 1/17/77; 1/31/77; 5/23/77; 11/7/77; 12/26/77;
New London River - 6/13/77
New Milford – 11/7/77; 3/6/78; 9/25/78; 7/8/79
New Weymouth, New Jersey - 12/25/78
New York - 1/3/77; 1/10/77; 1/17/77; 1/31/77; 2/14/77; 5/16/77; 5/23/77; 6/6/77; 6/27/77; 7/4/77; 7/18/77; 9/19/77; 10/17/77; 10/24/77; 1/2//78; 1/9/78; 1/16/78; 2/20/78; 4/10/78; 4/24/78; 5/8/78; 7/24/78; 9/4/78; 9/11/78; 9/25/78; 10/16/78; 11/13/78; 12/4/78; 12/18/78; 12/25/78; 1/1/79; 1/8/79;

3/5/79; 4/15/79; 6/2/79;
7/1/79; 8/4/79; 8/11/79;
8/18/79; 8/25/79; 9/29/79;
10/13/79; 10/20/79; 12/8/79
Newbury - 6/12/78; 6/19/78
Newent - 7/11/77; 12/26/77;
2/27/78; 5/22/78; 9/18/78; -
5/13/79
Newfoundland - 9/19/77;
9/29/79
Newport - 2/21/77; 6/20/77;
7/18/77; 7/25/77; 8/1/77;
8/8/77; 12/26/77; 10/10/77;
1/2/78; 2/6/78; 2/13/78;
3/27/78; 4/10/78; 5/15/78;
6/12/78, 6/19/78; 9/4/78;
11/13/78; 12/18/78; 2/26/79;
3/5/79; 4/15/79; 7/21/79;
10/20/79; 10/27/79; 11/3/79;
11/24/79
Niantic River - 3/14/77;
5/1/78; 6/12/78; 12/4/78;
1/8/79; 4/8/79; 6/9/7; 8/4/79
Norfolk - 12/25/78
North Bolton - 1/31/77
North Carolina - 2/21/77;
1/9/78; 3/6/78; 3/13/78;
6/19/78
North Kingston - 4/4/77
Norwalk - 7/24/78; 3/5/79
Norwich - 1/3/77; 1/10/77;
2/7/77; 2/21/77; 2/28/77;
4/4/77; 4/11/77; 4/18/77;
4/25/77; 5/2/77; 5/9/77;
5/16/77; 5/23/77; 5/30/77;
6/6/77; 6/13/77; 6/20/77;
6/27/77; 7/4/77; 7/11/77;
7/25/77;1/9/78; 1/16/78;
1/23/78; 2/13/78; 2/27/78;
3/13/78; 3/27/78; 4/3/78;

4/10/78; 4/24/78; 5/1/78;
5/29/78; 6/19/78; 7/17/78;
7/24/78; 9/18/78; 10/2/78;
10/9/78; 11/6/78; 11/13/78;
11/20/78; 12/4/78; 1/8/79;
1/8/79; 1/29/79; 2/5/79;
2/26/79; 3/19/79; 4/8/79;
4/29/79; 5/6/79; 5/20/79;
6/2/79; 6/23/79; 7/1/79;
7/8/79; 7/14/79; 7/21/79;
7/28/79; 8/11/79; 9/22/79;
9/29/79; 10/20/79; 10/27/79;
11/17/79; 11/24/79; 12/22/79
Norwich East Society -
6/5/78; 2/12/79; 5/20/79
Norwich, First Society -
2/7//77
Norwich Landing - 1/10/77;
5/30/77; 7/4/77; 8/1/77;
8/8/77; 8/15/77; 8/22/77;
8/29/77; 10/10/77; 10/24/77;
10/31/77; 11/14/77;
11/28/77; 12/12/77;
12/19/77; 1/16/78; 7/3/78;
8/14/78; 9/18/78; 10/2/78
10/9/78; 10/16/78; 11/13/78;
3/19/79; 4/29/79; 6/2/79;
6/9/79; 7/14/79; 7/21/79;
9/1/79
Norwich Plain - 10/23/78
Norwich River - 8/1/77;
8/15/77; 8/22/77; 2/27/78;
6/12/78; 8/5/78; 11/13/78;
12/25/78
Norwich West Farms -
1/10/77; 6/2/79; 8/4/79

Old York - 12/25/78
Oyster Bay - 10/6/79

Paucatuck Bridge - 6/27/77; 7/3/78
Paugwonck in Colchester - 5/22/78
Peek's Kill - 8/22/77; 12/26/77
Pennsylvania - 1/9/78
Penobscot - 8/18/79
Philadelphia - 4/11/77; 12/19/77; 12/25/78; 7/1/79; 11/3/79; 12/29/79
Pine Island - 11/20/78
Plainfield - 4/4/77; 5/30/77; 6/20/77; 7/4/77; 7/11/77; 10/10/77; 10/31/77; 1/16/78; 5/15/78; 5/29/78; 6/12/78; 7/24/78; 8/14/78; 9/18/78; 1/15/79; 4/29/79; 7/21/79; 8/25/79; 11/17/79; 12/15/79
Plumb Island - 7/31/78; 4/8/79; 7/1/79
Plymouth in the Susquehanna Purchase - 10/10/77
Plymouth - 12/25/78; 5/27/79
Point Judith - 4/3/78; 2/26/79; 7/1/79
Pompret - 2/21/77; 2/28/77; 3/21/77; 10/24/77; 11/14/77; 11/21/77; 11/28/77; 12/26/77; 1/2/78; 1/30/78; 2/6/78; 4/10/78; 4/17/78; 7/17/78; 9/4/78; 11/6/78; 11/27/78; 3/26/79;6/2/79; 7/8/79; 7/21/79; 10/20/79; 10/27/79
Poquatanuck, Norwich - 2/12/79; 7/28/79; 8/11/79
Poquatanuk Village - 1/10/77

Poquatanuk Cove - 9/29/79
Poquatuck River - 8/11/79
Port L'Orient, France - 3/13/78 2/19/79
Post Road - 5/23/77; 4/17/78
Preston - 1/10/77; 2/21/77; 5/9/77; 5/16/77; 5/23/77; 6/20/77; 8/22/77; 11/28/77; 12/5/77; 12/12/77; 1/16/78; 5/15/78; 5/22/78; 5/29/78; 6/12/78; 7/17/78; 7/24/78, 10/9/78; 1/8/79; 3/19/79; 4/22/79; 5/6/79; 5/20/79; 5/20/79; 6/16/79; 7/21/79; 8/11/79; 8/25/79; 9/1/79; 9/22/79; 12/1/79
Preston, North Society - 5/16/77; 10/10/77; 5/29/78; 6/5/78
Preston, South Society - 5/15/78
Providence - 5/9/77; 5/23/77; 6/20/77; 7/18/77; 9/19/77; 12/19/77; 1/16/78; 3/6/78; 11/13/78; 12/25/78 2/26/79; 3/5/79; 6/16/79
Providence Bay Plantations - 1/9/78
Providence River - 4/3/78

Quaker Hill - 1/29/79
Quebec - 1/31/77; 9/29/79; 10/13/79

Reading - 9/25/78
Red Bank - 11/24/79
Rhode Island - 1/3/77; 1/10/77; 2/14/77; 3/14/77; 3/21/77; 4/4/77; 4/25/77;

319

5/23/77; 6/6/77; 7/11/77;
7/18/77; 8/22/77; 8/29/77;
10/10/77; 10/24/7; 11/14/77;
11/28/77; 4/10/78; 5/15/78;
5/22/78; 9/4/78; 11/13/78;
1/1/79; 7/21/79; 7/28/79;
9/22/79; 10/20/79; 11/3/79;
12/15/79
Richmond, Rhode Island -
11/28/77; 5/15/78
Roacher Lot– 11/21/77
Rocky Hill – 2/27/78;
8/18/79
Rope Ferry– 11/14/77;
11/28/77
Rope Walk in New London -
5/29/78

Sachem's Head in Guilford -
6/20/77; 3/5/79
Sag Harbor - 2/5/79; 2/26/79;
3/26/79
Salem, Massachusetts -
5/27/79
Salem, New Jersey -
12/25/78
Salem - 12/25/78
Salisbury - 10/23/78
Sandy Hook - 3/26/79;
8/18/79
Saybrook - 2/21/77; 3/7/77;
4/11/77; 4/18/77; 5/23/77;
7/4/77; 7/11/77; 8/1/77;
8/29/77; 3/20/78; 4/10/78;
6/26/78; 7/24/78; 8/5/78;
9/18/78; 12/4/78; 1/22/79;
4/29/79; 5/20/79; 7/28/79;
8/11/79; 9/15/79; 9/22/79;
12/8/79

Saybrook, Chester Parish -
1/31/77; 1/31/77
Saybrook Ferry - 2/7//77;
4/18/77
Scarborough - 2/12/79
Scituate, Rhode Island -
6/6/77; 8/22/77
Scotland – 12/26/77; 7/24/78
Shetucket Bridge - 1/22/79
Shetucket River - 8/14/78
Simsbury - 4/8/79
South Carolina - 4/25/77;
1/9/78; 1/23/78
South Kensington, Rhode
Island - 5/2/77; 8/29/77;
10/3/77; 10/24/77; 9/22/79
Southhampton - 5/15/78;
3/26/79; 4/8/79
Southhold - 4/24/78; 3/12/79
St. Croix - 4/25/77
St. Eustatia - 2/21/77
Stamford - 5/23/77; 7/24/78
Stonington - 1/3/77; 1/10/77;
1/17/77; 2/14/77; 2/21/77;
2/28/77; 3/21/77; 4/4/77;
4/11/77; 4/25/77; 5/2/77;
5/9/77; 5/16/77; 5/23/77;
5/30/77; 6/13/77; 6/27/77;
7/4/77; 7/18/77; 8/1/77;
8/8/77; 8/15/77; 8/22/77;
9/5/77; 9/12/77; 10/10/77;
10/24/77; 11/7/77; 11/14/77;
11/28/77; 12/5/77; 12/12/77;
1/16/78; 1/23/78; 2/6/78;
2/13/78; 3/13/78; 3/20/78;
3/27/78; 4/17/78; 6/19/78;
7/3/78; 7/24/78; 7/31/78;
8/21/78; 9/4/78; 9/11/78;
9/25/78; 10/2/78; 10/23/78;
11/13/78; 11/27/78;

12/11/78; 12/18/78; 1/1/79;
2/5/79; 2/12/79; 2/26/79;
3/5/79; 3/12/79; 4/29/79;
5/13/79; 5/20/79; 6/23/79;
7/1/79; 8/11/79; 8/25/79;
9/1/79; 9/22/79; 10/20/79;
11/3/79; 11/17/79; 11/24/79;
12/15/79; 12/29/79
Stonington, North Society - 4/4/77; 5/2/77
Stonington Point - 5/23/77; 7/11/77; 8/8/77; 9/12/77; 9/19/77; 11/14/77; 11/28/77; 12/19/77; 4/1/79; 6/9/79
Stratford - 5/9/77; 3/6/78; 7/24/78; 9/25/78; 12/4/78
Sturbridge - 6/27/77
Suffolk county - 4/24/78
Surinam - 12/8/79
Susquehanna Purchase - 10/10/77
Swansey in New England - 3/20/78

Teneriff - 6/26/78
Thompson's Wharf, Westerly - 8/11/79
Tiffany's Point - 4/11/77
Tobago - 9/15/79; 10/20/79
Tolland - 10/2/78; 4/29/79
Tower Hill, New London - 1/17/77; 5/16/77
Tower Hill, South Kingston - 5/2/77
Trenton - 1/3/77

Updike's New Town, Rhode Island - 5/23/77

Uxbridge, Massachusetts - 5/30/77

Vermont - 10/13/79
Vineyard - 12/25/78
Virginia - 1/9/78; 12/25/78; 1/29/79; 6/23/79
Voluntown - 6/20/77; 9/5/77; 5/29/78; 8/14/78; 9/18/78; 4/29/79; 5/20/79; 5/27/79; 6/9/79; 10/13/79; 11/17/79

Walnut Hill, Lyme - 4/11/77
Warren - 3/5/79
Warwick - 12/25/78; 5/6/79
Waterman' Point, Norwich - 6/20/77
Wequequock Cove – 1/23/78
West Simsbury - 7/4/77
West Indies - 3/7/77; 3/21/77; 4/25/77; 5/30/77; 7/18/77; 11/14/77; 11/21/77; 11/28/77; 12/19/77; 12/26/77; 1/16/78; 4/17/78; 6/5/78; 2/26/79; 4/8/79; 4/22/79; 8/18/79; 9/22/79; 11/24/79
Westerly - 2/14/77; 2/28/77; 3/21/77; 6/27/77; 7/3/78; 4/29/79; 8/11/79; 9/22/79
Wethersfield - 5/2/77; 12/26/77; 2/27/78 7/3/78; 7/10/78; 7/17/78; 12/25/78; 10/20/79
White Beach, New London Harbor – 3/6/78; 4/10/78
White Plains - 7/31/78
Wickeposet Reef - 1/16/78

Willimantic river - 4/25/77
Windham - 2/21/77; 3/7/77; 4/4/77; 5/9/77; 5/16/77; 5/23/77; 6/27/77; 8/29/77; 9/5/77; 9/19/77; 10/31/77; 11/14/77; 12/19/77; 1/16/78; 1/23/78; 3/13/78; 3/27/78; 4/10/78; 5/1/78; 7/3/78; 7/10/78; 7/24/78; 8/14/78; 9/11/78; 10/2/78; 11/6/78; 11/13/78; 4/1/79;5/6/79; 5/20/79; 5/27/79; 7/8/79; 7/28/79; 8/11/79; 8/18/79; 8/25/79; 9/29/79; 10/13/79; 10/27/79; 11/17/79; 11/24/79
Windham County - 1/10/77; 4/18/77; 5/20/79; 5/27/79; 9/15/79
Windham, Canada Society– 11/21/77
Windham, Second Society - 10/31/77; 6/26/78; 7/24/78; 11/27/78

Windsor - 6/9/79
Winthrop's Neck, New London - 6/9/79
Woodbury - 9/25/78; 4/15/79
Woodstock - 3/7/77; 4/4/77; 5/2/77; 5/30/77; 12/26/77; 2/27/78; 4/10/78; 8/14/78; 11/27/78; 5/20/79; 7/21/79; 10/20/79; 11/17/79
Woodstock First Society - 5/1/78
Woodstock, North Parish - 3/12/79
Woodstock, West Society - 8/11/79
Worcester - 7/10/78
Workington - 2/12/79
Worthington - 4/29/79
Woter's Cove - 8/5/78
Yarmouth - 12/25/78

GENERAL INDEX

Allen's Wharf – 12/5/77
Articles of Confederation and Perpetual Union between the States – 12/19/77

Baley's *Ovid* - 1/17/77
Battle of Bennington - 11/13/78
Battle of Trenton - 1/3/77
Braddick's Passage Boat - 4/3/78; 12/25/78
Brooklyn Meeting House in Pomfret - 3/26/79
Buca's Family Physician - 7/3/78

Champion and Deming - 4/4/77
Chapman's Ferry - 10/17/77
Chappel's Tavern - 10/27/79
Church & Hallam - 1/31/77
Committee of Correspondence - 9/15/79
Committee of Inspection and Observation - 1/10/77, 1/24//77; 4/25/77; 8/29/77
Committee of Supply - 4/18/77
Connecticut Gazette -7/24/78; 12/11/78; 2/26/79; 4/1/79; 5/27/79; 7/1/79; 11/24/79; 12/8/79
Continental Congress - 4/4/77; 12/19/77; 1/9/78; 1/30/78; 3/13/78; 4/3/78; 12/11/78; 10/13/79; 10/20/79; 10/27/79

Council of Safety - 2/28/77; 4/25/77; 11/7/77; 12/11/78; 8/11/79; 9/29/79

Dilworth's Spelling Book - 1/16/78; 3/13/78
Distilhouse, New London - 8/22/77; 1/10/77
Don Quixote - 1/17/77
Dr. Watt's Divine Songs for the Use of Children - 7/25/77

Emmons' Tavern - 12/4/78
Essays on the Character, Manners and Genius of Women - 1/17/77

First Church of Killingsworth - 2/28/77
First Church in Norwich - 3/27/78
First Church in Preston - 6/16/79
Fort Griswold - 7/1/79; 9/1/79; 9/22/79; 12/1/79
Fort Saybrook - 8/11/79
Fort Trumbull - 3/7/77; 9/26/77; 3/13/78; 7/1/79; 11/17/79; 12/15/79
Freebetters New England Almanac - 1/10/77; 12/12/77; - 10/13/79

General Assembly - 9/12/77;
11/14/77; 11/21/77; 3/27/78;
4/17/78; 8/14/78; 9/11/78;
4/15/79;5/20/79; 6/16/79;
7/8/79; 10/20/79; 11/24/79
Gilbert and Miles - 3/26/79
Golden Ball - 2/7//77; 4/18/77;
5/30/77; 6/20/77; 6/16/79
Green & Spooner - 7/25/77;
3/13/78; 7/17/78

Hartford Paper Mill Lottery –
3/13/78
Hessians - 3/14/77
Howland & Coit - 10/2/78

John Matthews & Co. - 2/21/77
Johnson's Plays, 1/17/77

Lathrop & Coit - 3/27/78
Leavens Tavern - 10/9/78
lotteries - 4/7/77; 5/23/77;
2/6/78; 2/20/78; 3/13/78;
4/10/78; 4/24/78; 8/14/78;
11/6/78; 12/11/78; 1/22/79;
3/12/79; 10/27/79

Malbone's Farm - 6/2/79
Mendon Hospital - 5/9/77;
6/6/77
Miner's Tavern - 11/13/78
Mrs. Bigelow's Tavern -
1/31/77

Nathan's Cellar - 12/11/78
New London Gazette– 5/16/77;
11/28/77

Newgate Prison - 4/18/77;
4/8/79

Old Coffee House Wharf -
6/23/79
Oneida tribe - 3/14/77

Palmer Meeting House -
10/24/77
Pennsylvania Gazette - 2/26/79
Portage Bill - 1/1/79
Prison Ship *Good Hope* -
8/25/79

Rodman and Woodbridge -
11/24/79
Rodulphus & Co. - 2/7/77;
2/21/77
Rope Ferry - 4/1/79

Salisbury Furnace - 4/18/77;
4/10/78
Sign of the Stage Boat -
11/13/78
Small pox - 2/14/77; 2/21/77;
2/28/77; 3/7//77;/ 3/21/77;
4/11/77; 4/18; 77; 5/9/77;
5/16/77; 7/11/77; 3/27/78;
5/15/78; 6/12/78; 6/19/78;
12/25/78; 1/29/79; 2/19;
79;3/5/79; 3/26/79; 4/8/79;
4/15/79; 6/9/79; 6/29/79;
10/27
Society of Marlborough -
12/29/79
Stafford Furnace - 11/10/79
Susquehanna Purchase –
1/23/78

The Free Mason's Companion - 1/17/77

Union School - 11/13/78

Wait's Writing Room - 5/13/79; 11/17/79
Wilks' Jests - 1/17/77
Yale College - 10/20/79

INDEX OF VESSELS

Adelgonda Louissa - 1/24/77
Adventurer - 5/20/79; 9/15/79; 10/20/79
Alfred - 5/30/77; 10/10/77; 7/17/78; 2/19/79; 2/26/79; 10/20/79
Amazon - 2/21/77; 3/14/77; 3/21/77
American Revenue - 1/31/77; 2/7//77; 4/25/77; 7/18/77; 8/8/77; 1/30/78; 5/8/78; 6/12/78; 12/11/78; 12/18/78; 1/1/79; 4/8/79; 5/27/79; 6/16/79; 7/21/79; 7/28/79; 10/20/79 8/18/79; 8/25/79
Amherst - 10/10/77; 11/7/77; 1/16/78; 6/23/79
Argo - 8/11/79; 9/15/79; 10/20/79
Argyle - 10/20/79; 11/24/79

Badger - 10/13/79
Beaver - 3/13/78; 6/19/78; 7/17/78; 1/29/79;2/5/79; 2/12/79; 4/15/79; 4/22/79; 5/20/79; 5/27/79; 7/8/79; 9/8/79; 9/29/79; 12/8/79
Bellona - 5/27/79
Betsy – 11/14/77; 5/22/78; 7/3/78; 9/18/78; 9/25/78
Blaze Castle – 12/26/77
Braddick's Passage boat - 3/19/79
Brilliant - 5/29/78
Britannia - 2/21/77; 6/20/77; 7/11/77

Bunker Hill - 4/22/79

Carlotta - 4/22/79
Carolina - 8/11/79
Chance - 11/3/79
Charlotte - 5/27/79; 7/28/79
Charming Sally - 9/19/77; 10/20/79; 11/24/79
Clinton - 7/1/79
Columbus - 4/3/78
Confederacy - 11/13/78; 12/4/78; 3/19/79
Cyrus - 10/9/78

Daphne - 9/29/79
Defense - 4/18/77; 4/25/77; 5/30/77; 1/16/78; 8/14/78
Defiance - 5/20/79; 10/6/79; 10/13/79; 12/1/79
Delancey - 5/22/78
Dispatch - 11/6/78; 12/11/78; 5/20/79; 5/27/79
Dispenser - 7/3/78
Dolphin - 10/20/79; 11/24/79
Dory 4/17/78; 5/8/78

Eagle - 1/24/77; 2/21/77; 2/5/79; 2/12/79; 4/8/79; 5/20/79; 6/2/79; 6/23/79; 9/29/79; 10/20/79
Elliot - 9/15/79; 10/20/79
Endeavor - 9/15/79; 10/13/79
Experiment - 7/3/78; 8/18/79; 10/6/79; 10/20/79; 11/24/79; 12/15/79

Fanny – 12/26/77
Ferguson - 8/8/77; 9/5/77
Fly - 10/13/79

Galactia - 10/10/77
Game Cock - 4/22/79; 9/1/79
Gates - 9/29/79
General Sullivan - 4/8/79; 7/28/79
General Gage - 7/31/78
General Mifflin – 11/21/77
Generous Friend - 6/20/77; 7/11/77; 9/5/77
George - 5/22/78
Good Hope - 8/25/79
Governor Trumbull - 11/13/78; 12/18/78; 4/22/79
Greyhound - 3/14/77; 8/18/79

Halifax - 7/4/77; 10/10/77
Hancock - 4/15/79; 5/20/79; 5/27/79; 6/16/79; 7/28/79; 8/18/79; 9/1/79; 9/29/79; 12/15/79
Hannah - 9/15/79; 10/20/79
Happy Return - 7/11/77
Harlequin - 8/11/79; 10/20/79
Hawk - 11/6/78
Hero - 5/20/79
Hornet - 7/3/78; 9/18/78; 5/20/79
Hunter - 2/12/79; 5/20/79; 5/27/79

Industrious Bee - 7/17/78
Industry - 5/8/78; 5/22/78; 11/6/78

Jacob - 5/22/78
Jenny - 12/1/79
John - 9/19/77; 10/10/77; 5/27/79
Jolly Robbins - 11/6/78
Judith - 12/25/78
Juno - 12/18/78

Katherine, - 5/22/78
King George - 8/11/79

Lady Erskine - 5/27/79
Lady Trumbull - 2/12/79
Lark, Ship - 3/14/77
Little William - 9/15/79; 10/20/79
Lively - 10/20/79; 11/3/79; 11/24/79
Lord Howe - 7/21/79
Lovely Lass - 5/8/78; 12/4/78
Lydia - 9/25/78
Lyon – 3/13/78; 5/29/78

Marquis of Rockingham - 12/18/78
Middletown - 11/27/78; 1/1/79; 2/5/79; 2/12/79
Mifflin - 4/17/78; 5/8/78; 5/15/78; 8/21/78
Morning Star, - 5/22/78
Mosquito - 8/11/79
Mulberry - 5/20/79; /27/79

Nancy - 3/27/78; 7/3/78; 9/18/78; 7/14/79; 8/18/79
Nautilus - 7/8/79
Neptune - 6/26/78; 7/28/79; 8/25/79

New Broom - 8/14/78; 11/13/78
Niger Frigate - 7/25/77; 2/7//77
Norwich Packet - 3/19/79

Oliver Cromwell - 1/10/77;
1/17/77; 2/7//77; 4/18/77;
7/18/77; 9/19/77; 10/17/77;
10/9/78; 3/19/79; 4/1/79; 8/4/79;
8/25/79
Admiral Keppel - 10/9/78
Oliver - 5/27/79
Otter - 7/21/79; 11/3/79

Peggy - 5/22/78; 9/15/79
Peter - 2/12/79
Phebe - 5/20/79; 5/27/79
Pigeon - 11/6/78
Plymouth - 12/25/78
Polly and Hannah - 5/22/78,
Polly - 6/20/77; 5/22/78; 4/8/79;
5/6/79; 5/20/79; 5/27/79
Proteus - 6/23/79
Providence - 2/26/79
Prudence - 5/20/79
Putnam - 3/20/78; 5/1/78;
5/20/79; 7/1/79

Rachael - 4/1/79
Raleigh - 10/10/77; 2/26/79
Randolph - 10/10/77; 4/17/78
Ranger - 2/5/79; 2/12/79
Refugee - 11/6/78; 3/5/79;
4/8/79; 5/6/79
Renown - 3/26/79; 4/8/79
Resistance – 7/25/77;
12/26/77;9/26/77; 4/17/78;
6/12/78; 12/4/78
Retaliation 11/14/77; 11/21/77;
9/15/79; 10/6/79; 12/8/79

Revenge - 8/8/77, 9/19/77;
10/10/77; 11/14/77; 11/21/77;
11/28/77; 5/8/78; 6/12/78;
6/26/78; 7/3/78; 7/10/78;
7/17/78; 7/24/78; 9/25/78;
11/6/78; 12/4/78; 1/8/79;
2/12/79; 2/26/79; 4/8/79;
7/21/79; 7/28/79; 8/11/79;
9/15/79; 10/6/79; 10/20/79;
11/3/79
Rural Felicity - 7/1/79

Sally - 5/27/79; 7/1/79; 10/6/79;
10/20/79; 11/24/79
Saratoga - 7/1/79
Scorpion - 10/24/77
Sea Flower, - 5/22/78
Senegal - 10/16/78
Shelah - 10/6/79
Shemburg - 6/9/79
Speedwell - 5/22/78,
Spencer - 12/29/79
Spy - 1/3/77; 7/25/77; 8/1/77;
8/8/77; 9/19/77; 4/15/79
Stellar - 8/11/79
Strumpet - 9/15/79; 9/29/79;
10/20/79
Success - 6/20/77; 7/11/77;
7/17/78; 12/1/79
Swan - 7/4/77

Thomas and William - 2/12/79
Three Friends - 5/20/79; 5/27/79
True Blue - 1/24/77, 2/21/77
True Love - 6/26/78
Trumbull - 3/7/77; 7/18/77;
9/5/77; 2/20/78; 4/17/78; 5/8/78;
6/2/79
Two Brothers - 6/20/77;
10/17/77; 9/25/78

Unicorn - 7/28/79
Union - 10/20/79; 11/24/79

Venus - 11/6/78; 1/1/79; 5/27/79; 9/29/79
Victory – 12/12/77

Walpole - 9/15/79; 10/13/79
Warren - 6/26/78; 7/24/78; 6/2/79; 6/23/79; 7/8/79
Washington - 9/1/79; 10/6/79

Washington and Gates - 7/21/79; 11/3/79
Weasel - 11/6/78
Weymouth packet - 10/17/77
William – 10/10/77; 11/7/77; 8/11/79
Wooster - 7/1/79

Yarmouth - 4/17/78
York - 9/25/78
Young Cromwell - 9/15/79; 9/29/79

Heritage Books by Richard B. Marrin:

Abstracts from The Clarksville Standard
(Formerly The Northern Standard*)*
Volume 7: August 6, 1859–May 25, 1861

Abstracts from the New London Gazette*:*
Covering Southeastern Connecticut, 1763–1769

Abstracts from the New London Gazette*:*
Covering Southeastern Connecticut, 1770–1773

Abstracts from The Connecticut Gazette
(Formerly The New London Gazette*):*
Covering Southeastern Connecticut, 1774–1776

Abstracts from The Connecticut Gazette
(Formerly The New London Gazette*):*
Covering Southeastern Connecticut, 1777–1779

*A Glance Back in Time: Life in Colonial New Jersey (1704–1770)
as Depicted in News Accounts of the Day*

Going to Court in Texas: Riding the Circuit, 1842–1861

New Jersey During the Revolution, as Related in the News Items of the Day

The Paradise of Texas, Volume 1: Clarksville and Red River County, 1846–1860

Passage Point: An Amateur's Dig into New Jersey's Colonial Past

*Runaways of Colonial New Jersey: Indentured Servants,
Slaves, Deserters, and Prisoners, 1720–1781*

Heritage Books by Richard B. Marrin and Lorna Geer Sheppard:

Abstracts from The Northern Standard *and the Red River District [Texas]:*
Volume 1: August 20, 1842–August 19, 1848

Abstracts from The Northern Standard *and the Red River District [Texas]*
Volume 2: August 26, 1848–December 20, 1851

Abstracts from The Clarksville Standard
(Formerly The Northern Standard*)*
Volume 4: 1854–1855

Abstracts from The Clarksville Standard
(Formerly The Northern Standard*)*
Volume 5: 1856–1857

Abstracts from The Clarksville Standard
(Formerly The Northern Standard*)*
Volume 6: 1858–1859

Fireside Fiction by Richard B. Marrin:

The Retaking of America

www.ingramcontent.com/pod-product-compliance
Lightning Source LLC
Chambersburg PA
CBHW060109170426
43198CB00010B/829